EATING AS I GO

EATING AS I GO

SCENES FROM AMERICA AND ABROAD

Doris Friedensohn

Photographs by Carol Kitman

THE UNIVERSITY PRESS OF KENTUCKY

Publication of this volume was made possible in part by
a grant from the National Endowment for the Humanities.

Scholarly publisher for the Commonwealth,
serving Bellarmine University, Berea College, Centre
College of Kentucky, Eastern Kentucky University,
The Filson Historical Society, Georgetown College,
Kentucky Historical Society, Kentucky State University,
Morehead State University, Murray State University,
Northern Kentucky University, Transylvania University,
University of Kentucky, University of Louisville,
and Western Kentucky University.
All rights reserved.

Editorial and Sales Offices: The University Press of Kentucky
663 South Limestone Street, Lexington, Kentucky 40508-4008
www.kentuckypress.com

10 09 08 07 06   1 2 3 4 5

Maps by Alex Thor at the University of Kentucky Cartography Lab.

Library of Congress Cataloging-in-Publication Data

Friedensohn, Doris.
Eating as I go : scenes from America and abroad / Doris Friedensohn ;
photographs by Carol Kitman.
p. cm.
Includes bibliographical references and index.
ISBN-13: 978-0-8131-2402-5 (hardcover : alk. paper)
ISBN-10: 0-8131-2402-6 (hardcover : alk. paper)
ISBN-13: 978-0-8131-9164-5 (pbk. : alk. paper)
ISBN-10: 0-8131-9164-5 (pbk. : alk. paper)
1. Food—Anecdotes. 2. Travel—Anecdotes. 3. Cookery, International.
4. Friedensohn, Doris. I. Title.
TX357.F75 2006
641.3—dc22   2006012095

This book is printed on acid-free recycled paper meeting
the requirements of the American National Standard
for Permanence in Paper for Printed Library Materials.

Manufactured in the United States of America.

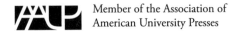

Member of the Association of
American University Presses

For Eli

Elias Friedensohn, 1924–1991

CONTENTS

ACKNOWLEDGMENTS

"More vinegar, please," my husband, Eli, scrawled on the pages of some early sketches for this book. Be real, he meant. Show the underside of adventurous eating along with the thrills. If only he had lived to see where his advice and love have propelled me.

This project dates back twenty years and encompasses a wide and varied terrain. It's a pleasure to acknowledge many debts I have incurred along the way. My agent, Cecelia Cancellaro, believed in this project and found the right home for it. Joyce Harrison, editor in chief of the University Press of Kentucky, has enthusiastically supported the book I wanted to write; she has been a source of good cheer at every stage of the process. Jena Kim brought sweet order to my files and much-needed technological savvy. Donna Bouvier, my discerning copyeditor, turned the final round of editing into a very smooth ride.

In the mid-1980s, grants from the New Jersey Department of Higher Education to the Garden State Immigration History Consortium and to Jersey City State College (now New Jersey City University) supported my first efforts to examine how Americans eat. The result was an exhibit, Eat! Eat! Food as Family and Cultural History, produced in collaboration with photographer Carol Kitman. I thank Carol for a year of indefatigable eating-and-working and for many years of food-enlivened friendship. Carol's photos from the 1987 exhibit add luster and connecting links to the stories recounted here.

Several pieces, revised for this volume, have been published elsewhere. Earlier versions of "Yom Kippurs at Yum Luk," "The Politics of Couscous," "Buddhist Delights," and "The Penultimate Passover" appeared in *People of the Book,* edited by Jeffrey Rubin-Dorsky and Shelley Fisher Fishkin (Madison: University of Wisconsin Press, 1996). A version of "A Kitchen of One's Own" appeared in *Through the Kitchen Window: Women Explore the Intimate Meanings of Food and Cooking,* edited by Arlene Voski Avakian (Boston: Beacon Press, 1997). And a version of "Chapulines, Mole, and Four Pozoles" appeared in *Pilaf, Pozole and Pad Thai: American Women and Ethnic Food,* edited by Sherrie Inness (Amherst: University of Massachusetts Press, 2001). In addition, shorter versions of "A View from the Fortress Polana" and "Georgia on My Mind" appeared in *Women on Campus* (Jersey City State College, Spring 1995 and Fall 2004 respectively). Ideas for

bookGoddess 5

8175 main st apt 1
buffalo ny 14221

bg5@mail.com

Packing Slip

Order id: 058-8107148-5829112

Purchased On: 27-Jul-2006 16:59:14PST

Amazon Marketplace Item: Eating As I Go: Scenes from America And Abroad [Paperback] by Friedensohn...

Listing id: 0713A073307

Condition: Used - Like New

Comments: ISBN: 081319645, as shown. Penciled price, rest unmarked, minimal shop wear. Ships next business day.

Quantity: 1

Buyer Name: susan d summa

Shipping method: standard

Shipping Address:
Susan D. Summa
Atelier
210 E Houghton St
Santa Fe, NM 87505

ACKNOWLEDGMENTS

"Opakapaka and Poke, Too" were tried out in "As Good as It Gets: Working in a Liberated Zone," *The Academic Forum* 8, no. 1 (1999), published by New Jersey City University. Parts of "The Real Senegal" and "The Politics of Couscous" first appeared in "*L'étrangers:* Two (Food) Tales from the 1970s," *Radcliffe Culinary Times* 8 (Spring 1998).

Fulbright lectureships to Tunisia (1978–79) and Portugal (1987) gave me the leisure to explore two vibrant cuisines; they also provoked a heightened self-consciousness about eating as an American abroad. Sabbatical leaves from Jersey City State College during 1990 and 1996 provided time for writing and lecturing abroad. Casa Don Miguel, an artists' retreat in Patzcuaro, Mexico, offered me a tranquil month (November 2000), which I devoted mostly to practicing my Spanish and savoring the Casa's cooked-to-order Mexican meals. On three separate occasions, I had the good fortune to spend time at the Salzburg Seminar's Center for the Study of the United States. I am grateful to Ronald Clifton, who directed the center, and his wife, Gwili, for extraordinary hospitality over the years and for making those visits so rich and companionable.

In the early 1990s, Joy Oh and Christine Lordi began introducing me to their favorite Korean food markets and restaurants. I thank them for this ongoing education and especially for their appetite for friendship.

Chefs James Bulger and Robert Brown at the Community FoodBank of New Jersey's Food Service Training Academy opened their program to me and opened themselves as well. I am grateful to them, to other staff members, and to the many students (some identified by their first names, others by pseudonyms) who cheerfully tolerated a nosy visitor in their kitchen.

I have a large, food-loving family, and many of its members appear in these pages. My parents, Bess and Joe Platzker, would not have followed where my appetites led. But they would have appreciated these reports from near and far as my way of doing American studies and being an American in the world. Shola Friedensohn and Adam Friedensohn are sources of joy, wisdom, and excitement in my life. I relish sharing meals and swapping food tales with them and with Hal and Debbie Platzkere, Lin Lerner, Laura Baum, Sapana Shakya, Marsha and Cy Worby and their splendid clan, and the youngest generation of eager Friedensohn eaters: Tara, Emily, Sonam, and Rahula.

Although writing is a solitary activity, eating is an endlessly sociable subject. Everybody has an opinion about my eclectic palate and the connections between eating, travel, and self-knowledge. Readers of these sketches question my food passions and fears, my political correctness as an eater, and the particular stories

ACKNOWLEDGMENTS

I've chosen to tell. Dare I say that friends and colleagues have chewed over my pieces at meals, on the phone, while traveling, and by e-mail. For their insights and suggestions, I am delighted to thank Jane Baum, Claudia and Bert Bial, Henry Bischoff, Michael Cowan, Delight Dodyk, Ann Fitzgerald, Edwige Giunta, Rita Jacobs, Carol and Larry Kaplan, Misako Koike, Paul Lauter, Karen Lystra, Nancy Melser, Batya Monder, Ferris Olin, Jean Pfaelzer, Adelaida Reyes, Deborah Rosenfelt, Gayle Samuels, Yael Tal, Ben and Mary Ann Whitten, Roberta Wollons, Cy and Marsha Worby, Eric Worby, and Norman Yetman.

Once a month for the past seven years, I have read portions of this book to members of my writers' group. Our ritual gatherings, with coffee and cookies, made writing less lonely. It's my pleasure to thank Phyllis Arenfeld, Marc Bernstein, Joe Chuman, Theresa Forsman, and Patricia Lefevere for their camaraderie, shrewd questions, and constant encouragement.

I am fortunate in my closest collaborators. They have been reading versions of these pages for years. There would be no book without the intellectual acumen, sensitivity to language, abiding friendship, and generosity of Stanley Bailis, Blair Birmelin, Rachel Brownstein, Marilyn Halter, Alice Kessler-Harris, Irene Ramalho Santos, and Barbara Rubin. I owe a special debt to Stanley, my e-mail correspondent par excellence. His discussions of how culture works and his incisive, ongoing commentary have inspired me and kept me wondrously entertained.

INTRODUCTION

A few years ago, when she was visiting New York, my granddaughter Emily, then nine, proposed that we have lunch at La Bicyclette, a French bistro she remembered from an earlier visit. "We could eat Italian," she said, "but the restaurant is noisy and you wouldn't like it. Or we could have sushi, but my Grandma Jane took us to a Japanese restaurant last night." Emily is a discriminating restaurant goer. Had I pressed her further, she might have suggested an Indian place where the dal reminds her of lunches at home in Kathmandu, or a Peruvian hole-in-the-wall where everyone orders garlicky roast chicken. Her brother, Sonam, then seven and a half, agreed with Emily. "The French restaurant is really nice," Sonam said, "and I can have *crème brûlée* for dessert."

When I was Emily's age, I hadn't set foot on a plane. There was no television at home to transport me into remote African villages where women haul water in earthenware jugs and grind millet by hand for the family's stew. We learned of current events by reading several daily papers and listening to the radio; except for war-induced shortages and victory gardens, food was not considered newsworthy. When I gobbled up my hamburger and mashed potatoes but left the spinach, my parents reminded me of "the starving Armenians." While we were safe in New York, Hitler's army was marching through Europe, slaughtering millions of innocent people. American GIs were over there, defending liberty. We children could help the war effort, my father would say, by joining the clean plate club—no foolish complaints and no waste.

In my Jewish, semi-kosher family, eating was not the path to global education. My brother and I learned world capitals and state capitals as well as the names of mountains, rivers, and valleys by playing Geography, where the last letter of a place becomes the first letter of the next place to be named. When we kids were taken out for a Sunday or holiday lunch, the destination was often the locally renowned Tip Toe Inn. I loved the big, airy dining room, the double layer of thick white tablecloths, and the formally attired waiters, who presented the menu with a flourish. The place was famous for its not-too-lean corned beef and its peppery pastrami sandwiches, served hot on platter-sized plates covered with white doilies. Choosing between these two succulent specialties was anguish.

The foreign restaurants I remember from my childhood on the Upper West

۱ were mostly Chinese. My parents approached them with cau-
t the forbidden pork and shellfish. Irish pubs dotted the area,
٬ns for male drinkers in flight from women and children, or so
..ᴄ ⱳᴇ৲ᴇ ৲old. When my mother treated me to lunch during one of our regular
shopping expeditions, it was usually to Chock Full o' Nuts for a thrifty cream
cheese and nut sandwich followed by a whole wheat donut and chocolate milk.

I was eleven the first time I ate in a French restaurant, Fleur de Lis in the West
Sixties. For years my French teacher had been training our class for this peak experience. Her lilting "*Bon jour, mes élèves, comment allez vous?*" held the promise
that France (and its New York surrogates) would one day be ours. At Hunter College Elementary School, French and art history were as critical to our training as
English and math. When the great day finally came, I still wasn't sure which *four-
chette* to use with *la salade*, but I did know how to ask for bread and butter in
properly accented French, and I knew the difference between *boeuf, poulet,* and
poisson. As for *crème brûlée,* it would be another decade before I had my first unforgettable taste.

One powerful trajectory of my history as an eater is outward bound. As a young
woman headed for a career in American studies, I despaired of being a provincial
American. Chinese, French, Greek, Mexican, and Indonesian cuisines beckoned
to me like mysterious suitors. Alert to difference in ways I only vaguely understood, I pursued pork sausages, suckling pig, squid, strong cheeses, brains and
tripes, rice noodles, and anything with rosemary or cumin. Each rendezvous with
an unfamiliar food was a way station on the express route to a cosmopolitan
life—or so I wisecracked to friends.

A reader in a rush might think, mistakenly, that this is the tale that shapes my
book. It's true that a promiscuous appetite often motivates my travels, even in my
own suburban neighborhood. But I haven't signed on as a culinary tour guide.
Countless chefs, restaurant critics, journalists, and food scholars do that job, and
do it elegantly. They direct the readers' attention to ingredients and their sources,
the cooking process, the finished dish, the order of the meal, and the vital connections between food, terrain, history, and culture.

I have a different objective. I use food as a point of departure. I use it—
shamelessly, some might say—to reflect on my moorings, my life as an American,
changes in American culture, and my experiences as an American in the world. I

am alert to the ways eating brings people together and keeps them apa_
ish food taboos with which I grew up, for example, are intended to unite family
and clan while excluding others. I've always fancied myself, naively perhaps, as
belonging to the party of inclusion. In food markets and restaurants, whether on
the Upper West Side of Manhattan or in a Tunisian village, I struggle to connect
with strangers. Around the table—at an artists' club in Mozambique, with colleagues in the Republic of Georgia, and at home in Leonia, New Jersey—I mon-
itor intimacies with new acquaintances, old friends, and my closest relations. At
the edge of these encounters, and sometimes right in the center, are politics and
economics, religion and gender. What we eat informs each experience. Ditto for
where we gather and under what circumstances. All these concerns belong to the
social surround of eating—my focus wherever I go.

Let me put it another way. Food is the occasion for my learning rather than
what I am principally committed to learning about. At the end of the road lies my
reckoning with myself. Perhaps, as I cross the finish line, a well-fed existential ac-
countant will help me tote up the fruits of a wider purview and a fortunate life.

Eating as I Go spans four continents and fifty years. And what a half century it has
been! Martin Luther King's "I Have a Dream" survived his assassination. Vietnam
splintered America. A huge new population of immigrants, largely from Asia and
Latin America, enriched America's labor force, talent pool, food supply, and dining options. Multiculturalism as an inclusive national ethos replaced the ideology
of the melting pot. Feminism transformed our private lives and our politics. Corporate capitalism flourished. Globalization, facilitated by the new information
technologies, increased the gulf between rich and poor nations and between the
haves and the have-nots in the United States. Communism collapsed. The United
States stepped up from a world power to The World Power.

America's changing demographics are on vivid display in Hudson County,
New Jersey, where my university is located. And so are the foods of the world.
Participants in all the great waves of immigration and migration to New York
have crossed the Hudson River into the gritty towns and cities facing Manhattan
Island. Among them have been Germans, Irish, Italians, Jews, and Slavs; African
Americans moving north and Puerto Ricans leaving their island; and, since 1965,
immigrants and refugees from the Caribbean, Latin America, and Asia.

In 1985, with photographer Carol Kitman, I set out to investigate Hudson

County's immigrant and ethnic food markets and restaurants. While Carol juggled four cameras, I talked to shopkeepers and waiters, cooks and bakers, cheese, chocolate, and sausage makers, and eaters of all ages and backgrounds. Some of our subjects were Asian and Latin American immigrants; others were second- and third-generation European ethnics and African Americans. No matter what questions we asked, no matter who answered them, our informants celebrated family foodways. Eating "traditional foods" was critical to their sense of identity and well-being. Food entrepreneurs talked about sustaining ethnic community traditions. But many also looked outward, beyond their own groups, with pride. America was changing. And their businesses, they believed, were changing the way America eats. The resulting photo exhibit, Eat! Eat! Food as Family and Cultural History, reflects these encounters.

On sabbatical in 1990, I continued exploring the transfer of old-world foodways to the global villages of northern New Jersey. I intended to chart the transformation of a region's eating styles in response to the increasing variety of its peoples, products, and cuisines. Henry Bischoff, an immigration historian, joined me in that initial effort. While we lunched on Portuguese *bacalhau*, Korean *bibimbop*, Filipino *pancit*, and Middle Eastern pita and falafel, Henry and I regaled each other with food memories.

My own stories about eating teased me—in the car, in the shower, at the supermarket, and at home over cocktails with my husband, Eli. I envisioned a short piece describing my origins as a rebel eater. "Yom Kippurs at Yum Luk," about feasting on egg foo yung on the holiest day of the Jewish year while my parents and relatives fasted and prayed, almost wrote itself. A few weeks later, I drafted a follow-up sketch—"A Kitchen of One's Own," about my emancipation from family foodways at age twenty-one.

There was no turning back. Each meal, restaurant visit, and food shopping expedition was a research opportunity. Failed meals and boring company at the table—even long lines at the supermarket—were redeemed by links to a larger narrative. Formerly simple questions—What shall we eat? Where shall we eat?—became as dense with interpretative possibilities as the dreams I used to examine with my analyst. The first-person narrative I had fallen into, a meditation on my own experiences as an eater in the context of a changing America, became the project I wanted to pursue. This book—a braiding of memoir, traveler's tales, and cultural commentary—is the result.

INTRODUCTION

With so many ethnic and national traditions represented in the United States, twenty-first-century Americans have access to a vast global smorgasbord. Of course, the access is uneven—a function of economics and geography, as well as imagination and persistence. As a lifelong resident of Greater New York, I take this access for granted. But it's also a challenge: to understand how culinary diversity is transforming my American life and the lives of those around me.

At my doorstep (or within a ten-minute drive) are ethnic markets, supermarkets, green markets, and a hundred specialty food stores. E-markets provide whatever the neighborhood lacks. When eating out, I respond to the lure of Brazilian barbecue, Korean noodles, and bistro French along with tapas, Tex-Mex, and Turkish kebabs. Cookbooks describing cuisines from every corner of the world, as well as American adaptations of those cuisines, encourage me to improvise in the kitchen. I can stay close to home and dine as a world traveler. In an era of rampant globalization, we are what we choose to eat, unless we happen to be poor, young, sick, or incarcerated.

My choices are my history. Decade after decade, I have sorted out, eliminated, revised, and added to my repertoire. Over the past twenty years, my friends and I have canonized arugula and portobello mushrooms along with kimchi, couscous, grilled tuna, goat cheese, and granola. Generally we prefer our breakfasts healthy and our dinners ethnic. For lunch we consume oversized salads, designer pizza, barbecue in a pita pocket, and tortilla wraps bulging with roast chicken, imported cheese, and grilled veggies. In between bouts of indulgence, we exercise and diet.

Our liberal culture celebrates choice. But what are the real meanings of multicultural culinary opportunities? What's to be learned from tasting unfamiliar foods or from analyzing one's appetites and culinary adventuring? In appreciating a cuisine, how important is it to know the language? (The mouth is made for speaking and eating; perhaps skill with the former facilitates the latter.) More important, what effect does appreciating a cuisine have in fostering intimacy and community between people of different backgrounds?

I think about my friends Joy and Christine, Korean immigrants who have been introducing me to Korean cooking for over a decade now. Eating in Korean restaurants and shopping in Korean food stores with them has brought Korea into my everyday suburban life. This experience of Korea-in-America sent me off to a literary conference in Seoul in 2002. When it's my turn to introduce Joy and Christine to the American way of eating, I take them to Chinese, Thai, and Indian restaurants, and to upscale Whole Foods, where the lunch buffet is international, hybrid, and healthy. Sampling new cuisines and mixing cuisines, Joy and Christine feel like worldly Americans, or perhaps like their native-born American friend.

Even as I relish our culinary diversity, I struggle to keep my soft multiculturalism in perspective. The food hype and the slick ads about eating together mask deep rifts relating to class, race, gender, religion, and national origin. In the parking lot of my supermarket, a man in a torn jacket asks for $2 to buy coffee. Close to half the children in New York City's public schools are eligible for free lunches. In the rich state of New Jersey, more than 500,000 people depend upon the Community FoodBank of New Jersey and its affiliated agencies for food support. I don't have to visit my local soup kitchen to be reminded that eating is not an equal opportunity activity.

Nor is the kitchen (usually) a place of shared burdens or just rewards. Even when cooking is seen in the context of family intimacy and nurturing, routine labor crushes creativity. I fight to hold fast to the joyful aspects of meal making without turning into a kitchen slave. As I grow older and my household becomes smaller, I am content to shop around for what others have cooked. Thank goodness for feminism—and an adequate income. I can make this choice without apology or too much guilt.

Like it or not, I am often a culinary tourist. In Mexico, I yearn for both safe foods and strange foods; in Hawaii, I search for glamorous restaurants and hideaways where the locals eat. In South Africa, I am happy eating in an artsy neighborhood famous for its Greek, Italian, French, Mexican, and Brazilian bistros. In Nepal, the pursuit of adventure leaves me anxious about my digestion and bowels.

Several trips abroad are professional junkets. I was an American studies Fulbright lecturer in Tunisia and Portugal and a consultant on academic programs about the United States in Mozambique and the Republic of Georgia. Wherever I go, there's no escaping who I am: a well-fed American woman, a *gringa* whose privileges attach to the power of her pocketbook and nation. Sometimes I know very little about my hosts and their societies. Eating and drinking are part of my education. When things go well, my hosts and I trade intimacies and deflate stereotypes. Other times, even though we eat chicken and drink beer together, we trip over differences in language, culture, and power.

What teases the palate teases the mind. The small dramas of the dining room, restaurant, market, and kitchen ripple with geopolitical, economic, psychological, sensual, and spiritual tensions. These are my materials, my "scenes from America and abroad."

INTRODUCTION

This volume of memoirs is organized topically and more or less chronologically. "More or less" is important, because memoirs are about memory, and memory is no friend of chronology.

Our roots are always with us, and so are our early rebellions. The opening section of this book, "Delicious Acts of Defiance," highlights the latter. I remember the food wars I waged against my middle-class Jewish family in the 1950s as the droll side of a seemingly interminable struggle for independence. The food ghetto, delineated by my mother, was the enemy. I recall my liberation as a graduate student, cooking chili, paella, and casserole-roasted pork. In defiance of Jewish prohibitions, I designated the pig as king in my kitchen. While the Free Speech Movement was freeing my tongue and unisex clothes were freeing my body, I added food to my list of new freedoms. After we made love in his studio, Eli, my husband-to-be, introduced me to Chinese duck feet and pork jowls. Eli and I were food mavens together, *compañeros* in experimentation and resistance.

In "Crazy Salad" I examine aspects of ethnic, multiethnic, and kitsch ethnic eating in contemporary America. New Jersey, the Garden State, where I have lived for the past thirty years, is America's most crowded state; it is also one of the most diverse. Shopping and dining where little English is spoken—often in my own suburban community—I am a foreigner on native soil. At the Phil-Am in Jersey City, Carol Kitman and I follow the lead of Filipino immigrants as we fill our plates. At the eclectic Café Europa, in my favorite high-end mall, I cannot resist a kitschy Mexican cheese quesadilla served with sour cream, guacamole, and salsa. I wander around Han Ah Reum, a vast Korean supermarket, wondering how long it will take to transcend the strangeness I feel, even after a decade of eating Korean foods with Korean friends.

"A Global Appetite" blends a traveler's food tales with those of an Americanist working abroad. During a Fulbright year teaching American studies at the University of Tunis, I'm introduced to couscous as an emblem of national identity. Lecturing and consulting on American culture in Austria, Mozambique, and the Republic of Georgia, I probe the connection between eating with colleagues and understanding their experiences and milieu. Eating mole in a Mexican village, I contemplate the impact of Bloomingdale's and Pier 1 on the residents' sanitation and sense of community. Personal connections preoccupy me. I try to understand my encounters with strangers in relation to the superpower I represent and its academic surrogate, American studies.

While my friends and I can choose to eat organically or inventively or in an eco-friendly fashion, many Americans must scramble for food. "Cooking for a Change" links eating, poverty, and social policy. What the poor eat is generally not a matter of choice. For students at the Food Service Training Academy, many of them ex-cons and recovering addicts, learning to cook is a gift they give themselves. It's also a marketable skill—a meal ticket. Their training involves cooking lunch for workers at the Community FoodBank of New Jersey, where the school is located, and themselves. My time at the Food Service Training Academy is a trip to another country, barely a half hour from where I live. As the academy's self-styled writer-in-residence, I talk with students about food, race, crime, drugs, and getting by. The deck is stacked against all of them, especially the black men with prison records. Can they change themselves and the lives of their families through cooking?

"How do you eat?" the father of my Nepalese daughter-in-law asks me when I tell him that I live alone. Friends and relatives come to my house, I say, and I eat at their houses; but this is only a partial answer. My concluding section, "Eating Alone," fills out the story. When I first learned that my husband, Eli, had cancer, I imagined myself eating alone, joyless and bereft. He died in 1991. The plant-filled dining room facing the garden is still my favorite room in our house. In the years since Eli's death, I've come to relish my freedom to eat (and drink) to excess or hardly at all. Despite the loneliness, I've found that living alone has a lovely simplicity. Visitors, while deeply welcome, disturb the peace. Eating alone in Tokyo in a restaurant where no one speaks English, I experience a heightened interest in everything around me—including myself. Eating alone in the suburbs, I reckon with my losses. I also revel, unexpectedly, in the company of strangers.

Part 1

DELICIOUS ACTS OF DEFIANCE

YOM KIPPURS AT YUM LUK

New York, 1950–1953

My favorite egg foo yung is the one I ate religiously—in an ammonia-scented Cantonese dive on upper Broadway—every Yom Kippur during my high school years. At Yum Luk, three crunchy "omelets," neatly stacked and bulging with bean sprouts, onions, and diced roast pork, rose high above a sea of gluey brown sauce. Sweet and salty, crisp and moist, garlicky and pungent: the tastes fused in my nose before the first bite reached my mouth. When we initiated the ritual, more than fifty years ago, my friend Ruth and I devoured the exotic concoction in a record three and a half minutes. I can still see us, giggling and fussing with our chopsticks, shoveling it in.

The moment and the meal were heavy with meaning. After a morning in the synagogue, dutifully mouthing prayers, we had opted to violate the cardinal rule of the Jewish Day of Atonement: *Thou shalt not eat.* It was not mere hunger that impelled us. To appease a growling stomach, a hot fudge sundae or a chocolate malted would have served quite nicely. No. The occasion offered grander possibilities. While the rest of the Jewish community was suffering through the obligatory fast, we would feast on forbidden foods.

Of course we were desperately afraid of being caught. Suppose a friend of our parents'—out for a breath of air between prayers—chanced to pass Yum Luk just as we were emerging from the restaurant? Suppose my chopsticks slipped and some of that sticky sauce stained the pale yellow orlon sweater I was wearing? There would be hell to pay—not from the all-knowing God of our ancestors, whose being and behavior were matters of indifference to us, but from our parents, who would not fail to appreciate the enormity of their daughters' rebellion. God might avert his eyes or remain silent, but we would hear from Them and feel the fullness of Their wrath.

No risk, no gain, the saying goes. As a teenager I assumed that fighting my family was natural and necessary—even as I often played along with them. "We're people who can discuss things," my mother liked to say. "Your father and I were educated to think for ourselves." Indeed, my New York–born, college-educated parents had rejected their immigrant parents' orthodoxy as Old World and hide-bound. Their own practice as Conservative Jews, however, was riddled with contradictions. These contradictions both delighted and enraged me. They certainly didn't make for satisfying discussions. For example, there were the "innocent" bacon, lettuce, and tomato sandwiches we all indulged in when eating out. Ham, however, being somehow more categorically gentile, was taboo. Occasionally, in an uncharacteristically relaxed mood, my mother would allow me to order a clean-looking ham and cheese sandwich at Chock Full o' Nuts, frowning darkly when I did.

How is it, I wondered, that some forbidden foods are less evil than others? What delusion or double standard accounted for the BLT exemption? Could it be that bacon strips are so removed in their cooked form and appearance from the corpus of the pig as to sever their connection with the "unclean" animal? Is it that the cooked-to-a-crisp slices are obviously beyond contamination by trichinosis? Perhaps for my mother, observing the spirit of *kashrut*, the Jewish dietary laws, at home allowed for "rewards" in restaurants, where the modern Jew could, on occasion and in moderation, relax for a minute and be cheerfully naughty?

In a period and an environment in which so many risks were either unthinkable or much too dangerous, food was my frontier of choice. Sleazy Yum Luk signified "no" to God, "no" to my parents and their Jewish holidays, "no" to piety, parochialism, and the protective custody of Jewish law. Yum Luk beckoned like a way station for the outward bound. Yom Kippurs at Yum Luk were delicious acts of defiance, the beginning of a long history of infidelities to the culinary tradition in which I was raised.

A KITCHEN OF ONE'S OWN

New Haven, 1958–1962

The first kitchen I called my own was the one I shared with fifteen other female graduate students on the second floor of Yale University's Helen Hadley Hall. The building, which opened its doors in 1958, the year I entered graduate school, was a tasteless concrete box. But our sparkling virgin kitchen offered ample compensation. Light poured into the big room through a wall of picture windows and onto six round, blond wood tables. U-shaped spaces at the north and south ends contained a built-in stove, a double sink, a large refrigerator, and cream-colored Formica counters with cabinets above and below. As soon as I unpacked my clothes and bedding, I rushed out to stock my half shelf in the south refrigerator and my half shelf in the south pantry.

For two years at Helen Hadley Hall, I abused three frying pans and a glass-covered Corningware casserole. I produced omelets with ham, bacon, onions, and cheese; rice dishes with ham, bacon, eggplant, onions, and shrimp; and salads with ham, bacon, onions, tuna, hard-boiled eggs, and shrimp. When I wanted to show off to new friends, I experimented with coq au vin and arroz con pollo.

Liberation from family traditions began with the one-dish dinner. At last I could dispense with the omnipresent tomato juice and grapefruit for openers; the trinity of meat, potatoes, and vegetables; and the trailers of salad (iceberg lettuce and tomatoes with Russian dressing), fruit, and Danish pastry or pie. Enter simplicity. And farewell to the whole marching band of propriety and health!

Casseroles and other one-dish concoctions ran counter to my mother's deepest convictions about good, clean cooking. I could hear her warning me: Beware of dirt you cannot see. When the final product disguises the parts, you eat at risk. The poor depend on blending to stretch the precious meat or fish; they season elaborately with garlic and spices to cover the inferior quality of ingredients. Blended foods are not simply bad for the body but repulsive, disgusting.

Bad is beautiful, especially when we are young. The point of leaving home is to be bad in peace. Finally, at the advanced age of twenty-one, I had no one (who counted) spying on my love life, my sleeping habits (including where I bedded down), or my eating patterns. In New Haven, my sexual and culinary freedom ran on separate tracks. I did not entertain male companions at Helen Hadley Hall; instead, I would go to their rooms, as the men's places offered more privacy for trysting and drinking. And I rarely cooked for them. For cooking and eating in, I staked out the territory alone or with my female friends. After years of eating forbidden foods at the tables of others—in neighborhood Chinese joints and in Greenwich Village pizzerias with red checkered tablecloths and candles in Chianti bottles—I embraced my own outlaw cookery.

Packaged ham and bacon—and occasionally one-pound tins of delicious Polish ham—smoothed the way. But shrimp fried rice gave me my comeuppance. I remember hesitating halfway down the row of canned fish in the supermarket and studying the cans of medium shrimp. Fresh shrimp are too expensive, I rationalized, too hard to find in this strange town, too time-consuming and difficult to shell and devein. But I wasn't fooling anybody, least of all myself. In buying canned shrimp, I had opted to let someone else do the gritty finger work and inhale the perfume of fresh, raw shrimp. I had opted for a safe, sanitized product that might just as well have been tuna. With time, I promised myself, I would cook more honestly.

Adventurous eating was not a simple matter during those years at Yale. New Haven in the late 1950s and early '60s was a provincial place, sharply divided between Ivy and Other. Living in the midst of the university, I knew little of the town. At first, I was busy enough and snobbish enough not to be curious. Without a car, I did my shopping on the way home from the library and bookstore—at a market of such unalloyed WASPiness that even Italian sausages were *hors de combat.*

In the Other New Haven, even in the chilliest weather, products of the sunny Mediterranean were readily available. Vast sections of the town, beginning a mile or so from the university, were Italian; and New Haven's pizzerias—large, boisterous places, with oversized booths for six and eight—were among the city's most renowned institutions. The trip to Wooster Street for Pepe's or Sal's thin-crusted, aromatic cheese and sausage pizzas was a gustatory event. There were no tricks and no compromises: just the mouth-scorching mozzarella, the olive oil dripping down our chins, and the pile of filthy napkins on chipped Formica tables. These pizzas were the stuff of legend then. Today they are enshrined on the food pages of the *New York Times.*

Competition with Wooster Street came not from my still-immature skillet, but from the soirees hosted by my friends Mary Ellen and Burhan. Mary Ellen's Louisiana hospitality set the stage for Burhan's Middle Eastern kitchen savvy. Both were lawyers in their mid-thirties, pursuing graduate law degrees and reshaping their careers. Mary Ellen, tall and handsome, turned knotty legal issues into lively parlor talk. When they entertained together in Mary Ellen's tiny apartment, Burhan was the cook. Long before most of us could imagine *pita* as a household word, Burhan fed us baba ghanoush, falafel, and silky smooth hummus. A short man with a round face and thinning hair, he would wait for us to gather around—assuming our roles of audience and support staff. Then he would begin stirring extra-virgin olive oil into ground chickpeas and tahini, adding just the right dash of lemon and fresh garlic and swirling the mixture with Syrian bread brought directly from Atlantic Avenue in Brooklyn.

On stage in Mary Ellen's kitchen, Burhan was transformed from a modest Jordanian attorney to Clark Gable with a mixing spoon. He bestowed hugs on his favorite women, among whom I was happy to be counted, and claimed kisses in return. His maroon knitted vest held the sweet scents of cinnamon, thyme, and oregano. A hush would descend as he supervised the transfer of marinated lamb, onions, and peppers from bowl to skewers to oven. Often he would pause to admire his handiwork. Then he would launch into tales of high living as a junior diplomat at the United Nations—with dirty politics all around. Burhan often said that diplomacy, like cooking, was a fine art, but not for the weak at heart. These days, he would add flirtatiously, his heart was in his cooking.

The kitchen at Helen Hadley Hall was showing signs of neglect. A patina of grease stains had settled on the inside of the oven and the broiler. Week-old milk, loosely wrapped chunks of cheese, and open cans of tuna fish befouled the refrigerator. Even more distressing was the need to guard my private stock of coffee, eggs, butter, and beer. Snippy signs announcing "You're not welcome to my sugar" appeared on the cupboards. I found myself avoiding the kitchen when suspected offenders were present.

In the fall of 1960, two friends and I moved into a dilapidated gray-shingled house with a travel agency on the ground floor. The pride of our roomy fourth-floor walk-up was an old-fashioned, eat-in kitchen. Canary yellow walls promised a tropical lift even on the grayest winter days. There, Ruth Ann from upstate New York and Isabel from southern California—both Protestant and distinctly non-ethnic—introduced me to "real" American food. I learned from them about breakfast sausages and baked pork chops, Indian pudding, buttermilk biscuits, avocados, and chilled artichokes with mayonnaise. And I let them nurture my hankering for real American booze: bourbon on the rocks, old fashioneds, manhattans, mint juleps, and Almaden by the jug.

Ruth Ann, with short, red, curly hair and a joshing manner, sang show tunes as she ferried chicken parts from egg to flour to breadcrumbs to frying pan. Isabel, blond and grave, preferred chopping onions and slicing tomatoes in silence. In the kitchen, liberated from reading and paper writing, I always wanted to talk. Good talk—whether about love or money, preparing for comps, or the news— was reason enough to hang out at the big table in our sunny common room; it was often more satisfying than cooking. I was clumsy with a paring knife—to cut an apple I required a cutting board—and impatient with prepping. I was also the least methodical worker of the group, and the most cavalier with recipes.

Ruth Ann, Isabel, and I were all proud of our hearty appetites. And our flat bellies. Dieting was not an issue. Nor were food allergies, food restrictions, food fears, or weird food needs.

The three of us attacked the stove with amateurish abandon: *boeuf bourguignon* for birthdays, chili for crowds, paella for small parties, and pasta when the budget was blown. We all leaned on James Beard for basics, Julia Child for sophistication, and *Marion Tracy's Casserole Cookery* for one-dish curried lamb chops, chicken stewed in sherry, and shrimp more or less Newburg. It was a generous diet for three graduate students without family money or serious jobs.

The late 1950s and early '60s at Yale were good years for graduate study, even for women. Generous government grants and Yale University fellowships covered our tuition and expenses, and the future seemed promising. Each of us had been admitted to a relatively small graduate program. I was the only woman in my American studies cohort of ten. (There was one woman in the previous class and one in the class that followed mine.) The expectation was that we would complete our PhDs and find good teaching positions—unless, of course, we married and dropped out of school to support or follow our spouses (or, heaven forbid, we became pregnant) before getting degrees and finding jobs.

In the summer between my third and fourth years at Yale, I discovered French bistro cooking in New York's theater district. My guide to the romantic hideaways producing this fare—e.g., Pierre au Tunnel, Le Beaujolais, and Chez Napoleon— was a pleasure-loving, tennis-playing political scientist. Between tennis outings and trysts in a Westchester motel, we ate lustily: *escargots, cervelles au beurre noir* (calf's brains in brown butter sauce), *tripes à la mode de Caen, rognon de veau* (kidneys) *en casserole, ris de veau* (sweetbreads) *au gratin*, and *rôti de porc poêlé* (casserole-roasted pork). And we drank heartily, which led me to be careless with my diaphragm (a common contraceptive choice in those years). An unwanted pregnancy and an abortion in Puerto Rico followed. Eating as the French do and getting pregnant were not connected, much as it amuses me now to think otherwise. I blamed myself and the man. My culinary passion for innards remained uncompromised.

Back in New Haven, regular forays into continental cuisine seemed a proper foundation for three not yet worldly American women who would be Yale PhDs in European history (Isabel), Russian literature (Ruth Ann), and American studies (me). In the early 1960s, we certainly envisioned cooking for husbands, lovers, and friends—for other, more worldly academics, male and female, who would take the measure of our culinary accomplishments. The meals we planned and the dishes we perfected would prepare us for the social side of world-class, fast-track academic life—or so we imagined from our peripheral, graduate-student outposts.

Of course, we never uttered such notions to one another in any but the wryest of terms. Who, me? Enhance my social mobility through cooking? You've got to be kidding! But what woman in those years didn't think such thoughts? And what aspiring female academic—especially at a chauvinist Ivy League university where we were few in number and not quite first-class citizens—did not wonder whether she would make it alone or coupled and what trade-offs might await her in the role of faculty wife?

We were more venturesome at the stove than we were in our scholarship and more self-preserving than in our sexual lives. In the kitchen, we could fail without risking our friendship. The few fights we had were not about food. We could give vent to ambition and "waste" a Friday afternoon and a Saturday preparing a twelve-hour cassoulet; and we could just as easily drift into no-fuss franks, beans, and packaged biscuits. Food work was communal, creative, and comforting. Cooking together, we brushed aside anxieties about the strenuous road ahead.

MARRIAGE MEXICAN STYLE

New York and Juarez, Mexico, 1966–1969

"*Dos margaritas,*" I said, showing off my Spanish. "*Lo mejor que tiene,*" the best that you have. In 1969, Eli and I didn't know brand names of tequila or whether Cointreau made a richer drink than Grand Marnier. We had been nibbling fiery peanuts, and a fresh taste was required immediately to cool down the chili powder and garlic. But we also needed something special to mark the occasion. Had we been drinking on the U.S. side of the Rio Grande, without spicy nuts, Eli probably would have ordered Beefeater martinis, straight up, with onions, very dry. He might even have intimated to the English-speaking bartender that only two hours earlier we had met with a poker-faced Mexican justice of the peace and come away with a certificate of marriage. The ceremony, in Spanish, had taken three minutes.

In the era before Starbucks and Match.com, couples met on the subway, on blind dates, at the weddings of mutual friends, or even at work. Ours was a faculty cafeteria romance. I remember my first glimpse of Eli, tall and lanky with long sideburns framing a craggy face, waiting for a tuna sandwich and coffee. A Jewish Abe Lincoln, I thought, intense but approachable, at ease in his body. He was wearing a dark brown corduroy Norfolk jacket, forest green corduroy pants, a blue work shirt, and a red cotton tie—the crossover look of the painter as professor.

I was thirty years old with a new PhD—in the 1960s, a wonderful union card—and a job in the English Department at Queens College, CUNY. That morning, munching a stale cheese Danish, I was sitting with a crew of 11:00 a.m. coffee klatschers. The company compensated for the Danish. With students excluded from our no-frills campus sanctuary (until "democratization" took hold the following year, in 1968), the talk was alternately playful and recondite. At the table, a classicist, a French scholar, a couple of film buffs, Eli, and two painter friends traded scholarly tidbits, gossip about exhibits, and trivia. I watched him as he gave his full attention to whoever was speaking—this was a man not afraid to be generous. When he claimed the floor, he spoke with gusto. He looked at me twice, appreciatively, I thought. The sight of his well-shaped hands, with a bit of paint under the nails of his right forefinger and thumb, stirred something in my belly. I laughed a lot and waited for the artist to make his move.

Eight stories above the northwest end of Chinatown, light flooded into Eli's cluttered studio. Beneath us, on Canal Street, truck drivers leaned on their horns and ambulance sirens wailed. Smells of stale Chinese frying oil, mingling with exhaust, wafted upward. The movable walls of Eli's "courtroom" smelled of glue and veneer and oil paint. They vibrated from violence intensified by satire. As I fingered the identical ceramic faces of judges, jurors, and prison guards, I wondered what perverse notion of justice the painter intended to convey. Then, holding the cap pistol attached to Eli's "assassination machine," I peeked in at the presidential target and released a volley of shots. Is this what Eli's vision implies—that none of us can resist the temptation to play assassin? Should I be as frightened by the artist as I am by the insight?

He had begun painting the assassination of President McKinley in the summer of 1963, Eli said, six months before John Kennedy was murdered. He had stopped the project after that awful November day in Dallas. How did it feel, I wanted to know, to be so prescient about American history? Paralyzing, he said, as though he had been practicing voodoo. The "tea lunch" we had planned to cap off the afternoon was forgotten.

The work may have been deeply strange, but Eli was not. He spoke directly to me, in a voice that went from soft and earnest to fiery. He handled words with respect. A devout New Yorker, he nevertheless claimed Paris as his true love. He entertained me with tales of his sabbatical in Rome, drinking espresso and grappa with Italian friends in small cafés but never in their homes. I told him about studying German in Austria and drinking beer all through the summer with a dashing Swiss anti-Semite.

There, with Eli in his studio, it was important for me not to be trivial. Surrounded by the assassin Czolgosz's judges, I described my illegal abortion. I raved about Ben W, my brilliant analyst and the author of several books on psychoanalytic psychotherapy. Eli asked if I had noticed his three paintings hanging in Ben's office, gifts from the artist a decade earlier to his analyst. Imagine: two people on the verge of an affair, sharing the same psychoanalyst! Eli opened a bag of pretzels.

Between sips of Taylor's New York State sherry, we clung to each other. A red-orange glow hung over Canal Street when we left the studio at 6:00 p.m.

After that visit, Eli and I rarely met in the faculty cafeteria. We lunched at least twice a week and on weekends at coffee shops in Chinatown, where protocol required that we wipe our spoons with paper napkins and drop the napkins on the floor. The more napkins on the floor, Eli assured me, the more authentic—i.e., Chinese—the eatery. Romance was not in the venue but in eating together. We talked food as we talked history, psychoanalysis, and art.

We became regulars at Hung Ho, in the basement under the bank on Mott Street, where the counter was always crowded with aging Chinese men. Seated at a Formica table near the front door, we could see all the varieties of dim sum in glass-enclosed steam units. Eli liked to order for the two of us: har gao (shrimp dumplings), beef noodle with hoisin sauce and a sprinkling of scallions, and taro crescents. The taro crescents were my favorite: ground pork in a light, soft pastry made of ground taro root, slightly crunchy at the surface. When we finished the first round, the waiter would stack our dishes and we would order again: duck feet, steamed pork dumplings, gluey tripe, and inch-long spare ribs in a delicate brown sauce. Save room for dessert, Eli would remind me, and we would head around the corner to another greasy spoon—and the best roast pork buns in Chinatown.

In the fall of 1968, a big year for social revolutions, I gave up my small, dark Upper West Side apartment and moved into a larger, brighter one (only two blocks away) with Eli and the younger of his two children, eight-year-old Adam. Shola, Eli's daughter, was a senior at Brandeis.

During the weeks and months that followed, my mother, who lived two blocks away, began each telephone call with an anxious "What's new?" Nothing, I would say, assuring her that she would be the first to know when something happened. "Something" was the transformation of Eli's separation into a formal divorce. When it became clear that divorce would not be in the cards for some while, we planned the Mexican alternative—for our own comfort as well as my mother's. This way, she would have news for all of those relatives and women friends when they asked, ever so carefully, how Eli and I were doing.

Our marriage-night margaritas, as it turned out, were perfect: frothy, well chilled, and a touch more sour than sweet. A delicate pale green, they were presented in oversized martini glasses, the rims crunchy with kosher salt. "To my love," Eli toasted. "*A mi amor*," I said, tearing. "*A l'amour*," Eli said. "*A l'amour*."

Menudo rojo, a tripe stew, was on the menu, and we both leaped at the opportunity. Uncooked tripe is rubbery and unpleasant to handle; in the first hour or so of boiling, it gives off a harsh, barnyard smell. Most of our friends, revolted by the idea of tripe, wouldn't even sample a forkful. "Tripe on your wedding night!" we could imagine them shrieking. In Chinatown tripe is recommended for hangovers. Could this Mexican *menudo* serve as a talisman, we wondered, protecting us from the consequences of happy, weary margarita-madness?

It must have been 10:00 p.m. when we stumbled to the phone and managed, finally, to get my mother on the line. "We've done it," I announced, running my fingers through Eli's mop of black hair as I spoke. "On Saturday?" she responded. "You got married on Saturday?" I told her that they didn't perform marriages in Mexico on Sunday, and on Monday Eli and I had classes to teach.

In New York, two weeks later, my mother insisted that I accompany her to the printer. The text of our marriage announcement, when she finally worked it out, declared that Doris Platzker and Elias Friedensohn were married in Juarez, Mexico—in February 1969. The day was missing. She had tossed in bed, my mother said, thinking about her rabbi. She imagined him opening the announcement, frowning, and rushing to consult his calendar. Whatever would he think when he discovered that Mrs. Platzker's daughter (who no longer went to the synagogue) was married on a Saturday? My mother, as it turned out, worried in vain. Her concern with propriety so befuddled her—and me—that we both forgot what we both knew perfectly well: Jews often marry on Saturday, after sundown.

Soon enough, my mother returned to her senses. After another visit to the printer, she invited two hundred relatives and friends to a gala, post-wedding party at a Westchester country club. She embraced Eli, as my father had before he died, for his many gifts, but also because of another artist named Elias, a dear, dead friend, whose etchings adorned her living room. In time, she managed to forget about our unsanctified status.

Seventeen years later, when Eli finally got his New York divorce, we were married again, this time by the mayor of our suburban town. We brought two bottles of

Champagne Veuve Clicquot to the mayor's chambers and our friends Blair and Bob as witnesses. On our way to the ceremony we spotted a witch with a wide-brimmed hat parading along the avenue. Right behind the witch, a black cat, holding hands with a pumpkin, shouted "Happy Halloween!" The mayor, who had appeared in his Frankenstein costume at the bank earlier in the day, wasted no time getting down to business. We exchanged vows in a record forty-five seconds. Over champagne, with no reason to rush, the five of us compared wedding stories. Afterward, with our witnesses in tow, we repaired to an Italian restaurant, where men sporting diamond pinky rings talked real estate and waste management. We celebrated with oysters on the half shell, osso bucco, and more champagne. And we did not call my mother.

DINNER PARTY PROTOCOLS

New York, 1969

When the doorbell rings at 6:45 on a sour Friday evening, I am busy slicing onions and holler to Eli to get it. The bumper-to-bumper traffic following a Friday afternoon meeting at the college has left me frazzled and pissy. Now all I want is to get the liver and onions into the skillet and onto the table before my martini catches up with me. Adam, with a nine-year-old's mix of curiosity and closed-mindedness, has already checked out the menu and registered his disappointment.

Laughter in the front hall disrupts my kitchen musings, and I strain to identify the intruders. Holy shitcakes! The remaining olive in my martini is no comfort as I register the presence of Evelyn and John B, two of Eli's artist friends. Sculptors with a brownstone in Brooklyn Heights, the Bs devote entire evenings to reviewing prestigious museum and gallery shows. In between reviews, they gossip ferociously about their competitors—and some of their friends—in the New York art world. Eli, who shares this world, enjoys comparing notes and matching wits with them. I enjoy the first twenty minutes before my irritation sets in.

Evelyn, at thirty-two (my age), speaks with the authority of an aging movie queen: ludicrous, dull, unoriginal, pretentious, she labels one show after the next. While Evelyn is all acid and angles, John, a decade older (like Eli), is rounded and soft-spoken. Her nastiness combined with his indulgence make me wish to end a visit with the Bs forty minutes after it has begun. We had a similar evening at their house two months earlier. I did more than my fair share of clearing the table and visiting the bathroom until I could mention the sitter's curfew. Then, as we took our leave, mellow with cognac, I hugged Evelyn warmly—and invited them for dinner at our place.

Washing my hands and summoning a smile, I am grateful for a number of particulars. First, we have not yet demolished the liver and onions. Second, Eli and I haven't abandoned our street clothes for jeans and work shirts. Third, the table hasn't been set for a telltale three. And fourth, I'm only on my first double martini.

It's 1969, a hang-loose time. But these friends of Eli's do not inspire candor or wry confessionals. I bring out Planters peanuts and Greek olives, melba toast and cheddar cheese. I pour generous shots of scotch for the men and bourbon for Evelyn before retreating to the kitchen. Liver and onions! Whose awful idea was this? The usual expletives are inadequate to the occasion. Fortunately, the main dish can be stretched by treating Adam to a peanut butter and jelly sandwich in front of the TV in his room. I drop a few more imperfectly caramelized onions and a can of potatoes into the frying pan. Reaching for an extra *je ne sais quoi*, I add a splash of dry vermouth, an extra shake of thyme, and a decorative camouflage of chopped parsley. For the rest, I'm on automatic: green salad, espresso, chocolate mints, and cognac. We will drink a lot and get by.

Since that night over thirty-five years ago when I was caught short by Evelyn and John, I have made few dutiful dinners. Obligation is antithetical to the joy of cooking. From time to time, when failing to repay an invitation is more vexing than doing so, I break out in mental hives. I forget to buy bread or skimp on the meat or overcook the beans. I start drinking too early. I lean on Eli to make and serve coffee. My hangover the next morning is both punishment and penance.

New York, 1977

For our friends Abby and Julian, distinguished medical researchers, the dinner party is a polished performance art. When Abby calls, three or four times a year, to invite us to one of their soirees, she embellishes the invitation with a set of abbreviated vitas. There will be the Carnegie Hall soloist, the Pulitzer Prize–winning historian, several university chairs, a multilingual psychoanalyst, and a pair of foreign dignitaries. Of course she hopes for Eli, the painter, to complete the roster.

Arriving at Abby and Julian's large Park Avenue apartment, we are immediately ushered into the study. Floor-to-ceiling bookshelves surround two sofas covered in off-white silk brocade. There's a French period desk in one corner, and a mirrored bar opposite the sofas. In the center of the room three physicians are comparing notes on the variety of wildlife in the Serengeti. Herbert, a psychiatrist who makes exquisite silver jewelry, beckons to me. "Not bad, not bad at all," he says, pointing to the pre-Colombian bronze lovebirds I am sporting on my black cashmere sweater. I'm proud of the piece, from the Museo de Oro in Bogotá. I remember thinking how, after a tough week of academic consultations, mostly in Spanish, I deserved a treat. "Eli indulged me," I tell Herbert, "with this symbolically loaded object." The jewelry-making shrink, who adores his own wife, reaches over to finger my birds. A uniformed maid serves us hot pastries filled with crab. The pastry is light and properly flaky, the crab delicately flavored with red pepper and lemon. Thinking that a dozen of these pastries would make a great dinner, I accept a hefty scotch on the rocks from Julian.

As others arrive, crowding the study, Eli and I take our drinks to the living room. A platter with small rounds of sturgeon and salmon topped by fine-grained black caviar beckons to me. On side tables next to gold brocaded chairs are freshly baked cheese sticks and a bowl of giant cashews. Eli, also focused on the scrumptious hors d'oeuvres, smiles mischievously at me with his eyes. The Ts' cocktail hour is a class act, we agree.

"No, I'm not a painter," I say in response to a query from one of the scientists, "just a garden-variety academic. I was a dean for five years, and too young to know what hit me. Now I'm free of those burdens," I add, "and back in the classroom." The second double scotch is kicking in. Between the booze and the snacks, I am losing my appetite along with my self-consciousness.

The living room has a familiar aspect. Five of Eli's paintings preside over the space. All have a mysterious figure or figures caught in a web of light or shadow. If pressed, Eli likes to explain that the figures "are seeking the silence within." The formulation is bait. Eloquent on the subject of his oils and watercolors, Eli has wide-ranging interests. Most of the time, he'd rather talk about other artists' work than his own. And that's part of his charm for Abby. The two of them go way back, some thirty-five years, to New York's High School of Music and Art, where both distinguished themselves not only in art but also in English, science, and French. Talent counted, but so did discipline and competitive zeal. Abby began collecting Eli's work even before his first big New York show in the late 1950s. Now, having the painter in her parlor adds value to the art.

Linking the cultures of art and science is an obsession of Abby's. At these soirees, practitioners of the fine arts and researchers on the biomedical frontier take graceful potshots at one another. The scientists in Abby and Julian's circle pride themselves on never missing a New York performance of the Tokyo String Quartet or a major exhibit at the Met. While they fall naturally into gossiping about NIH grants, they relish matching interpretations of Mozart or Michelangelo with those of the artists in the crowd.

Abby, who runs a multimillion-dollar lab at her hospital, orchestrates her dinner parties down to the final chocolate truffle. She plans meticulously, envisioning the several parts and connecting links. In truth, she enjoys the relative simplicity of these evenings. For more than two decades, she and Julian have practiced and synchronized their routines. Both are the smoothest of hosts. The party is unfailingly twelve in number, divided into two tables, with one host at the head of each. Couples, the organizing principle of these soirees, are always separated. As I look for my place card, I'm hoping that my table companions will not dismiss my new field of women's studies (new to me and new in the mid-1970s) as agitprop for bra-burners or an updated version of home economics.

The evening's spread, displayed on carved silver trays and Limoges dishes, is, as usual, continental: rollatini of veal with capers in a brown sauce, potatoes Anna (finely sliced and baked in a sauce of cream and cheese), and stuffed tomatoes surrounded by mushrooms and shallots. Our places are set with glasses for red and white wines, St. Julien and Vouvray respectively. A warm, crusty roll sits on each bread plate.

Julian, at my left, holds forth provocatively about the high cost and dubious value of hospital care for prostitutes with VD. "Why should we spend thousands of dollars at a shot to clean these women up, when they'll go right back to the streets? Where's the social benefit?" he asks. When I speak about the forces entrapping women in sex work, Julian dismisses my concerns as falling outside the hospital's purview. After a decent interlude, the man to my right grabs the floor with his favorite subject, the ethical problems of psychiatrists who work with homicidal patients. Both men exude self-confidence. Each is delighted to entertain questions, but neither expects a nonscientist at the dinner table, especially a female, to affect his views. I rush to savor the veal and potatoes before both are too cool to please.

The meal makes a polished statement: proper victuals for prosperous, sophisticated New Yorkers. At Abby and Julian's, the typical guest has seen the natural wonders and major ruins of six continents. The women come bedecked as if for an evening at the opera, where they would surely be seated in the eighth row center of the orchestra. The men are properly buttoned down. Season after season, I am the only woman in black pants or a black jumpsuit. And season after season, Eli is the only man with a white turtleneck or a bright purple shirt dressing down his navy suit. On such small rebellions, identities hinge. And the same goes for food. At Abby and Julian's, a proper dinner is continental, and form always holds.

Or almost always. It's five months since our last Park Avenue dinner, and Eli and I are at the airport in Buenos Aires waiting for a flight to Rio. We scribble postcards, repeatedly interrupting one another to show off a clever turn of phrase. The man sitting next to me, pale and gray with a Central European face, observes us closely. "You're from New York?" he asks me in Spanish. He's been to New York many times, for medical conferences. He's a neurologist and knows many New York doctors quite well. "Perhaps we know some of the same people," he ventures, "*queridos amigos*, dear friends who work at Columbia Presbyterian and who have recently given an excellent paper together at a meeting I organized in Buenos Aires. Are you acquainted with the doctors T, Abby and Julian, brilliant researchers, a perfect couple, so charming to be with?" We nod. "Would you be so good as to give them my kindest and warmest regards?"

Yes, it's a "small world" story, one that will be ideal for the Ts' next dinner party. When I ring them up two weeks later to pass along the Argentine doctor's regards, Abby's flat voice signals news of her own. "Julian and I have separated," she says, "and we'll soon be divorced."

THE PENULTIMATE PASSOVER

New York, 1989

I can always count on a certain phone call in early March to bring out the worst in me. Once again, it is Gerry, my eighty-eight-year-old aunt, phoning about plans for the forthcoming family seder. She is having the usual "interesting" group at her house, and she certainly hopes that Eli and I will be free and can join them. The older she gets, the more elaborately Gerry spins out the requisite forms of politesse—gentility cloaking her command that I participate in the holiday ritual. "Which night?" I ask, using the question to delay for a few seconds my inevitable acquiescence.

It's hard to be gracious about such directives from on high with their subtexts of filial piety and Jewish survival. This year, though, my tone in accepting the invitation is perky enough—for I am off the hook. My mother, for so many years a stalwart seder-maker but ailing now at eighty-six, will have a seder to go to— and I am spared the burden of providing for her.

Of course, my mother's seders were also unwelcome events: occasions for endless fussing over food, prayer, and the prescribed order (the word *seder* means order) of drinking, eating, and washing. We were frequently twenty or more at the table—and feeding this crowd required at least a week of concentrated activity: planning; cleaning; storing the regular dishes, silver, and pots and making room for the two sets of each used during Passover; shopping; and cooking. My mother, who did most of this work herself, commissioned me as her lieutenant for the final stages of preparation and serving.

At our seder table, the Party of Tradition and the Party of Modernization negotiated for primacy. The tradition, as once practiced by my maternal grandparents and championed by my mother, required that prayers be *chanted* in Hebrew—an arcane skill, possessed only by (some few) males of my mother's generation. Generally, my mother's youngest brother presided. He would wend his way through the story of the exodus from Egypt, murmuring for stretches in his old-fashioned Hebrew. Then, as if seized by the occasion, he would pour his rich voice into laments of pure anguish and hymns of exaltation. Try as I always did, it was difficult to resist joining him for the moment of release represented by his final, operatic hallelujahs.

The Party of Modernization, aggressively captained by Gerry, advocated a participatory ethos and practice. So the chanting I did not understand and therefore did not mind was balanced by a round of readings in English—an English convoluted enough to confound its revelations of God's mysterious and wondrous ways. How was it, I would inquire of no one in particular, that He who had been so vigilant on behalf of the Jews when they were slaves in Egypt could have slept so soundly during our darkest hours in twentieth-century Europe?

Actually, I was usually too busy during my mother's seders—dashing in and out the kitchen, checking on the chicken soup and potato pancakes, carrying, fetching, and gossiping with cousins I rarely saw—to fret too much about God. I was more likely to fret about my mother, his unfortunate surrogate. Had I not been so faithless, I might have been more tolerant of her seder stress: anxieties about the quality of the meal and the correctness of the ritual; anxieties about propriety and hospitality and control. I would also have been more tolerant of her dependence on me—for labor I did not relish, for good cheer and unflappability under fire.

Let Gerry worry now. At least at her seder, I am free to be a guest and an onlooker—well, almost free. My duties this year are to bring the chopped chicken liver for hors d'oeuvres and the *choroseth*—apples, walnuts, cinnamon, and red wine mixed together (like mortar for bricks) symbolizing the Israelites' "labor of affliction" under the pharaohs of Egypt. "Do you know how to make *choroseth*?" Gerry asks me, preparing to dictate instructions in the event that my half century of sedering should have left me without this very basic skill. Concerning the chicken liver, she credits me with knowing, or being able to find, the right kind of ready-made product.

I give some thought to both assignments. There was an intriguing recipe I had seen for sephardic (deriving from the Spanish and Italian Jewish traditions) *choroseth*, using dates instead of apples. I imagine the deep sweetness of the chewy mixture and know how stubbornly it will cling to the teeth. Will this exotic alternative do for Gerry's seder? Or will the two finicky old ladies and even the laid-back younger folks feel cheated if their familiar apple-nut snack is not available to stave off hunger halfway through the predinner service? Uncertain, I take the path well trod. Ditto for the chopped chicken liver. After contemplating duck paté, mousse of foie gras, and paté de campagne, I settle for Squire's rabbinically supervised kosher classic.

Perhaps I am weary of testing the muscle of tradition. Perhaps I am appalled by the recognition that, in our family, the muscle is flabby indeed. My octogenarian mother and aunt have frail bones and failing eyesight. They are making their separate peace with Passover.

At eighty-eight, Gerry's age, the mere act of making a seder is blessing enough. So I ought not to have been surprised by the rather gentle white wine (Israeli and kosher) that was poured into our glasses for the kiddush ceremony and prayers. True, we had liberated ourselves in the late 1960s from Manischewitz's deadly sweet burgundies. But *white* wine for the Passover seder is something else. Had nobody been assigned to bring a red for the occasion? Had one of my younger cousins decided that a kosher white would be chic and welcome? Or had Gerry herself opted for the "lighter" drink—especially since she no longer drinks red, and since she, rather than her brother, is presiding? To think that I hesitated to bring a sephardic *choroseth*.

Without an old-school male to chant the prayers, democracy wins by default. The reading of the service will be shared: a paragraph per person of the awkward English text, around the table again and again. Gerry, who is awaiting cataract surgery, struggles to read, then gives up. My mother, who has left her glasses at home, reads poorly. I too have left my glasses at home, but I borrow Gerry's and read theatrically, as if to my students. Eli, who has no need of reading glasses, claims to have left his at home and declines to read. The others, more relaxed than Eli and I about their roles in this gathering, take their turns without comment.

We are reaching the end of the line. Even one of Gerry's fine dinners of thirty years ago—when she produced beautiful standing rib roasts and flawless legs of lamb—could not have erased the pathos of this event. The chicken soup, which looks lusty, is not only salt, pepper, and fowl free, but seems also to have been infused with a broth of carrots. The main course, proudly presented as chicken Hawaiian, has been left in the oven an extra hour so that the requisite golden glaze covers a dozen desiccated breasts. Dessert, traditionally Gerry's forte, is a leaden nut cake (homemade with Passover products) topped with a distressed-looking layer of impossibly bitter chocolate.

It used to be that the family gathered for the seder to do God's work—and also its own. That edifice of ritual has crumbled. Nowadays at Passover, Eli and I reluctantly take our places at the table of the older generation: we drink wine, make entertaining dinner conversation, and wait to be released from our filial obligations. Four parts cynicism, one part piety. Our demeanor dishonors the occasion more than it honors the family. We spare our children this burden of duplicity: they are elsewhere, and grateful.

There will come a time soon when this deathwatch is over and I will be forced to add up my losses. When the last Passover has come and gone, will I dissolve into nostalgia and embark on a frenzy of ritual cooking? When spring arrives and Passover products appear in the supermarket, will I find myself researching the seder meal of the Venetian ghetto in the seventeenth century? When these ladies are laid to rest, what will I do with a lifetime of resistance to the bully power of religious ritual and family authority?

Turn my emotional swords into plowshares, perhaps. Say yes to history and family without confusing family with deity and piety. Do the ritual work that pleases me most: repeat the gala Thanksgiving family feast—for our children, their friends and companions, and for Eli's sister and brother-in-law and their clan—in the season of the Paschal Lamb and in memory of the Israelites' departure from Egypt.

The menu will be open to discussion. Adam and Laura, my son and daughter-in-law, will propose a pair of Thai and Chinese dishes. My nephew Eric and his wife Gul Rukh may offer us curries from her native Bangladesh. My niece Paula, who works in Guatemala, will have a bean stew to contribute, and my niece Laura and her Salvadoran husband, Carlos, may recommend a spicy fish with chiles. My stepdaughter Shola, Eli, and I will wish to complement this intensely flavored fare with something delicate and mild (French, perhaps); and Marsha and Cy, my sister-in-law and brother-in-law, world travelers who now live in Reno, Nevada, will surely amuse us with a campy western creation. If the *New York Times* runs another feature on Passover around the world, someone may even propose a sephardic date, fig, and nut compote or a bitter salad of dandelions.

A common cuisine is not required to cement this family. However, a passion for cooking and eating—and for creating beautiful foods—is a powerful force among us. Most of us relish the union of handwork and headwork. We relish the juxtaposition of the exotic and the familiar, the fluid process and the unpredictable products. In this collective endeavor—invested with the special histories and passions of each one of us—resides our newly minted ritual.

BUDDHIST DELIGHTS

New Paltz and Woodstock, New York;
Leonia, New Jersey, 1988–1990

A large white tent shimmers in the September sun. Beneath it twenty round tables are covered with sparkling white cloths and whimsical bouquets of fall flowers. Overhead, the sky is clear and big. On the western edge of the horizon, the Shawangunks (a.k.a. the "Gunks"), where my son, Adam, has climbed for more than a decade, loom like citadels of mystery and spirit.

When the flute and continuo strike up a William Byrd processional, Eli and I take our places among the assembled wedding party. The rabbi, with his guitar, embroidered silk Rastafarian beanie, flowing white robe, and rainbow-colored *tallith*, leads us up the grassy hillock. Adam and Laura, who were married privately three months earlier, are about to repeat their vows in the presence of family and friends. They stand, tall and glowing in their wedding gear, beneath a ceremonial *chuppa*. The *chuppa*, or wedding canopy, a bright blue silk "flag" resplendent with male and female symbols and icons from the Jewish and Buddhist traditions, flaps in the breeze, like Buddhist prayer flags in a new configuration. Max, Adam's Indonesian martial arts teacher and friend, made it especially for the occasion.

Behold Buddha's children at their Jewish wedding—seeking blessings wherever they are to be found. Adam, Laura, and the guitar-playing Woodstock rabbi have a common idiom. They invoke the primacy of spirit, the unending quest for wisdom, openness to God, and devotion to the manifold aspects of creation. The parts of the marriage ceremony flow and fit together, harmonies of the psyche powered by celestial energy.

When Adam and Laura informed us that they were willing to let Laura's parents make a big Jewish wedding, we anticipated difficulties. So we were not exactly surprised when Adam broached the subject of Indonesian hors d'oeuvres with us. "It's important to have our friends, the Palars, make the hors d'oeuvres," he announced. "You'll appreciate the extraordinary food, but it's more than that. When Indonesians cook for you, it's like a gift. They do it with such love." Predictably, the notion of Indonesian hors d'oeuvres upset Laura's observant father.

He insisted that the laws of *kashrut* be honored: no pork, no seafood, and, when he considered it further, no unkosher meat.

I know about food wars, and I certainly wanted to avoid the front lines of this one. The wedding belonged to Adam and Laura, and to Laura's parents by virtue of the power of the purse. Eli and I relished our role as celebrants on the sidelines. But how could we not recognize ourselves in Adam's defiant spirit? How could we not enjoy his rebellion, support his need for a symbolic statement—one that gave his soul-nourishing foods a place alongside the foodways enshrined by his in-laws? Yes, we were delighted to locate ourselves on the Buddhist-Indonesian side of the family and pay for the hors d'oeuvres along with the music.

I'm reminded of our first visit to Adam and Laura's place in Woodstock almost two years earlier. On the stove, all four burners were going. Our hosts bounced back and forth between Indonesian, Thai, and Chinese cookbooks on the counter and shrimp, beef, and eggplant dishes on the fire. Spring air wafted through the screen door, diffusing the jumbled odors of curries and lemongrass. A neat row of sliced scallions sat quietly, like a seventeenth-century Dutch still life, between dirty dishes and open condiment jars.

In the living room, plates and chopsticks were laid out on a large square coffee table. It was the only piece of furniture in the room. "Like the table? I just finished staining it last week," Adam said as he and Laura carried in two steaming dishes, a sizzling frying pan, and a pot of rice. The kids settled themselves on the floor on opposite sides of the table, and Eli and I awkwardly followed suit.

Laura's creation was a colorful curry of shrimp, rice thread noodles, and parsnips. "Thai coconut curry," she said. "Delicate, not hot." Adam, at ease at the stove, announced that his recipe for "five-element beef" was made with betel nut, coconut, peanuts, lemongrass, an intense green curry paste, and a sour lemon curry paste. Counting six elements, I wondered which one was Adam's addition, his personal mark on the dish. "Very ambitious," Eli remarked, bending forward to sniff the beef. "The Szechuan eggplant looks muddy," Adam said. "But it's got the right smoky taste—and great heat."

They offered the feast to us unencumbered: no napkins, no beverages, no appetizers, and no dessert. "We're down to bare bones in the pantry," Adam confessed. Bare bones, but a rich Asian statement. This is our world, the meal announced. Laura's Chinese dish honored her Chinese painting teacher and the Chinese tradition of landscape painting in which she and her teacher work. The Indonesian beef, Adam's proud achievement, honored his Indonesian martial arts teachers and their Buddhist community outside Jakarta, where he had studied. The colorful curry pointed to Bali, where the two were thinking of relocating.

Like most of their closest friends, Adam and Laura regularly participate in Buddhist ritual teachings, retreats, and the affairs of their "lineage" in the United States. The only space in the Woodstock house on which they have lavished attention is a shrine room, where ancient and modern *thonkas*, traditional Tibetan woven hangings, surround precious silver and brass ceremonial objects.

Adam has a contracting and construction business; Laura struggles to sell her paintings at street fairs. Both have recently separated from other partners. Together they have set up housekeeping without a real bed, chairs, or a simple stereo. Living in Woodstock among hippies, peaceniks, and spiritualists, Laura, twenty-five, and Adam, twenty-eight, are seeking their path. The world of the spirit beckons, entwined with the oddball pleasures of lotus root, tamarind, dried mushrooms, quail eggs, and dalian (a fruit that smells like rotting cheese).

I remember another occasion, on a muggy Saturday afternoon several months after the Woodstock visit, with Adam and his four-year-old daughter, Tara. In a crowd of Asian food shoppers, we stood before an "island" of impeccably ordered Japanese pickles: shocking pink garlic cloves, salmon colored ginger, inky black seaweed, emerald green spinach, all displayed in neat plastic containers, with toothpicks alongside, for tasting. Adam, after sampling three varieties of green seaweed, urged Tara to taste the ginger. "Don't be afraid, honey," he coaxed. "You've had this at home with your mom and also with Laura and me."

We are not in a hurry. Yaohan, the famous Japanese food emporium, is deliciously cool and full of surprises. The store, on the edge of the Hudson River opposite Riverside Church in Manhattan, attracts Asian and Asian American food shoppers from all over the metropolitan area—and Asian tourists as well. Earlier in the day, Adam had proposed making sushi for dinner. He knew I would acquiesce. Now, with four kinds of pickles in the shopping cart, we move toward the fish department. Approximately forty feet of display cases are loaded with raw tuna, salmon, mackerel, squid, octopus, scallops, clams, abalone, shrimp, and sea urchin roe. Such beautiful ingredients! After surveying the options, Adam chooses tuna, shrimp, red salmon roe, and his great favorite, uni: a mustard yellow, slimy roe of sea urchin. We add a bag of Japanese sushi rice (short round grains that are sticky when cooked), a package of dried sheets of seaweed, a tube of wasabi (green "horseradish," to be mixed with soy as a dipping sauce), and a nine-inch-square bamboo mat for rolling the rice and seaweed mixture. At the cash register, I repress a gasp and write a check for $60.05.

In the mall adjacent to the supermarket, we find ready-made maki (rice with slivers of vegetable and pickles, rolled in sheets of seaweed and cut into rounds). Ambling from stall to stall, we admire skewers of yakitori (pieces of meat, seafood, or vegetables cooked on an open grill) and small pastries filled with bean paste. Had we not already had lunch, we would have ordered steaming bowls of udon noodle soup and passed an hour at a window table watching sailboats zip past loaded tugboats on the Hudson River.

Adam shares my fascination with Yaohan: the combination of high-tech food merchandizing and high-quality goods in a sanitized yet visually compelling setting—like bathroom showrooms or the unused kitchens of those who are too rushed or too rich to eat in. In this postmodern emporium, there are no culinary perfumes. At Yaohan the art of Japanese sushi making abuts the science of packaging with plastic. Even fresh fish, fruit, and baked goods have lost their olfactory characteristics in this brave new world of late-twentieth-century food technology.

From Yaohan to my kitchen is a voyage back in time. Making sushi is hand-work, and Adam has great hands. As it turns out, he has been his own sushi chef only once before, with unremarkable results. However, since his last venture Adam has been reading Shizuo Tsuji's *Japanese Cooking: A Simple Art* (with an introduction by M. F. K. Fisher), a wonderful book that he bought for me but immediately took to Woodstock on long-term loan.

This time, in my kitchen in Leonia, everything works. The rice is properly gluey and gently vinegared. The seaweed rolls are neat, firm, colorful, cut at sharp angles, and arranged on wooden boards. With a final flourish, Adam has carved a tomato to resemble a rose and placed a parasol-like carrot in a stump of wasabi. Turning our backs on the chaos in the kitchen, we escape to the dining room and eat to excess. Adam has demystified sushi-at-home. One day, perhaps, I'll give it a try.

After the wedding ceremony, the hors d'oeuvres are presented on two huge, groaning boards, each about twenty feet long. One table is unalloyed New York in the Zabar's tradition: smoked trout and baked salmon, warm *brie en croute*, and

ıpura vegetables. The second table, presided over by the proud
of Indonesian offerings: chicken curry, a spicy beef stew, fine
ıs and bean sprouts, cabbage in a hot vinaigrette sauce, lettuce
with peanut sauce, and thin, freshly fried lotus seed crisps. Adam, eager to
interpret, reminds me that an Indonesian meal is a balance of spicy and bland,
crisp and soft, dry and wet. I find myself wishing that someone had put together
a descriptive menu of the Indonesian dishes or, failing that, had labeled them in-
dividually. Without names, these foods will be lost to me in a few weeks.

Several of our friends, adventurous eaters all, mistake the Indonesian fare for
the wedding dinner and return to it for seconds and thirds. Later, at the round
tables under the tent, they give short shrift to attractive plates of grilled fish, pasta
salad, green beans, and tomatoes with feta cheese. I give three silent cheers for the
upstart Asian appetizers.

Modern weddings are generational struggles. Against parents' assertions of
faith and community, the new couple seeks both their own connections to the
past and a separate path. Perhaps Eli and I deprived Adam and Laura of some
longed-for struggle with us because we give so little obeisance to tradition. Our
own, Mexican-style marriage and the gala, ceremony-free country club party that
followed suited us perfectly. Yet ceremony is important to Adam and Laura. Buddhist rituals shape their daily lives and give coherence to the community they
have chosen to live in. Adam, like many of his friends, has replaced our secularism
with a perfervid spiritualism. In his devotions, he is closer to the traditional Judaism of Laura's parents than to Eli's and my anticlerical position.

What distinguishes Eli and me and our children from our forebears, in religion and food, in work and family life, is our consciousness of choice. My parents
and their parents and all of our ancestors understood that ritual sustains a people,
creates identity. The decision not to eat at the tables of "others" is one they made
to keep their covenant with God. I inherited the proscription without the faith to
support it.

Eli and I suffer with our choices and exult in them. We pressure ourselves to
choose carefully but not too prudently, and we lacerate ourselves when our choices are rash or cowardly or ungenerous. We encourage our children to make their
own way, but we respond archly or irritably when they take too many unfamiliar
turns in the road. For the wayward descendants of Abraham and Sarah, weddings,
like all tribal confrontations, are simultaneously blessed and unsettling.

THANKSGIVING IN THE GARDEN OF EDEN

New York and Englewood, New Jersey, 1990

I shift the heavy shopping bag, brown paper in white plastic, from my right hand to my left, flexing the tired muscles before I press the elevator button marked "8." The tall, burly man who has come in after me inspects my parcel, sniffs for telltale odors, and then abruptly glues his eyes to the elevator door. "Happy holiday," he says unexpectedly, exiting on three, and I just about manage a "You, too" before the door shuts and he is gone. I check my watch, knowing full well that it is already 7:00 p.m. and that I am uncharacteristically late. On the eighth floor, I rush down the familiar corridor, past the nurses' station and the patients' kitchen, toward 827, where Eli is waiting.

We lower the table, which Eli has already cleared, and swing it around between the bed and the chair. Our holiday feast—two containers of miso soup and two handsomely boxed deluxe sushis—will just about fit. I open a bottle of hastily chosen Mondavi Chardonnay, pour some into a plastic cup, and place the bottle discreetly on the floor. I pour some of Englewood Hospital's best water for Eli, and we toast to his return home in less than twenty-four hours and to many more Thanksgivings together.

Our typical Thanksgiving consists of twenty family members for the big feast, most of them bedding down in our house for a chunk of the long weekend. But this year, a birth, an extended honeymoon, and a pair in Central America who can't come north in November open up the holiday to alternative arrangements: some minor surgery for Eli and a quiet interlude for recovery.

The week before Thanksgiving, instead of joining our neighbors in an orgy of frantic food buying and provisioning, Eli and I shop unhurriedly for hospital gear: a good Walkman, a 600-page World War II thriller, sheepskin slippers to replace his torn ones, and a pair of medium-weight long johns. We even have unhassled time for tennis—Saturday, Sunday, and Monday—before delivering Eli into his surgeon's hands on Tuesday morning.

The members of our clan are elsewhere and accounted for—except for my eighty-seven-year-old mother in Manhattan, who relies on us for holiday celebrations. I have promised her that we will have a Thanksgiving lunch in the city. Correction: my proposal is for *a* lunch on Thanksgiving Day, not turkey and trimmings surrounded by noisy extended families at a holiday-priced restaurant, but something mildly unconventional. Just the two of us. I envision a Chinese duck or crispy chicken along with pan-fried noodles and sautéed broccoli or asparagus with black mushrooms. No wild experiments, just a conservative bird and side dishes.

When I pick her up at her apartment at 1:30 on the dot and steer her toward Broadway, my mother admits to being a little bit hungry. A good sign. For this elderly woman who has just about ceased to cook for herself, a "little bit" hungry means that she will eat whatever is placed in front of her. I am seriously hungry, but determined to eat moderately in order to save room for the planned evening sushi with Eli. As my mother and I wait for the traffic light to change, I debate whether to order wine or beer with the meal. I imagine the smell of garlic frying in peanut oil, mingling now with fresh ginger and sesame oil; greedy fingers reach for the plastic chopsticks, and I smack my lips in anticipation of the soy-flavored fowl.

But I am rushing things. The Hunan Balcony, on the corner of Broadway and 98th, which never misses a day of business, is, to my surprise, closed this Thanksgiving day, as are the two Szechuan restaurants on Broadway and 97th. How curious! Have the owners of these 365-day-a-year establishments met together over scotch and soda and decided to shut down for this holiday? Has market research shown that North Americans will not eat Chinese food on Thanksgiving? Is the daughter of one of the owners being married this evening at a classy Westchester country club to the son of another owner, with everyone who is anyone in the industry in attendance?

Continuing south on Broadway, I worry about my mother in her spring raincoat and thin dress. She no longer thinks about the weather when dressing and doesn't appreciate having someone else do the thinking for her. At 95th and Broadway, I hesitate in front of a downscale Chinese-Cuban Comidas Criollas y Chinas. The place is crowded but sleazy. My mother, when her vision was sharper, would never have considered setting foot in such a place. But now she asks if I want to give it a try. "Chilly?" I ask. "Tired of walking?" Certainly not, she insists. The day is perfect and she needs the exercise. Another ten blocks down Broadway and four more closed Chinese restaurants feed my conspiracy theory. Their owners are organizing and calling the shots. Rich now, they are enjoying the American holiday and abandoning my mother and me to fend for ourselves.

We give up on the Chinese and take a table at Eden Rock, a simple storefront eatery with a Middle Eastern menu. A half dozen ready-made salads sit on large trays in a glass case, and I waltz my mother over to examine our options. Everything appeals to me, especially the extravagant mountain of lentils dressed with glistening, dark brown onions. The walk and the wait have pushed our appetites into overdrive, and I order without restraint: appetizers of hummus, baba ghanoush, cucumbers in yogurt, and the lentil salad, to be followed by platters of chicken and ground beef kebabs with green salad and rice pilaf. It will be much too much. The waiter, a warm and smiling man, knows that I know. He knows that I am amused that he knows.

Why not go for it? Everything is blessedly cheap. Besides, I have saved a small fortune by not feeding the family, and I am taken with the waiter and the restaurant. Both the menu and the place itself have an oddly nonspecific regional identity, yet the food is neither kitsch nor yuppified. No dish is identified by country of origin, and there are no calligraphic markings on the menu or symbols anywhere to indicate whether the establishment is Muslim, Jewish, or Christian. As I dip into the salads and kebabs, I listen to two waiters talking to each other in Arabic and a third who I feel certain is speaking to his young son in Hebrew. Impossible. I must be mistaken. Even on the Upper West Side of Manhattan, where the beautiful mosaic holds surprises of its own, this combination is unlikely.

On the cassette player, a Middle Eastern vocalist sings what is probably a lover's lament. Arabic or Hebrew? What am I hearing? I need to know. A Jew in the Middle East needs to know in whose tent she sits in order to enjoy her lunch. Our waiter, whom I ask, carefully, about the country of origin of the music, answers by asking me—after the briefest hesitation—whether I like it. I do—sincerely. But more than the music, I like my game with the waiter and his with me: each with a boxer's caution and an attraction for the simpatico other. The music, he tells me, is Egyptian. And why, I ask, is the restaurant named Eden Rock? After the Eden Rock in Lebanon, he counters, a famous restaurant. I picture a posh, sprawling place, surrounded by cedars, facing the sea—with a bomb through the roof and forty smashed windows. My plate is half full, but I am suddenly weary and desperate to get back to New Jersey. I tell the waiter that I am ready for "the bad news"—the check—and I see his eyes go dead for ten seconds until his brain programs in the more familiar term.

My circuits keep buzzing. I wonder whether the "Rock" in Eden Rock refers to a geological or a musical form or whether the allusion is to God's steadfastness in the rough sea of life. Whatever "Rock" may mean, on this disorienting Thanksgiving afternoon with my mother failing, Eli in the hospital, and the Middle East inflamed once again—this time by Iraq's invasion of Kuwait—it is Eden that truly counts. Garden of innocent pleasures, peaceful abode. Eden on Broadway. Eden in our waiter's twinkling glance and graciousness when he returns with the bill. In this improbable oasis, having feasted on foods of the war zone, I watch the filtered November light caress our table and slip abruptly away.

Part 2

CRAZY SALAD

EAT (ETHNIC)! EAT (AMERICAN)!

The Phil-Am, Jersey City, New Jersey, 1986

I watch the tiny, wizened woman on the line in front of me selecting her lunch. She points an arthritic forefinger first to *pancit* (Filipino noodles), then to a chocolately brown pork adobo (pork belly marinated in vinegar, garlic, and soy sauce), then to a sculptural wedge of *chicherones* (pork cracklings), and last to golden-brown fried bananas. When the man behind the counter gestures encouragingly toward the fried plantains, the woman responds with a cackle and shake of the head. The two have been chatting nonstop in what I recognize as Tagalog. "You know my weakness," I imagine her saying, "but this body has limits."

Then, at the cash register, a matronly employee folds the old woman into a gentle embrace. Over my shoulder I see Carol adjusting her camera. She motions to me to step out of the shot she is framing: the Filipina customer, with a selection of her national foods, getting change from a woman who could be her daughter. Distracted—or should I say absorbed—by the scene before me, I move too slowly. The moment has passed. It's often that way: I linger, trying to graft a narrative onto an image, while Carol maneuvers to get the image on film.

We are at the Phil-Am, a Filipino food store and cafeteria-style restaurant in Jersey City. Pig heaven, I call it. Soon Carol and I will be sitting opposite each other at a small, black Formica table. We'll be stuffing our faces with three kinds of Filipino-style pork, including my favorite, suckling pig with a super-crisp crust. If need be, there will be a second plate for *chicherones* (served with a thimbleful of vinegar in a white paper cup) and fried plantains. We're eating as we work because eating is central to our work: documenting the local food institutions of some of northern New Jersey's immigrant and ethnic communities.

When Carol finally loads her tray, putting her camera aside (a second camera hangs on her neck and two others are stashed in a canvas bag), the storefront restaurant is just about full. We squeeze into a table between an African American mother and her young daughter and a thirty-something Filipino couple. He's a stockbroker, he says after I introduce myself as someone who studies immigration; his wife works as a secretary at the United Nations. "We live in Queens," she says, "but we come here for Filipino products. Sometimes we run into old friends,

Filipinos who have moved to Summit and Short Hills." Almost ten thousand people of Filipino descent live in Jersey City, enough to keep business lively at the Phil-Am and the Filipino bakery a few blocks down the street.

When I ask the African American woman, Elaine, if this is her first visit, she tells me that she comes often. "The food's like a mix of Chinese and Spanish," she says, "and it's cheap. We don't have to know the names of dishes." "We can just point," her daughter, seven-year-old Shayla, adds. "And everyone speaks English."

Jersey City is the Times Square of our ethnographic field: a vital, tawdry hub in a twenty-five-mile global village on the Jersey side of the Hudson River, facing the Statue of Liberty and the World Trade Center. Newly arrived Indians, Pakistanis, Egyptians, and Filipinos rub up against immigrants from Cuba, Colombia, and Iran. The newcomers bring their food, entrepreneurial energy, and expectations into an urban mosaic of African Americans, Puerto Ricans, and Irish, Italian, and Polish Americans who cohabit, often uneasily. Poverty and violence are the underside of this mix: people from different traditions, often with limited resources and suspicious of their neighbors, must compete for opportunities for themselves and their families.

Inside the Phil-Am, a boisterous informality prevails. Filipinos on their own turf shrug off their troubles and welcome outsiders. If Carol and I don't weaken from flatulence or too much fat, we will capture some of these dramas of continuity and change. Carol's photos and my narratives will locate the Phil-Am in the context of other ethnic food markets and restaurants in Hudson County. Our work on the traveling exhibit Eat! Eat! Food as Family and Cultural History is supported by grants from the New Jersey Department of Higher Education.

During that first visit to the Phil-Am almost twenty years ago, I hardly knew where to focus. On center stage was the emotional drama between an aged Filipina customer and Phil-Am's Filipino employees. For the old woman, being at the Phil-Am evoked a world left behind and memories threatening to fade. Her age commanded respect. Her humor evoked affection. In Manila, perhaps, among her own countrymen and women, relations between the old woman and the workers might have been less emotional.

The Filipino stockbroker and his wife provided us with a secondary plot. Stealing a few hours from their busy schedules, the couple had battled bridge and tunnel traffic to fill their car with Filipino groceries, and they grabbed a sentimental home-style meal in the process. I imagined them orchestrating a show-and-tell dinner for their Filipino and non-Filipino colleagues, celebrating their culinary roots. With their unaccented American English and fluency in Tagalog, the couple embodied Phil-Am: bicultural, at ease in two worlds.

Inevitably, the outsiders grabbed our attention. The only blacks in the small, Asian-filled dining room, Elaine and Shayla were having a seemingly untroubled eating adventure. At the Phil-Am they were in another country. Carol's photo of the two of them eating noodles was a favorite of mine. While I appreciated the Phil-Am's role in sustaining immigrant Filipinos and their descendants, I relished its openness to non-Filipinos. More evocative than newspaper articles about the Philippines or tapes of Filipino music, here were smells and tastes from that distant place. In downtown Jersey City, proximity held out the promise of exchange and the strange made familiar. This is the global village's gift to us, I thought: the glossy side of multicultural America. I wondered whether Shayla's second-grade class might have had a unit on the Philippines. And if they did, would Shayla have told her classmates that she really liked Filipino *pancit*—and that maybe one day she would eat it over there?

A "unit" on the Philippines! How shallow the phrase sounds to me now, twenty years later. In the shadow of 9/11, long after Shayla's high school graduation, I imagine a military recruiter at the nearby Hudson Mall persuading a restless young woman and her best friend to enlist in the U.S. Army. "Do something exciting," the recruiter might say. "Join an elite unit and see the world." "Unit," indeed.

Eat! Eat! opened in April 1987 at Jersey City State College (now New Jersey City University), where I had been teaching since 1973. The college was a ten-minute bus ride from the Phil-Am, a neighboring institution, so to speak. Our working-class, multiethnic student body was the typical audience envisioned for the show. These viewers, with very few exceptions, were not likely to be familiar with *pancit*. They weren't reading the food section of the *New York Times* or *Gourmet* magazine, nor were many of them watching the Food Channel. In 1987, food was not yet a hot topic.

To show the Phil-Am, Carol and I chose a horizontal photo (enlarged to twenty by thirty inches) of the restaurant's female cook at the stove behind the cafeteria counter (page 54). An animated Filipina woman of forty-five or so, the cook was proud to be turning out the same dishes that defined her family as Filipino. Moreover, she was proud to be a woman at the core of this business. Had she taken a break from sautéing vegetables in the huge wok shown in the photo, she might have complained to the elderly woman customer that the day's pork adobo was a bit on the fat side. Or she might have boasted that the fried flounder with green beans and peppers was fresh from the market that very morning.

Pat's Place, Jersey City, 1986

"Where are the best soul food restaurants in the neighborhood?" I remember asking several African American colleagues. Jersey City in the mid-1980s was more than 20 percent African American. An extensive black ghetto sat on the college's eastern flank. "Try Pat's Place for breakfast," a friend suggested. "On Martin Luther King Jr. Drive. It's just minutes from here."

Deserted buildings and boarded-up shops lined the avenue. A boldly painted mural depicted black power and civil rights leaders (Dr. King among them) urging African Americans to throw off the shackles of oppression. Parked in front of the mural, Carol and I sat silently. Rage and hope, the two themes of the mural, were intertwined in struggle. I remembered a story told by the president of my college, a white scholar of African American history, about Martin Luther King Sr.'s visit to Jersey City on the occasion of the street's dedication. As the president described it, King looked around in dismay. He said to the local pols, "Is this the best you could do to honor my son?"

Approaching Pat's Place, Carol and I were uneasy. Would we find a parking spot near the restaurant? Would the camera around Carol's neck and her camera bag attract the attention of unemployed men on the street? Crime data for the city supported our anxieties about safety, but those were not our only concerns. How would people at the restaurant respond to our interest? Would they resent our inquiries? Would they feel used—manipulated for dubious "white" purposes? Carol and I were all too aware that black Americans have long been forced to tolerate suspicious and hostile whites; there would be justice in whatever discomfort might await us.

Red checkered tablecloths gave Pat's Place a warm, cheery glow. The dense, smoky smell of bacon filled the air. Three middle-aged men at the counter swiveled around to inspect us as we entered, and then turned back to their joshing and coffee. The manager and two other male customers stopped their discussion of a Jets game to see what we "wanted." I was reminded of Hemingway's story "A Clean, Well Lighted Place": Pat's Place was an oasis, a respite from the disarray and devastation on the street.

The cameras were our goodwill ambassadors. Jeanette and Evelyn, secretaries in their twenties, smiled and posed for Carol as I wrote down their addresses (page 55). Like so many people we met, they responded more readily to the camera than to my questions. Maybe it was the sort of attention they could understand, that and the dream of being seen. Enjoying the privacy of their table, the women had come halfway across Jersey City for a late breakfast of scrambled eggs, grits, and fat, crispy sausages. "There aren't too many places like this, you know, cute and friendly," Evelyn said, "where we can forget about things and be treated nice." We promised to send them prints and announcements of the exhibit. They promised to come to the opening.

Jersey City, 2004

In the late 1980s and early 1990s, the rotting docks that lined Jersey City's waterfront, remnants of a once vibrant shipping industry, were gradually replaced by new, gated communities marketed as "the Gold Coast." Ten minutes from the Phil-Am and Pat's Place, young professionals look out from their terraces at the New York harbor and the famous—though now towerless—skyline. Chic Italian bistros, art galleries, and trendy clothing shops have followed them, along with the reconstituted Jersey City Museum. On the eve of the 2004 election, the Gold Coast thrives.

The Phil-Am, when I drop in on a cloudless October Sunday, is spiffier than I remember it. Good commercial lighting and broad aisles showcase an immense variety of canned, bottled, and dried Filipino products. The cafeteria-style restaurant, however, has been reduced to a take-out counter: pork stews, a tired-looking *pancit, chicherones*, baked fish, and a rice dish. In the storage space where the restaurant once was, two middle-aged Filipina women bend over a makeshift table, stuffing doughy buns with seasoned pork.

The changes in the Phil-Am do not spell loss to the Filipino community. On the contrary, Filipino-owned food businesses have multiplied. Farther east along Newark Avenue are two full-service Filipino restaurants and three additional food markets. The Philippine Bread Shop, expanded from the mid-1980s into another cafeteria-style restaurant, is full of young people. They no longer rent videos and CDs, but four English-language Filipino newspapers are for sale at the front of the shop. The Maynila, two doors down from the Phil-Am, has a cafeteria setup just like the one Carol and I documented—Formica tables, Styrofoam plates, and cheap plastic cutlery. The place is filled with a Sunday lunch crowd, 90 percent Filipino. Every table is occupied. Inhaling the sweet smells of soy-grilled pork and fresh ginger, I line up for take-out. In my car I devour a skewer of roast pork, licking the barbecue sauce off my fingers.

It's a short ride from the Phil-Am and the Maynila to Martin Luther King Jr. Drive. Brilliant sunlight gives the bleak street—barely changed over two decades—a hyperreal, celluloid appearance. Empty stores and buildings with broken windows blend with grungy mini-markets and launderettes. Almost every block has a storefront church: Christian Rationalism, Heavenly Temple Church of God in Christ, Living Word Community Center, St. Stephen Holmes Church, Full Will of God Christian Academy, and Jehovah's Witnesses. A neat sign in one window reads "Active, Vitamins, Incense." Another pair of signs announces "King's Nails" and "Sadam Long Nails." A new branch public library, in attractive red brick, has a wrought iron fence surrounding an inaccessible lawn. A billboard pleads, "Don't Abandon Your Baby."

I see the ghost of Pat's Place in an empty brick storefront with a faded red awning and the words "May May's Kitchen" surrounded by Chinese characters. Young guys with dreads and wide pants are hanging out. Two middle-aged women in dark suits and bright scarves head home from church. Perhaps they are the older sisters of Jeanette and Evelyn, resilient still in the face of the surrounding joblessness, addiction, and AIDS. The two young women in our photo of Pat's Place would now be in their early forties. I imagine them with responsible jobs, each with a child or two, still close friends. Right before I turn onto MLK Drive, I can see them relaxing on a Friday night at the wine bar of Pat's New Place, waiting for their table and the special rack of lamb for two.

Laico's, Jersey City, 1973–2000

With Pat's New Place not an option, perhaps Jeanette and Evelyn were dining at Laico's, in an Italian American bistro about a mile away. Restaurant reviewers who discovered this neighborhood eatery in the 1990s called it a local treasure. They were right. Hidden away in a frame house on a residential, working-class street, Laico's was "my place" for twenty-five years: the site of hundreds of meals with colleagues and twice as many libations. Although it was only a five-minute drive from the college, we never went to Laico's for a quick lunch. We went to relax. We went for that first sip of a noontime scotch that rushes to the head and loosens the tongue.

Laico's, pleasantly dark on even the brightest day, was also the place for Hudson County politicians, contractors, and deal makers. A bar dominated one side of the walnut-paneled front room. Seated at banquette-style tables, we were often squeezed between schoolteachers and social workers, couples in their thirties or senior citizens who ordered dinner at 5:00 p.m. Whites, blacks, and especially neighborhood Italian Americans recognized one another as regulars (page 56).

"Laico's?" I would whisper to Barbara in the midst of an infuriating meeting of the college senate. I can still hear a smug male math professor savaging women's studies as "subjective," as if nothing he taught reflected cultural biases. And I can hear the social scientist with a reputation for harassing women students referring to our feminist work as unscientific and marginal. Just thinking about a scotch—and an order of garlicky, grilled portobello mushrooms—was enough to get us through the self-serving palaver.

Colleagues for twenty-five years, Barbara and I often needed to escape, bitch, and strategize. We treated Laico's as an extension of the office. Relaxing there, we did our best work. Drinking scotch in the 1970s, Chablis in the 1980s, and pinot grigio in the 1990s, we scribbled notes for new courses. We planned exhibits, selected guest speakers to bring to campus, and speculated about which feminist-friendly colleagues might be ripe for collaboration. We also wrote grants—for oral and photo history research and cross-cultural dialogues. Even if the yellow pads were on the table, personal talk came first: movies not to be missed, family troubles, friendships tested and unraveling. Barbara, famous for her numerology readings, would often report on whether the planets were better aligned for international travel or domestic affairs. Our birthdays, mine in November and hers in May, explained some differences in temperament as well as our rare compatibility. Laico's was what Jersey City offered by way of the icing on our friendship. We celebrated birthdays there, along with awards, promotions, and the precious grants that released us from teaching.

From the 1970s to the millennium, our Laico's rituals remained constant. As soon as orders were taken, waiters served a family-style salad along with hot, crusty garlic bread. For lunch we were loyal to the antipasti: portobellos with arugula, spinach, or broccoli rape with olive oil, and mozzarella with roasted red peppers. For dinner, I was partial to "shrimp francaise," fried in a light batter with butter and olive oil, and the gargantuan stuffed veal chop with mushrooms in red wine. Marge, our regular waitress, never rushed us. Jimmy, the bartender, was generous with the booze. And Mr. Laico himself often came by to gab and offer complimentary glasses of wine.

Laico's didn't put on airs. Side orders of pasta always came with tomato sauce. Mixed vegetables usually meant peas and carrots with a few cubes of zucchini. For years credit cards were not accepted. Nor were reservations. The atmosphere was festive with a minimum of fuss. In 1980, when we were hoping to turn our photo history exhibit Generations of Women into a book, Barbara and I invited a New York literary agent to lunch at Laico's. He came from the city in a stretch limousine that remained parked outside the restaurant while we ate. Hudson County is Mafia country, and stretch limos mean trouble as often as money. Everyone at Laico's was anxious and curious. When Mr. Laico appeared at our table, we introduced our guest. "We've brought him from New York for the ambience," Barbara said. Mr. Laico ran to the kitchen and said to his son, the chef, "Quick, call the exterminator. The professors say we have ambience."

Opening Day in the Gallery, April 1987

I am standing with Eileen, a former student and gifted photographer, in front of Carol's portrait of Fatima Abbasi (page 57). "Her eyes are so intense," Eileen observes, "that it takes a while to notice what she is doing with her hands—making dolma." The dolma—grape leaves stuffed with rice, lamb, pine nuts, and spices— and other appetizers, made at home by Mrs. Abbasi, are on the menu at Ali Baba, the family's Middle Eastern restaurant in Hoboken, New Jersey. "Are there two stories here or one?" Eileen asks. "Is the handsome woman with those pained, mascara-lined eyes telling the same tale as the hands that are folding stuffing into grape leaves?"

Fatima Abbasi's eyes speak to the anguish of exile. Her hands tell of adaptation, of an immigrant's effort to rebuild her life in New Jersey. Jerusalem Muslims, the Abbasis abandoned their home and olive groves after Israel's triumph in the 1967 war and moved to Jordan. In 1974 they moved again, from Jordan to the United States. When Carol and I visited the Abbasi household in North Bergen, where the photo was taken, we heard both stories. The family left Jordan, Mr. Abbasi explained, because he feared "the influence of the street" over his sons. Their close-knit family was at risk, he said, though he did not specify the threat. In America, he believed, he would have more authority as head of the household.

Indeed, migration and a family food business created a tight circle of interdependence. Ali Baba is a family undertaking. Mr. Abbasi does the buying; Mrs. Abbasi prepares specialty items, including hummus and baba ghanoush; and two of the Abbasis' five sons, all college graduates, run the restaurant. The olive oil used for dressing the dolma and the salads comes from the Abbasi family's olive trees on the West Bank. Like many successful ethnic restaurants, Ali Baba looks outward, toward a varied, mostly non–Middle Eastern, clientele. Located on a hip commercial street in Hoboken, close to the Stevens Institute of Technology, the restaurant attracts artists, students, and scientists, including many Jewish aficionados of Middle Eastern cuisine.

I contemplate the image of Mr. Haddad, the owner of a mini-market named the Great Cairo (page 58). He looks quite affable, posing with an Indian customer, even though the two of them communicate mostly by pointing. Of course, the photo would tell another story altogether if the customer were, like Mr. Haddad, one of the ten thousand Egyptians living in Jersey City. Perhaps the young Indian woman in the photo would prefer to be shopping four blocks down the street, in Little India. But the Great Cairo is closer to her home, and she is in a hurry. Clearly, the Egyptian merchant and his Indian customer have put on a good face for this photo. Two paper bags pass from his right hand to hers. The commercial transaction links them. That's a reality of urban culture: the zest and the sometimes ill-matched ingredients in our ethnic salad bowl. How sturdy are these linkages, I wonder. Too fragile to celebrate? Too posed? It's the job of the exhibit, I believe, to ask these questions, even when the answers are too complex or too elusive for the format on the wall.

My husband, Eli, accustomed to playing critic at art events, has planted himself in front of the photo captioned "Killing the Corned Beef" (page 60). He smiles mischievously at the cook in the photo, who chomps on a cigar as he removes an enormous corned beef from the steamer. "Brava to Carol for this one," Eli says. "This guy's not a poster boy for Eating Jewish. He's the hunter in modern dress, triumphant after the kill. Man as brute! He looks angry," Eli continues. "Business must be slow. Are there enough religious Jews left in the area to support a kosher restaurant? Do non-Jews eat there? Is his wife nagging him, back in the kitchen, about visiting her sister in Florida?"

I spot Maria, from Colombia, a former student who works at the college, standing in front of "Aquí es Colombia" (page 61). "Do you know this place?" I ask her. "I'd like to see the inside," Maria says, "the people serving and the customers eating *arepas* [cornmeal pancakes]. Maybe there's a waitress like the beautiful woman making grape leaves or like the Indian girl, also beautiful, eating a samosa. I'm disappointed. The sign on the store, 'Here is Colombia,' is cool. But a real Colombian store would be warm and lively. Everyone talking at once, the way we do at home. This picture doesn't tell people about my country."

I catch up with Eli again in front of "Mozzarella from Buffalo Milk" (page 62). "Look at the way the cheese maker's fingers press down on the mozzarella," he says. "The beauty of the shot," Eli continues, "is capturing this encounter between the man and the cheese, the maker and his object." I nod, wondering if Eli means "the artist and his subject." The drama of cheese making is what fascinated Carol and me: the daily routine, the primitive wooden spoon for mixing, and Victor Cannillo's red-roughened hands and arms. In comparison with Victor's cheeses, supermarket mozzarella in its plastic girdle is a dead object, a technologically produced imitation of cheese.

As the narrative suggests, there is an additional story attached to the cheese maker. He is a tall, good-looking college graduate, and the third generation of his family to work in this Italian American food business. After completing his degree, Victor interviewed for corporate jobs. But his heart belonged to the family shop and the craft of his ancestors. "Do you suppose he'll still be there ten years from now," I ask Eli, "when he's married with a couple of kids?"

My colleague Christine, who lives across the street from the college, requests a map. What she really wants, she says, is the full packaged tour: my safe route through an affordable food lover's Eden. I tell her that I'll work on the map.

A crowd has gathered in front of "Pumpkins at Ponticorvos" (page 63). I listen as two male students get competitive about the size of their own Thanksgiving pumpkins. In a culture where bigger is better, this response to the photo of a shopper inspecting a cluster of brilliantly colored pumpkins is natural enough. But it's not exactly what we had in mind. My caption refers to the pumpkin as an indigenous vegetable and a contribution of the American Indians to this country's cooking. Would any of our viewers pick up on the tension between Native American food traditions and our mythologized American Thanksgiving?

In an essay entitled "For Indians, No Thanksgiving," Native American novelist and critic Michael Dorris points out that when cultures clash, the winner controls the narrative. The American fantasy of Thanksgiving, Dorris observes, involves a tableau of grim-faced Puritan men, cheery, hard-working Puritan women, and a few vividly costumed Indians. The Indians bring their foods to the festival table and disappear after the last course is served. They puff on peace pipes and nod despairingly when agreements made with them are broken and their customs are outlawed. In modern times, Dorris writes, the descendants of those early contributors to the making of America sit at separate tables, embittered and shortchanged. The photo, with its oversized pumpkins and bright yellow gourds, tells the Thanksgiving story from the perspective of American bounty. Contemplating the photos, I realize I should have quoted Michael Dorris in the caption. Why didn't I?

Sometimes the thrust, or drift, of a project isn't fully visible until the end, when the work has a finished shape. Something of the kind has occurred with Eat! Eat! The images on the wall add up to America's fabled pluralism: Latinos, Middle Easterners, Asians, African Americans, and whites. Our human subjects are earnest, solemn, and smiling: dignified representatives of their respective communities. The entrepreneurs among them rejoice in the food business as a perfect marriage of ethnic self-affirmation and Americanization.

In designing the exhibit, Carol and I purposely made all of the photographs the same size (though some were some horizontal and some vertical). It would make hanging them easier, we thought, and create a harmonious appearance. Too harmonious, I realize now. The photos sit comfortably on the wall, one next to the other: a procession of marginalized peers, without pecking order or privilege. Like advertisements, they document working-class lives while blocking out evidence of class tensions, racism, neighborhood violence, fatigue, or fear of being unable to make ends meet. Clearly, the pictures celebrate. They celebrate democracy and difference, the work ethic and the contributions of immigrants and those of different ethnicities to American munificence. Some of the captions critique this tension-free version of America's salad bowl, but only gently and wryly. In the end, pictures always speak louder than words.

The hard-earned success of these ethnic food producers and consumers reassures us. With contentiousness affecting so many aspects of public and private life—abortion and affirmative action, gun control and the death penalty, immigration and taxes—eating creates a comfort zone. Eating, we escape our troubles. In the exhibit, ethnic eating is feel-good ethnicity: difference without subordination; difference as a reminder of lineage or perhaps even an invention of lineage for some who feel far removed from their places (often plural) and groups of origin.

If I ever do a sequel to Eat! Eat!, I promise myself, it will venture into the nasty politics of relations among ethnic groups and between particular groups and the so-called mainstream. It will consider the challenges to ethnic foodways from the mega–food industries, the supermarkets, and the fast-food outlets, as well as from the suburbanization of America. It will attempt to deal with economics and race along with olive oil, pumpkins, *pancit*, and corned beef.

Photos and Narratives from the Exhibit
Eat! Eat! Food as Family and Cultural History

The Phil-Am. Filipinos come from many parts of New Jersey and occasionally from New York to shop and eat at the Phil-Am in Jersey City. Rich and poor, young and old, professional and blue collar, most have emigrated to the United States since the late 1960s, and most are at ease in English. The restaurant, a modest self-service place with Formica tables, features *pancit* (noodle specialties), pork, rice, and vegetable dishes. Among the house favorites are *chicherones*, crisply fried pieces of the lining of a pig's stomach, dipped in vinegar and eaten with the fingers.

Breakfast Only. On Martin Luther King Jr. Drive in Jersey City, New Jersey, both the down and up sides of ghetto life announce themselves. Mixed among empty stores and sad-looking marginal businesses are active churches, neat new housing projects, and flamboyant murals celebrating African American achievement. The sign on one brick-fronted building reads "Pat's Place: Breakfast Only." Inside, hominy grits and fat, crusty sausages, traditional dishes of the black South, are served on large platters with eggs, toast, and home fries. Most customers, like the two young women shown here, are regulars.

Spaghetti Alle Vongole. Eating out in urban America often means eating Italian or Italian-style. For some of the regular patrons of Laico's, a heaping dish of spaghetti and fresh clams, accompanied by homemade garlic bread, may conjure memories of Grandma's kitchen or a recent trip to Italy. For others, pasta is neither humble filler nor exotic peasant fare but today's trendy item—and the dinner choice of tennis champions.

Fatima Abbasi's Dolma. Fatima Abbasi and her family came
to the United States from Jerusalem via Jordan in 1974. In
her modern kitchen in North Bergen, New Jersey, she
prepares many traditional Middle Eastern specialties for the
family's restaurant, the Ali Baba, in nearby Hoboken. In this
photo, she puts finishing touches on her dolma, grape leaves
stuffed with rice, lamb, currants, and spices, served with
homemade yogurt.

Inside the Great Cairo. Inside the Great Cairo, crammed shelves reveal the multiple functions of an ethnic mini-market. Customers can buy pita bread, canned juices, and beans from the Middle East, Hispanic (Goya) products, nuts and spices of all sorts, as well as Tide, toilet paper, Pampers, and paper towels. Middle Easterners can find several Egyptian newspapers and a variety of Arab-language audiocassettes and videos. South Asians from the neighborhood, like the young woman shown here, come to the Great Cairo to buy groceries and household supplies.

The Great Cairo. Outside, the Great Cairo sports stylish Arabic calligraphy and touches of graffiti chic. Jersey City, where the mini-market is located, has a population of ten thousand Egyptians as well as many other Arabic-speaking people. The Egyptian owner, who doesn't speak much English, says that his store reminds him of home.

Killing the Corned Beef. This particular corned beef is served lean, on rye with mustard—never as a grilled "Reuben" with sauerkraut, Russian dressing, and Swiss. The Goodwill Pantry in Bayonne, New Jersey, is a *glatt* (strictly) kosher restaurant and delicatessen, one of the few remaining in Hudson County. No milk products are served. The Jewish Sabbath is observed from Friday before sundown until Saturday after sundown. Evidently, no regulation prevents the cook from enjoying his cigar.

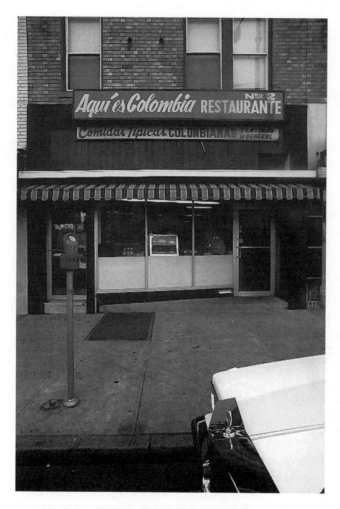

Aquí es Colombia. The sign, "Aquí es Colombia #2," beckons
first and foremost to Colombians. "*Comidas típicas
colombianas*," the sign underneath reads; in the spirit of
outreach, it continues, "*y latinas en general.*" Inside the narrow
West New York, New Jersey, restaurant, wedged between
businesses owned by Cubans, Dominicans, Italians, and
Arabs, one finds Colombian newspapers and magazines as
well as Colombian canned goods, corn meal, and freshly made
arepas (pancakes) served with a huge tub of Parkay margarine.

Mozzarella from Buffalo Milk. In southern Italy, mozzarella was once made with buffalo milk. Although buffalo milk has generally been replaced by cow's milk in the United States and in most of Italy, this is not the case at Cannillo's in West New York, New Jersey. In this photo, the mozzarella is made by Victor Cannillo according to the traditions of his ancestors. The family business is open 364 days a year, and Victor is there on most of them, readying the delicate cheese for retail customers and catering jobs.

Pumpkins at Ponticorvos. As Halloween approaches, pumpkins at Ponticorvos on Bergen Boulevard in Ridgefield Park get larger and larger. The customer in this photo may be wondering how large a pumpkin she can carry from her car to her kitchen and how much she will need for a pumpkin pie. Pumpkins are among our indigenous vegetables, a contribution of northeast Indians to American cooking. The Indians usually baked pumpkins whole in the ashes of a dying fire and then moistened the cooked pumpkin with honey, maple syrup, or fat. Sometimes they boiled pumpkin with meat for a stew or thick soup.

Samosas. In markets and bazaars all over their vast subcontinent, Indians snack on samosas: deep-fried turnovers or curry puffs filled with vegetables or potatoes that have been cooked with onion, ginger, garlic, and a sweet spice mix of coriander, cinnamon, cumin, cloves, cardamom, mace, and pepper. A proper samosa is crisp, pungent, aromatic, and easy to eat. The glowing young woman shown here has found samosas like those she remembers from her childhood in India at Shreeji's Bazaar on Newark Avenue in Jersey City's thriving Little India.

State-of-the-Art Pita. Harry Toufayan's state-of-the-art, automated pita bread factory in North Bergen requires the human eye and hand for quality control. Here, a worker recycles an imperfect unbaked pita. Toufayan, an Egyptian-born Armenian who emigrated to the United States in the mid-1960s, grew up in a family that ran a successful bread business in Cairo. Today his pitas, made of yeast, water, flour, and salt, are imaginatively marketed to appeal not only to Middle Eastern émigrés but also to Jews, joggers, grazers, and those who seek to market the croissan'wich.

King of the Roost. Chickens in the supermarket lack freshness and taste, customers report at La Pollería. In this Cuban-owned *pollería*, the smells are strong, the noise constant, and the only useful language is Spanish. Here the hens are confined but the roosters roam freely, sometimes fraternizing with frisky kittens. In this photo, above a warren of cages, the king of the roost flaunts his freedom.

Live Poultry Market. At La Pollería, a live poultry market in Union City, New Jersey, Spanish-speaking customers inspect the goods before moving confidently toward their fowl of choice. It's the job of this worker to prepare the live fowl for his customers' ovens and stockpots. Within two or three minutes, he will kill this chicken by hand in the back room, process it through three machines to remove its blood and feathers, bag it, and declare it ready to travel.

Sushi Artist. Heun Jeh Bang's father owned a restaurant in Tokyo. When the younger Mr. Bang came to the United States in the mid-1970s, he followed in the family tradition. Often, however, at Bang's American-style luncheonette in Jersey City, customers wondered why this Japanese man was dishing up Western omelets instead of something more "suitable." Today Bang practices the traditional art of sushi at Isumi, his Japanese-Korean restaurant.

***Isumi* Means "Fountain."** On commercial streets in Hudson County, Chinese restaurants abound; their fare is familiar to people of all backgrounds and ages. Japanese and Korean cuisines, by contrast, remain invisible to most "outsiders." At Isumi in Bayonne, diners like the young Korean couple here can enjoy sashimi, a combination of several kinds of raw fish served with pickled ginger, soy sauce, and wasabi. A Japanese and Korean husband-and-wife team run the restaurant. Mrs. Bang, the restaurant's cook, shown here with her customers, is Korean. "*Isumi,*" she and her husband explain, "means fountain: source of well-being, happiness, and good fortune."

Burgers. Russian sailors, the story goes, brought the recipe for steak tartare to Hamburg, where German cooks improved the dish by adding heat. Germans brought the hamburger to the United States in the 1880s. The hamburger on a bun is said to have made its first appearance at the St. Louis Exposition in 1904 when a vendor ran out of plates and substituted rolls. These frozen burgers at Burger King are evidence of late-twentieth-century America's love affair with mass-marketed beef.

Burger King on a Roll. Burger King and other similar fast-food chains serve America's common culinary culture. Like the fellow shown here, most workers are young, unskilled, and nonunionized and are paid a minimum wage. They are instructed to smile and be friendly. Burgers and fries arrive frozen from central distribution centers. They are computer managed and produced on a free-form assembly line. Computerized cash registers help speed the food to the customer.

Jewish Rye. You don't have to be Jewish, the famous Levy's ad instructed a whole generation of consumers, to love Jewish rye. Indeed, in supermarkets large and small, shoppers select from among an overwhelming array of packaged breads the flavor and ethnicity of choice.

Pizza as Performance Art. Nowadays pizza is as American as apple pie and—appearances to the contrary—more mass produced. While the owner of a Hudson County pizzeria is almost as likely to be Greek or Cuban as Italian, the materials for their pizzas come from the same cans of tomato sauce and the same plastic packages of preshredded mozzarella. In this West New York, New Jersey, pizzeria, pizza-in-the-making is theater, a prelude to the mouth-scorching first bite.

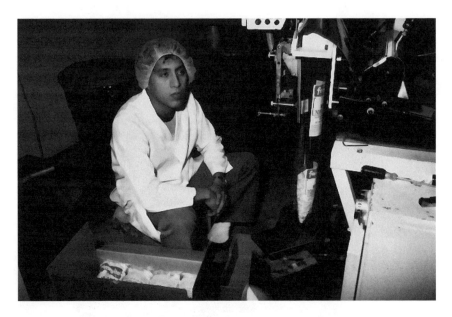

Famiglia. Daniel Inserra's new pasta factory in Jersey City bears the Italian name "Famiglia." But Inserra's pasta, designed in consultation with the French chef of New York's famous Le Cirque restaurant, is aimed at an upscale, postethnic market. In addition, "enriched" recipes are planned for school lunches and senior citizens' meals. The "beauty of the process," Inserra says of his new factory, is in the automated machinery. Perhaps the melancholy worker shown here fears that his days at the plant are numbered.

Pushcart Franks. Whatever the weather, Bobby Kalaidopoulos is out selling hot dogs on the corner of Newark Avenue and New York Avenue in downtown Jersey City. His customers are mostly young, black or Hispanic, and poor. The franks he sells are 28 percent fat. A Greek immigrant, Bobby came to Jersey City in 1975 to work for his cousin, who owns Helen's Pizzeria down the street. In 1981 he bought this Sabrett stand from his cousin and launched his own small business. Bobby's goal is to own a restaurant or pizzeria one day.

Long Beans at 440 Farms. This Asian shopper hasn't found her long beans at a Korean or Chinese store but at 440 Farms, an Italian American fruit and vegetable market in Jersey City. The Italian immigrants who established this business before the Great Depression began with a horse and pushcart. In later years, they sold a "standard" line of ingredients—onions and potatoes, peppers and tomatoes, oranges, corn, and zucchini—from a shed and refrigerated truck. Today, with Middle Easterners, Latinos, and Asians settling in the area, they also stock bok choy and *bacalhau*, malanga and mangos, okra, hot peppers, and fresh peanuts.

Wurst Works. The frankfurter-style wurst, or sausage, was invented in Germany in 1852. It appeared in German delis in the United States some three decades later. At Kocher's in Ridgefield Park, New Jersey, two tons of "authentic" beef franks are made each week, some for Kocher's own busy retail store and others to be sold in German-style shops that once made their own. On days when franks are not scheduled to be made, white-aproned butchers, often German speaking, can be found preparing liverwurst, specwurst, blutwurst, weisswurst, and other favorites of their pork-loving clientele.

OPAKAPAKA AND POKE, TOO

Honolulu, 2000

This is embarrassing. I am calling Alan Wong's, one of Hawaii's premier restaurants, at 11:00 on a Monday morning hoping to reserve a table for that evening. A New Yorker knows better. Alan Wong's received a James Beard award in 1996 as the Best U.S. Restaurant in the Northwest. The chef, Alan Wong, embodies the East-West hybridities for which his kitchen is famous. He is Japanese born, Hawaiian bred, and mainland U.S. trained, with Japanese ancestry on his mother's side and Chinese and Hawaiian on his father's. Wong's coffee-table cookbook, *New Wave Luau*, promises the likes of drunken duck on choy sum with mushrooms and roasted garlic smashed potatoes in a vertical presentation too dazzling to disturb either with chopsticks or a knife and fork. If I were phoning a restaurant of equal distinction in Manhattan, I probably wouldn't even get through to a receptionist; and if I did she would inform me quite snappishly that the first available reservation was three weeks from Tuesday. But Honolulu isn't Manhattan, my friend Marilyn protested earlier that morning, when I tried to wiggle out of making the call.

Now, on the other end of the line, a lilting "Aloha" greets me, fresh yet soft, like wind chimes or a muted guitar. I hesitate a second before asking about a table for two—on the early side, I quickly add, not wishing to sound disrespectful. There's pleasure in the receptionist's voice as she offers us a 6:30 seating at the chef's counter, facing the kitchen. It's the best way to enjoy Alan Wong's, she says, with four chefs cooking right in front of you.

Alan Wong himself slips into the kitchen without fanfare as we finish our first course: an artful ahi cake of eggplant layered with ahi tuna, onions, and tomatoes. The tuna and eggplant are silky in my mouth, buttery tastes balanced by a tart chile-lemongrass and goat cheese dressing. Eric, our server, alerts us to Wong's presence. It is part of his job, Eric explains, grinning boyishly, to make our visit a satisfying experience. He has given us his engraved business card, which reads

"Eric Leung, server," and has invited us to question him freely. When I ask his opinion about the exotic-sounding opakapaka, a pink snapper popular in Hawaii, he assures me that the house version, steamed with gingered vegetables in a truffle broth, is deservedly world famous. He adds, in case I require further encouragement, that the fish run leaner in the summer season. Eric is delighted by Marilyn's choice of another signature creation: grilled lamb chops (*carré d'agneau caramelisé*) with a macadamia-coconut crust, star anise sauce, and Asian ratatouille. To my question "Can an 'Asian accent' improve a French classic?" Marilyn flashes a five-hundred-watt smile.

We observe the famous chef, a chunky man with a calm, round face, oblivious to the kitchen ballet that swirls around him. He is preparing a loaf of smoked salmon with a creamy cheese, a Tuesday night special, he explains in response to our query. Marilyn and I both register a shock of (ethnic) recognition. Are we witnessing the mutation of Jewish New York's cream cheese and lox into a nouvelle Hawaiian–Pacific Rim delicacy? Eric, who probably hasn't heard that (some) New Yorkers have a genetically programmed cultural investment in smoked salmon, suggests we ask Alan Wong to autograph our menus. Politicians, tennis players, and rock stars acknowledge their fans in a similar fashion. We hesitate to interpose ourselves between the chef and his salmon. But our server, who knows the value of celebrity as well as the conventions of his workplace, prevails. When we move our menus toward Wong with apologies, he signs them with a flourish.

Honolulu, 1998

On my first visit to Hawaii in July 1998 I was a tourist with a mission. I was also an academic in transition, working in a liberated zone, as I liked to say. I remember my first awkward moment. Dr. Yoo, director of the Center for Asia Pacific Exchange (CAPE) in Honolulu, was introducing me to a group of Asian scholars at the center's eighteenth annual American Studies Forum. Reading from the vita I had sent him in the fall of 1997, he enumerated my degrees, publications, and teaching history. From my perch at the back of the room, I waved and smiled. I held the smile while twenty-two participants in the seminar Diversity in Contemporary America turned in their seats to acknowledge me.

The next morning I began the first session, as Asian protocol dictates, by handing out my card. As I did so, I made a confession. "All the particulars on my card are wrong," I said, "except for my name and the PhD attached to it. My institution has changed its name and e-mail address," I went on, "and I have just liberated myself from my institution." The word "retire" was too fresh—or too raw—to utter, but I was giddy with freedom. My students, aged twenty-four to sixty-four, looked grave. My tone was a touch too light. I hastened to reassure them that Hawaii was a fabulous field site for examining American diversity, on my own and in our sessions together. Unburdened, as it were, I was energized for work.

The eight-day forum was subtitled Collisions, Suspicions, and Coalitions. Most sessions focused on diversity's war zones: ongoing struggles by women, immigrants, and ethnic, racial, and sexual minorities for empowerment and respect. After discussing the achievements and costs of identity politics, I prodded the participants to experience the comfort zone of culinary multiplicity and munificence. The variety of foods and foodways in the United States, I asserted, is the soft side of diversity, the route beyond tense coexistence of embattled interests and cultures to creative fusion. The parts nourish and transform the whole.

I wanted to chase these Asian scholars down Diversity Road without leaving them in utter despair. Diversity, after all, is not a uniquely American phenomenon. By allotting the session's last laps to food, I hoped that the participants would cross the finish line smiling. Or, I hoped, at least they would learn something new about the United States and possibly themselves.

Eating in our fifty states, we Americans blur boundaries. In the restaurants of neighbors who are strangers, we devour pita and pasta, samosas and burritos, spring rolls and California rolls; we open up to difference without danger. How would the Koreans and Japanese who were attending the forum respond to our dietary *pluribus*? In a longer course, I might have handed out a list of "representative" restaurants with instructions to sample from columns A (ethnic), B (local/ hybrid), and C (fusion/Hawaiian regional), along with a set of questions for the explorers to mull over. My goal for this short course, however, was not to display diverse U.S. foodways. Since most of the participants had a scholarly connection to American studies, I preferred to spotlight their subjectivity in relation to food and diversity. What would they choose to eat? How would they interpret their choices? Without elaborate explanations, I asked the group to keep track of their meals—what, where, and why—and I promised to do likewise. During the closing session, listed in the course description as "Too Much Food for Thought: Eating, Ethnicity, and American Identities," we would see what meanings our data might yield.

Diversity eating has long been an addiction of mine. In pursuit of the meatiest moo shu pork long before that dish became a staple of every corner Chinese take-out, I scoured my neighborhood. If I missed trying one of the twenty-odd Chinese restaurants on Broadway between 72nd and 125th streets, it was because the place was too dark or the disinfectant too strong. Lasagna, French paté, paella, and suki-yaki also seduced me, not just as unfamiliar ethnic foods (we called them "foreign" when I was young), but as gateways to cosmopolitanism. Menus written in foreign languages conjured up romantic images of winding cobblestone streets, walled cities protecting ancient treasures, and serene Buddhist monasteries. They signaled an alluring world beyond the provincial confines of middle-class Jewish New York.

The Asian scholars in the diversity forum were not exactly at ease in my comfort zone. Almost immediately, the Koreans and Japanese sought out the foods of home. Most of the Koreans ate several dinners in Korean restaurants, and most of the Japanese did likewise. Both groups acknowledged the satisfaction they felt in encountering their own food traditions (sometimes well preserved, sometimes modified) in the fiftieth of the United States. When I am abroad, I almost never feel this way, although I know many Americans do.

During the sessions, some friendships were forged across national lines; and as a gesture of respect for their new friends, a few of the Japanese and a few of the Koreans crossed over to eat the cuisine of the other. I was aware that the foods of Korea have a presence in Japan, and vice versa. Still, I wondered, given the historic enmity between the two peoples, whether the border-crossers needed "friendship" to excuse their cultural transgressions.

More than half of the forum participants chose the Japanese or Korean breakfast (rice, soup, fish, and vinegary salads) on their hotel menu each morning. Almost everyone confessed to a daily need for rice. They all took advantage of the university cafeteria for lunch on days when classes were held, selecting a mixture of what they referred to as "Asian" dishes (rice based or with noodles) and "American" dishes (everything else: from pizza and couscous to pita-bread sandwiches).

Paradoxically, while the foreigners called everything they did not recognize as belonging to their part of the world "American," they were more precise when asked to identify "American" foods: burgers, fries, salads, and dry cereals, they all agreed. Some went on to mention fast foods and fat-free foods; a savvy Japanese professor with a PhD from the University of Hawaii added other contemporary American and distinctly Hawaiian-signature, fusion foods.

Forum participants understood that a course with "diversity" in its title required that they eat with at least a nod in that direction. Yes, they appreciated Hawaii's potpourri of culinary possibilities, in particular the range of Asian offerings. Intellectually, they honored choice. However, only a few liberated souls plunged into the fray. A mind-set of monocultural eating prevailed, except when necessity or convenience dictated otherwise.

Like the Asians, I ate as I usually do. So did my stepdaughter Shola, my companion on this trip. An artist and a cosmopolitan eater, Shola shares my passion for sashimi and salads of a dozen nationalities. And she shares my preference for small funky hotels, like the Manoa Valley Inn where we stayed, over larger, slicker, more anonymous places. The inn, a gothic structure built in 1915 and now on the National Register of Historic Places, has a genteel, neocolonial aura. Located off University Avenue, five minutes from the center of the University of Hawaii campus, the inn boasts a classic view of the Waikiki skyline—a solid wall of highrises that obliterates the beach and ocean.

Breakfast on the lanai (terrace) was informal but correct. The silver coffee service, delicate china cups, and platters lined with white paper doilies harked back to a time when guests would not appear for the morning buffet in cut-offs and bare feet. At breakfast here in Hawaii I'm a different person than I am at lunch and dinner; I feel closer emotionally to the foreign scholars at the forum. Early in the morning, my body is not yet open to the games my imagination and appetite subsequently conjure. It's not that I yearn for the foods of my childhood—the insipid cream of wheat or even the holiday morning French toast or smoked fish, canonical items for my parents. Rather, I am single-minded about wanting a "continental breakfast"—fresh fruit, croissant, yogurt, preserves, good butter, and plenty of strong coffee—like the one served at the inn.

After morning classes, Shola and I would grab a sandwich or a small salad and race off to the tranquil beach at Lanikai, twenty minutes by car but worlds removed from the touristic hubbub of Waikiki. We dined, as we would have in metropolitan New York, mostly in small ethnic restaurants—Chinese, Japanese, Thai, Vietnamese, Mexican, and Greek—that served well-turned-out, reasonably priced meals. After the day's exertions, we preferred eating in the (university) neighborhood or in Chinatown. No Waikiki glitz, no three-star chefs, no parking problems. In Chinatown we enjoyed dishes intended for Hawaii's large Chinese ethnic community; in our neighborhood, we were part of the residential and university mix, the ethnic-Asian-dominated rainbow that is Hawaii.

As an eater I am no less a creature of habit than the Japanese and Koreans who attended the forum. But that didn't seem to be the case at the time. Most of the Asian scholars were hard pressed to make sense of the cheerfully uncentered, open, multi-ethnic mode of eating I described as my own and about which I must have conveyed a certain moral superiority. Since the mid-1970s, my colleagues and I have been talking about American peoples and American cultures partly to avoid privileging the habits and values of white, middle-class society. This notion of the American *unum* as a permanent *e pluribus* was then only beginning to filter out of the academy and across oceans. It hadn't yet reached the non-American forum participants.

For the Asians, the foods of ethnic American minorities (especially Asian Americans) were not American. They were foreign, like their own foods. Thus, my (imperial) embrace of all these foods as belonging now, in some fashion, to America, like the global face of American peoples and the country's multiple cultures, seemed to them confused and chaotic. What had happened to the neat borders and simpler definitions of national cultures that still dominated their working vocabularies?

In a parallel vein I was surprised (and, dare I say, disappointed) by what I took to be the Asian scholars' timidity and lack of curiosity. We seemed to be polar opposites: the Asians, attached to their own culinary traditions, and the American, relishing her revolt against the confines of family foodways, celebrating her mobility in and around a globalized U.S. culinary mosaic.

It didn't occur to me then to tell the Japanese and Koreans that in their involvement with American studies they were the intellectually adventurous ones. After all, I limited myself to the study of my own continent and culture, while they allowed their minds to roam freely, to cross oceans. If only I had explained to them my suspicion that the parochialism of my career choice, in becoming a U.S. Americanist, was perhaps responsible for my roaming appetite. Like the foreign languages I relish speaking and the travel I crave, eating the world's foods—which are America's foods, whether in New York, Honolulu, or abroad—is a part of my balancing act, my unwillingness to be a provincial American.

The Asians understood their food predilections as authentic, tied to who they are. Secretly they must have seen my promiscuous palate as a character flaw, perhaps a cultural flaw of Americans generally: not knowing who we are, constantly reinventing ourselves. The result, one senior male professor came close to suggesting, is a culture of Gatsbys and golden arches: meretricious, deracinated, and grossly commercial. He might not have cared so much about what we are, he added, had he not feared for his grandchildren, with their obsessive attention to all things American.

Kauai, 1999

During the 1990s a cohort of talented chefs, Alan Wong among them, created what has become known as Hawaii Regional cuisine. Food writers sometimes call their "movement" Pacific Rim, Pan-Asian, East-West, or Eurasian. The chefs themselves, however, are adamant that their primary identification is with Hawaii. Some are island born, some are Asian immigrants, and some have relocated from Europe and the U.S. mainland. Yet in their kitchens and publications, all are Hawaii-proud cosmopolitans. They have built reputations for artistry by combining the freshest local products with the flavors and techniques of many national traditions. Describing his cooking, prize-winning chef Roy Yamaguchi, in his book *Roy's Feasts for Hawaii*, wrote, "My cooking is a blend of French, Italian, Thai, Japanese, Chinese, and Polynesian cuisines, with a few other influences thrown in for good measure."

The pioneers of Hawaii Regional cuisine have made it big. They write glamorous cookbooks and perform on the Food Channel. They are profiled in the *New York Times* and on the glossy pages of airline magazines as brilliant innovators; they are celebrated in Frommer's and Fodor's and Zagat's. For them, "Think globally, act locally" means marrying the best of Hawaii's produce and products with the techniques of the world's great (Asian and French) culinary traditions.

On my second trip to Hawaii, in the spring of 1999, I planned a tax-deductible ascent to this culinary Olympus. (Dinner at Alan Wong's a year later was the peak experience.) Among the chefs on my list were Yamaguchi, Sam Choy, Philippe Padovani, and Jean-Marie Josselin. Their fusion ambitions attracted me. So did the glamour of their establishments: the Hollywood-inspired fantasy of elegant eating as evidence of well-being. Beautiful food beautifully presented must be destined for beautiful people.

I remember a dinner at Jean-Marie Josselin's Beach House, overlooking the ocean at Poipu on the island of Kauai. Pink-purple ribbons of light shimmered in the evening sky. Marilyn, our friend Nancy, and I sipped Chardonnay in silence. Blissed out we were: the proper spiritual state for savoring the creations of a Paris-trained chef whose life changed when he found Hawaii. Josselin has a convert's passion for the Aloha State. In *A Taste of Hawaii: New Cooking from the Crossroads of the Pacific*, he celebrates the synthesis of the healthiest and most aesthetically appealing aspects of Asian, European, Polynesian, and Mainland American cuisines. What pleases our senses is also good for us, Josselin preaches. His wok-charred sea scallops with eggplant and a green curry coconut sauce—first heating, then cooling—did not disappoint. Nor did the old-fashioned pear tart with vanilla–macadamia nut ice cream. The smoothness and the firmness, the cream and the crunch were all synchronized in a perfect dessert.

A week later, still feeling nourished by emanations from the Beach House, I succumbed to a grand touristic folly. I purchased a time-share (for less than the cost of a decent used car, the saleswoman teased) directly across the road from Josselin's establishment. Every other year for one precious week, the Beach House would be my local restaurant. Or so I told myself. I did not tell myself that even the most celebrated dining rooms should be spared too much reality testing.

In the winter of 1999 I passed up my chance to use the time-share. Nor did I use it the following year, to mark the millennium. How do I explain this? The well-appointed Lawai Beach Resort, into which I giddily stumbled, resembles a mainland American watering hole. While there is no wrought iron gate with a security officer at the entrance, there is also no neighborhood: only the imagined community of other glossy-looking, big-spending U.S. tourists—the kind of people (with some of my own socioeconomic characteristics, I admit) I have never sought out.

Staying at Lawai Beach, I told myself, I'd be yearning for the "other" Hawaii. I'd want to drive off to Hanapepe and wander down its rinky-dink gallery row on the way to Waimea. Then, in Waimea, I'd want to stop at KJ's for sweet and sour pork and the down-home atmosphere. KJ's is a cafeteria-style restaurant boasting a bright blue linoleum floor. The proprietors, Joe and Paulette Grace, once owned a lunch wagon and catering service. Now their children, Kanani, Jonel, and Kamanu, manage the place.

When Marilyn, Nancy, and I stopped at KJ's for the second time, it was early evening and the TV was on. Two Polynesian men in their thirties, in surfers' shorts and flip-flops, watched the news as they ate; an elderly Filipina woman and her two middle-aged daughters, dressed in their Sunday best, lingered to catch a later program. Three little kids, members of the third generation of the Grace family, had their own entertainment; we watched them as they huddled around the computer, absorbed in a dinosaur game.

What a mixture of local foods at KJ's steam tables! Pork and cabbage, peppers with Portuguese linguica, shoyu chicken, sweet and sour pork, Filipino *pancit*, and Polynesian-style tripe were just a few. The three of us selected the first four items and snacked from a single Styrofoam plate. I ordered a small bowl of tripe and dealt with it alone. Marilyn asked for saimin, the classic noodle soup of Hawaii with chicken, seafood, and slivered vegetables. It was brought, steaming, from the kitchen. I picked up a plastic spoon and dug into Marilyn's soup. Nancy fixed on the banana cream pie, which she shared with Marilyn. When we ordered a second portion, Kanani, who was helping us, called for the pastry chef to come out of the kitchen; out stepped her nine-year-old daughter, DeeshanaLynn Tafiti. DeeshanaLynn, chubby with a shy smile, allowed us to take her picture holding a plate of banana cream pie. "She's really like Hawaii," her mother boasted: "a mixture of Tahitian, German, Portuguese, Samoan, and Hawaiian."

I wondered whether hanging around KJ's for a while would solve my Luau Problem. Young, pit-roasted pig, fussed over by beer-drinking friends and family and consumed under the stars, is one of my passions. The commercialized Hawaiian luau, however, is something else—a gaggle of mainlanders, as many as three hundred under a monumental tent, line up for their pig, taro-wrapped specialties, overdressed salads, and weak rum punch. The event (at $60 a head) includes a lecture with handouts and two hours of tourist-friendly hula. It's theme park eating in an ersatz living museum where tour organizers masquerade as docents. For a real luau, I need a world beyond tourism, a world that includes native Hawaiians and local people who out of generosity—and perhaps for some profit—are willing to absorb a mainland stranger.

The designation "local" is richly inflected. It refers to island-born and island-raised nonwhites. (Only those with Hawaiian ancestry can "correctly" claim to be Hawaiians.) Unpretentious and populist, "local" approximates the mythic *e pluribus unum*. In the realm of eating, "local" signals adaptation, the primacy of island realities, porous boundaries between otherwise distinctive groups. Like the omnipresent saimin (and poke, about which I'll have more to say later), local food, as Rachel Laudan evocatively describes it in *The Food of Paradise*, is creole food, the result of generations of improvisation and making do. It is the opposite of faceless, homogenized, supermarket staples. Of course it is American (starchy, fattening, and eclectic), and of course I include it in my comfort zone—unless Hawaiians would feel I was presuming too much.

Tourists may romp in "paradise," but my two friends and I enjoyed local food at the sufferance of locals. Hamura's Saimin Stand in Lihue is a down-at-the-heels sort of luncheonette with the status of a bona fide cultural institution. When the woman behind the counter served us our soup with disdain written all over her face, we understood. Maybe she was having a bad day. Maybe she thought we were slumming (and maybe we were) and were not worthy of their saimin and wouldn't like it anyway. Maybe she didn't give a hoot whether we liked it or not as long as they filled their stools each day and the cash kept flowing. (P.S. The saimin was tasty, but I wouldn't promote Hamura's to my mainland friends. Of course, they would go anyway, and I would want them to.)

Kauai, 2001

I finally tested Lawai Beach in May 2001. Shola, avid for hula as well as luau, accompanied me. Since I had arranged to pay for the time-share with automatic monthly credit-card deductions, I was spared the painful confrontation with myself that attaches to writing checks for a dubious enterprise. Still, I wondered how I would take to the other U.S. tourists at the pool, none of them, I imagined, reading a book I would care to borrow. Shola and I expected to swim and sun elsewhere. We planned long walks along a turbulent stretch of coast to watch the dolphins jump and the famous Spouting Horn erupt. The National Botanical Gardens were a mile up the road. A hula teacher whom Shola located on the Internet invited her to attend classes in nearby Koloa and Kapaa.

It was a fine plan, marred only by a return visit to the Beach House. The service was hurried that night, the crowd was noisy, and my grilled ahi tuna in a sauce of fresh tomatoes and ginger was sloppily plated and dull. Was Josselin's fancy establishment, like so many places, simply inconsistent? Could I have been so dazzled two years earlier by the waterside setting and the pink-purple sky that I misjudged the food? Had I ordered unimaginatively, wanting a light dish (after a big lunch) rather than an ambitious creation? Or was it something more perverse: with the Beach House so close at hand, had its glamour paled? Perhaps I had exhausted my ambition to collect world-class restaurant experiences along with a need to display my touristic competence—like good museum copies of jewelry.

After the Beach House letdown, Shola and I were eager to buy take-out and eat in—especially poke (pronounced "po-kay"), beloved as Hawaii's soul food. Poke, sold in ordinary food stores, fish markets, and neighborhood restaurants, is the most local of approaches to fish on the islands. It consists of small pieces of raw fish and seafood marinated in a mixture of soy sauce, sesame seeds, vinegar, salt, bits of cut-up vegetables, seaweed, or whatever the cook has at hand. (The "poke" treatment can be applied to vegetables as well.)

We stopped at Ishihara, a no-frills general store on the road to Waimea Canyon, shortly after noon the next day, thinking about ham and cheese sandwiches on whatever bread they were stocking. Lining up behind a pair of hefty, thirty-something contractors and two gum-chewing, working women, we considered our options. The guys ordered classic Hawaiian plate lunches: two scoops of rice in a Styrofoam box, covered with chicken in brown sauce, macaroni salad, and a few slices of bright yellow pickled radish. Cheap, filing, and fast, the plate lunch is available wherever locals eat.

The women took a different approach. From a selection of more than a dozen cold specialties, they chose salmon, tuna, and octopus pokes, a seaweed salad, a kimchi salad (made with cabbage), and two cans of Coke. We pointed to the same items in a refrigerated case of fifteen and substituted two bottles of water for the Cokes.

At a weather-beaten table in front of Ishihara, facing the road, Shola and I joined the two women. They smiled at us in an aloha-welcoming way without breaking the rhythm of their conversation. The younger woman, with a furrowed brow and raw-red hands, was complaining about her husband's bullheaded stubbornness. "Go your way, honey; he won't change," her companion kept repeating. "You do what you need to do, and don't look to him for saying yes."

"He's always into the bottle," the aggrieved wife lamented, "and he's either crushing my bones in bed or dead out, smelly and snoring." She glanced occasionally in our direction, confident that in the war between the sexes, we shared more than a taste for poke.

Our three containers of fish and two salads, which ran about $12, were enough for a light supper of leftovers that same evening, along with a bottle of Chardonnay, Finn Crisps, and a wedge of Brie. We returned to Ishihara two days later for another round of take-out: two ahi (yellowfin tuna) pokes, a salmon poke, and an intensely flavored snapper (opakapaka) poke made with ginger, sweet onions, and kimchi.

Poke invites invention by family cooks, merchants, and chefs. There are recipes galore, with canonical items based on tuna and salmon. However, the genre is open-ended and has lately been a focus for Hawaiian myth making. For the past few years, Sam Choy, the renowned Hawaiian chef and restaurateur, has been running Sam Choy's Annual Aloha Festivals Poke Contest, "pushing poke mainstream," as he puts it. His cookbook, *Sam Choy's Poke: Hawaii's Soul Food*, contains his favorite poke recipes from these competitions.

Tourists in general are not an ingratiating lot. I mask my own presumption with curiosity, glad-handing and forging ahead. One day I act like a member of an exclusive club, nurturing fantasies of entitlement that verge on the ridiculous. The next day I'm part of the madding crowd, stepping on toes without even noticing. A glutton for eating as experience, I pursue the chic and the simple, the global, the ethnic, and the luncheonette local. Occasionally, I get my comeuppance. The waitress's glance when I wrinkle my nose at her saimin is withering. Even if I'm right, I'm wrong. Can the good tourist unlearn habits and appetites of a lifetime? Is "good tourist" an oxymoron?

KITSCH ETHNIC

Paramus, New Jersey, 1995

It happens to me all the time. Shopping in the mall, I'm suddenly gripped by late morning hunger pangs that must be assuaged. My first thought is the Starbucks knockoff, where $2.75 will get me a disappointing cappuccino, which I'm likely to order rather than a perfectly acceptable regular coffee. After all these years, I still resonate to the mellifluous sound of the word *cappuccino*.

I remember standing at a coffee bar on the Via Veneto in Rome nursing a cappuccino. It was the end of my first year in graduate school, and I was eager for romance. A few feet away, a man with thick salt-and-pepper hair, fresh from his barber, ordered an espresso and smiled at me. A confident Italian man at home in the world. I did not imagine him then with a trim wife, kids, and a sexy secretary with whom he drank *Cinzano rosso* on Friday afternoons. But I did feel, incorrectly perhaps, that attention counts, even if the smile is more form than substance. Better the heated Italian forms, I remember thinking, comfortable with my stereotypes, than the cool indifference of northern Europeans. The cappuccino had served its purpose. I tilted my cup, savoring a greedy final sip of foamy milk. When I looked up, I was once again Mary Martin in *South Pacific* without Ezio Pinza: the Italian was gone, enfolded forever in the music of cappuccino.

This morning, however, more than coffee is called for. A bagel at the bagel shop would answer more directly to the gnawing I feel. But ever since bagelmania seized America more than a decade ago—severing bagels from their eastern European and Jewish origins—it's hard to find one that isn't too big or too soft, utterly tasteless or garishly overseasoned.

My body feels the heaviness of the bagel I have not eaten, and I consider running home for a salad and a few slices of fresh mango. But I've already fixated on Café Europa, where I'll surely order an oversized cheese quesadilla, served with salsa, guacamole, and sour cream. Of course, the quesadilla is more than my appetite warrants—and its lack of delicacy mocks my nostalgia for an "authentic" Mexican quesadilla, perfumed with *flor de calabaza*, squash flowers. "Three minutes," the Latino worker informs me, as he places a ready-made quesadilla in Café Europa's warming oven.

Enclosed by bistro-style tables, the wood-paneled Café Europa sits in the priciest corner of a high-end suburban mall. It features wraps with the flavors of the New World, North Africa, and Asia ("California," "Casablanca," "Teriyaki," "Chicken Fajita," and "Caesar"), paninis ("hot grilled sandwiches on Eastern European flatbread" with a similarly wide geographical spread), and transethnic salads. In addition, it offers beautiful chocolate cakes, cheesecakes, fruit pastries of a central European provenance, and decent coffee.

Europe still has a constituency among ladies who lunch at the mall and seniors who use the mall's interior streets as their free, all-weather health club. Hybrid Europe, with tentacles extending into Mexico, Japan, Brazil, and the American Southwest, is no less attractive. Perhaps the expansive reach of NATO and the European Union deserves the credit—or the blame—for Café Europa's transEuropean fare. Imagine, a magnanimous Europe mimicking an inclusive America! How can I mock a site of such (agreeably confused) political correctness? Even if the dark wood trim embodying "Europa" is more stage set than streetworthy, the place is my mall-entrapped oasis. It's my respite from getting and spending without the smell of grease and without the lines for fries and chicken McNuggets and other creations of America's homogenized culinary mainstream.

Paramus, New Jersey, 1990

Six-year-old Ruby and her mother, Dolores, are sharing an oversized Idaho potato stuffed to overflowing with chili con carne. I watch the pair from an adjacent table in the food court opposite the Hot Potato stand. Passing the Styrofoam plate back and forth, they finish the chili before attacking the potato. Finally only the limp brown skin is left, like a jacket abandoned on a bloody battlefield. Ruby pulls playfully on Dolores's red and black silk scarf and bounces in her chair. "Coke or California shake?" Dolores asks, picking up her daughter's signal. "You choose, and I'll have some of yours."

"You're a very good sport," I tell Dolores, unable to remain silent. After introducing myself, I say that I can't imagine my mother, a lifetime ago, putting her luncheon choices in my untrustworthy hands. Nor, for that matter, can I remember ever yielding so graciously to my son's requests. "Do you always like Ruby's selections?" "We usually do okay at the food court," Dolores replies. "Last week we had tacos with melted cheese at the Taco Maker, right over there," she says, pointing to a stall not far from Hot Potato. "And the week before that, we had shrimp fried rice with a roast pork bun at the Jade Fountain, on the other side, next to Nathan's."

Inevitably, they have their differences. "I just love spinach pizza with anchovies and olives," Dolores continues, "but when Ruby turns her big eyes on me and pleads, 'Double cheese, plea-ese, Mommy,' she wins. We had a fight at Molfeta's. It's Greek, right, so I wanted hummus and falafel with pita bread. Ruby was being stubborn. When she started crying for an onion bagel I almost lost it. 'We don't eat onion bagels at Molfeta's,' I told her. 'Bagels are Jewish. This is Greek.'"

I marvel at Ruby and Dolores's cheerfully experimental and egalitarian approach to eating at the food court. The routines my mother orchestrated for our shopping trips together might as well have been on another planet. On holiday afternoons, from the time I was about ten (in 1946), we would take the Broadway subway down to 34th Street and make our way east from Macy's and Gimbels to Altman's on Fifth Avenue. My mother would exhaust the two of us in her dogged pursuit of a well-made pair of shoes for me: oxfords, ideally brown, with strong laces, at a reasonable price. Afterward, she would offer me "a nice ice cream and a glass of milk" at Child's or Schraft's. In those darkened citadels of female correctness, ladies spoke in dulcet tones and wore pillbox hats and gloves even in summer. At Child's I encountered tea sandwiches, on white bread with the crusts trimmed, made with butter, watercress, and the thinnest slices of cucumber. At Schraft's, I became addicted to creamy, full-fat, coffee ice cream.

When our outings began in the morning and my mother was watching her pennies, as she would have said, we had lunch at Chock Full o' Nuts, in those days a paragon of cleanliness and efficient, "scientific" food management. There our routine was similarly fixed: two cream cheese and nut sandwiches on raisin bread, coffee for my mother, chocolate milk for me, and two whole wheat donuts. Occasionally, when I insisted, I was allowed to order an "impure" orange drink or one of Chock Full o' Nuts' famous frankfurters—all beef, the signs announced, and untouched by human hands. My mother's practice of Judaism did not require evidence of rabbinical supervision, only certain knowledge of no pork and no evidence of dirt.

From my childhood to Ruby's is a story of dramatic change in American life. My parents, teachers, friends, and relatives celebrated America as an exceptional nation, a true beacon of liberty in the world. New Deal liberalism, my parents believed, produced the most enlightened public policy. I came of age with the ideology of the melting pot, blind to its imperfections; Ruby's childhood is shaped by affirmative action, Martin Luther King Day, and Kwanzaa. I grew up being told what to eat, sheltered from the foods of non-Jewish immigrants and ethnics. Ruby is growing up with the culinary legacies of immigrants transformed into a national kitsch-ethnic cuisine. While I fought for choice, Ruby confronts too many choices at every turn: from multiplicity at the food court to the toppings on pizza, the flavors of bagels, and indistinguishable brands of cereals, sodas, candy, and snacks. I don't envy her that burden.

At Ruby's school in Englewood, first-grade students are routinely asked about their families' place of origin, the foods they eat at home, and the holidays they celebrate. Sometimes the children bring in different kinds of finger foods to discuss. They share Indian samosas, Colombian empanadas, Filipino spring rolls, Jewish knishes, and Middle Eastern falafel.

Six-year-olds like Ruby, going to school in multicultural communities, know something about eating their roots and their classmates' roots—as well as eating take-out from the local pizzeria and the local Chinese restaurant. In the face of this staggering diversity, I can't help wondering: Will Ruby grow up associating chili with Idaho potatoes and hummus and falafel with Greek cuisine? What will she make of the difference between the homemade products that her classmates contribute to multicultural celebrations and the kitsch-ethnic items at the mall?

Kitsch, as I use the term here, is a product of the commercial imagination. In the realm of food, it feeds on the nostalgia of certain ethnic groups and the sentimentality of others. Inauthenticity is its profitable hallmark. Taking their cues from pluralist politics, the food industries and their marketers are successfully transforming the culinary legacies of immigrants, refugees, and former slaves into a national kitsch-ethnic cuisine.

More American than apple pie, pizza is the queen of our kitsch cuisine, and I am as addicted as anyone. The economics of pizzamania are obvious. Cheap, available everywhere, ready to go, and easily devoured, pizza is the lunch and snack of choice for all but the moneyed, the snobbish, the big eaters, and the severely diet restricted. But consider this: even terrible-tasting pizza (doughy, with plastic cheese and thin, acidic sauce) is likely to come out of the oven smelling good, redolent of oregano and garlic and warm olive oil.

My own nostrils propel me, against all odds and in all sorts of venues, to nurture the fantasy of the succulent slice. The first blistering bite offers inconclusive evidence, but with the second, cooler and less aromatic, comes the knowledge that I've been suckered in yet again. Well, a slice costs only a dollar, or a dollar and a half, or two. I can afford to throw out the mess if I am feeling fastidious or cranky.

Nowadays, my friends and I take our pizza passion to an upscale bistro. There, at least, the dough will be properly thin and the sauce neither acid nor sweet. Perhaps the cheese will be local and the sausage imported from Italy. In such a pricey establishment, a complaint about the quality of the product may even get us a coffee on the house. Are we crossing a line here from everyday to elevated kitsch? Or are we somewhere else? If the ingredients are fresh and perfectly baked, if the pizza maker is a chef who trained with Alice Waters at Chez Panisse, and if the "slice" is an eight-inch oblong that costs $9.50, are we now in the realm of real food?

Fort Lee, New Jersey, 1990

On a hot summer afternoon in Shop Rite, no one watches as I fondle Gringo Pete's corn tortillas. Doubtless mothers with young children have flocked to the pool, and wage earners are still grinding it out. Two bent-over octogenarians search for the package of Mueller's macaroni that always fits so nicely on the third shelf of the cabinet to the left of refrigerator. I wonder whether their set-in-stone patterns are more efficient and somehow better for longevity than indecisiveness born of too many options?

Of the three brands of tortillas in the refrigerated area, only Gringo Pete's seem alive to the touch. Mission's tortillas look stiff enough to use as a dustpan after sweeping the kitchen floor, and Ortega's are garishly yellow, as if too much red dye number 2 had been dropped into the batch. But how can I buy a product with the name Gringo Pete's?

Perhaps it's just my "eastern" problem and I don't know Pete. Maybe all the folks in New Mexico have been listening to Gringo Pete on Santa Fe talk radio for the past five years now. Perhaps he's a local Paul Newman, doing his bit for children with AIDS, and I should be more than happy to eat his tortillas and support the cause.

Jersey City, New Jersey, 1989

The student cafeteria at my college resembles the food court at the mall. Pizza, tacos, burgers, chili, chicken fried rice, and Dunkin' donuts are all regular items on the menu along with the usual coffees and juices, ice creams, yogurts, and salad bar. At work, my ordinary fastidiousness about food yields to convenience and defeatism. I have saved a few minutes in the morning by not making a sandwich because I have shopped hastily and have forgotten sandwich bread, or because there is nothing to put on the bread except yet another round of boring tuna salad. I'm busy. Shopping on the run is a pain.

But who can bear the alternative—the cafeteria's greasy egg rolls, taste-free pizza, four kinds of leaden bagels, and a soupy chili with cardboard-like tacos? One bite of any of these is as bad as grading a pile of in-class essays. You get a mouth full of sawdust and nothing to eat.

Why are my colleagues and I not organizing to dethrone the institutional food-catering industries? Why is it that, year after year, we accept these insults in the guise of lunchtime convenience? In the process of teaching a first generation of college students how to make it in the system, have we forgotten how to buck that system? Are we so smug about our victuals at home—the pale pink veal and fresh Pacific salmon, mesclun salads, sweet cherry tomatoes from Israel, and French cheeses cut to our specifications? Or are we so beaten down by the higher education bureaucracy and by the erosion of our professional status that we regard the college workplace as inseparable from the food court and Burger King— just another sad offshoot of mass culture and mediocrity?

The problem is much larger than the university as an "industry" and my personal sense of displacement. Each morning, the newspapers inundate us with reports of billions of people subsisting on a dollar a day, increasing crime and drug use in our cities, and massive violence in Africa engendered by nationalism and racism. On TV every evening are soul-grating images of homelessness, malnutrition, and desperately ill people without access to health care. The globe reels from the forces of greed and heartlessness.

In this bitter time, it feels immoral to gripe about greasy egg rolls. It also misses the point. Still, the egg rolls are greasy and we do gripe. Next year in response to our complaints, the college will contract with a different caterer, and a new manager will add gyros and samosas to the traditional standbys. I'll eat in my office—a chaste yogurt or a tuna sandwich from the deli down the street—and I'll save my kitsch-ethnic bingeing for the food court at the mall.

KIMCHI PRIDE

Brookfield, Vermont, 2002

I load ten plastic containers and several Styrofoam-wrapped packages into the large red-and-white cooler: whole cabbage kimchi, radish kimchi, shredded daikon, spinach and cucumber salads, dried squid, sweetened dried fish, black soybeans, dried baby octopus, baby clams, japchae, scallion pancakes, and sesame chicken. Everything is double-wrapped in clear plastic, including the crack between the cover of the cooler and the base. I'd wrap my entire truck if I knew how. But to no avail. No matter what precautions I take, my Honda Accord will arrive at Rachel and Shale's place in central Vermont reeking of garlic, hot red pepper, ginger, and sesame oil. It will smell like another country, where I do my shopping: suburban Little Seoul, New Jersey.

My destination, sleepy Brookfield, Vermont, boasts a laid-back inn and a bistro-style French restaurant run by a New York expat couple. But it has no pharmacy, grocery store, or filling station, not even a 7-Eleven for an emergency bottle of Sprite. The summer crowd and the few resident cosmopolitans drive into Montpelier, about twenty-five minutes away, for the weekly farmers' market and a bustling natural foods supermarket. Dining out when the bistro is closed involves a half hour on the road and limited choices.

So when I offer to bring a dinner of kimchi (fermented vegetables and fish dishes mixed with red pepper, garlic, ginger, and sesame seeds) and other Korean specialties for a small gathering, Rachel is properly bemused. She and Shale have reckoned with kimchi only at a neighborhood restaurant on the Upper West Side of Manhattan and on excursions to Thirty-second Street west of Fifth Avenue, a stretch that Koreans have claimed as their own. "Will everything be spicy, seasoned to the max?" Rachel asks. "We're fine with the garlic and red pepper," she hastens to add. "Ditto for Ed and Curtis, who go for highly seasoned food as if it were prescribed for marathon training. But Gabriela is German, and her husband is from Maine."

Rachel is right to worry. Kimchi, which may be unexpectedly chewy or gooey, is an acquired taste for most Westerners, even for well-traveled, eclectic eaters. Many other Korean dishes are similarly challenging. I know. After a fifteen-year romance with Korean cuisine, I still haven't become accustomed to the overpowering odors and weird ingredients. Why, I wonder, do I persist in this uneasy relationship?

Leonia, Palisades Park, and Fort Lee, New Jersey, 1990

In 1990 Koreans suddenly became a presence in my small suburban town and in the nearby towns clustered around the Jersey side of the George Washington Bridge. Wherever we turned, they were opening restaurants and food stores, along with dry cleaners, camera shops, and martial arts studios. Eli and I, bored with bad Chinese and bland Japanese fare, began making the rounds of local Korean eateries, trying to get a handle on this pungent, foreign cuisine. No one was writing in English about the omnipresent kimchi and bulgogi (barbecued beef), and Koreans seemed diffident about explaining their food to non-Koreans. We needed help, more than waiters with limited English could provide.

I hoped for assistance from the glamorous Soojee, who buffed and polished my nails on Friday afternoons. Had Soojee remained at home in Seoul she would probably have been an assistant vice president for sales with a cosmetics company. Soojee had luminous skin, fine hair, a lovely oval face, and the aura of a Calvin Klein model. In 1989, when I first encountered her, Soojee had been in the States for three years. Gradually, she told me her story: six days a week doing nails, from 10:00 in the morning until 8:00 at night, then church on Sunday mornings and church picnics with the family on Sunday afternoons. "Work hard to buy house in good town," she explained. "My husband say no black neighbor. Good school for daughter. No drug trouble." The right suburban town, I understood, was a place with other middle-class Koreans, with Korean restaurants, food stores, and churches as well as sports facilities and college prep programs—essentially, a town like my own.

Emerging from the salon late one Friday afternoon, I caught sight of a white truck with large block letters announcing "Kim Chee Pride." Soojee's other world, I remember thinking. Soojee and kim chee, adaptation and tradition: two aspects of Korea in America. Kimchi (the more common spelling), usually made with cabbages and white radishes, is a mainstay of Korean cuisine. "Kimchi every day," Soojee once told me. "Kimchi is Korea."

Had Soojee's English been more fluent, she might have said that kimchi is an addiction for most Koreans, that no meal is complete without a few bites. She might have described the traditional, whole cabbage kimchi—a packet of crunchy-looking celery cabbage leaves (white at the base and pale green at the tips) slathered in a bright reddish mixture of radish, green onions, bits of black sponge seaweed, oysters, and red pepper paste. She might have connected kimchi to the traditions she wishes to pass on to her children.

Before I had Korean friends who could tell me these things, I relied on casual observation. The first Korean-owned vegetable stores in our area stocked several kinds of kimchi in jars of many sizes, and they offered a half dozen home-made varieties. Korean customers were avid for prepared kimchi, and shopkeepers did a brisk business with bottled and ready-to-eat items. All the Korean restaurants we frequented served at least one cabbage and one radish kimchi as an appetizer along with three or four other cold vegetable and fish dishes.

I was on sabbatical that year, writing at home. Eli, retired, was home, painting and writing. We were generally up by 6:30 a.m. and restless by 11:30. Driving a mile or so down the road, we entered an opaque Asian world, an English-free environment where the food was a conversation stopper and a conversation maker. Novelty propelled us. In Korean restaurants, the tastes were too new to us to be good or bad, only more or less surprising, more or less subtle, more or less mouth-scorching. After a half dozen forays into our local Little Seoul, Eli began lusting for the garlic and ginger, the low cholesterol intake, and the healthy balance between vegetables and meat.

At Keum Ho, we became regulars. Although no one expected us to eat kimchi, they brought it to the table as a matter of course, along with small dishes of cooked spinach, bean sprouts with sesame oil, cool (pepper-free) shredded white radish, tiny sardines, and cubes of tofu. On most visits, Eli and I were the only white customers. Everything was served at once, or as soon as the kitchen prepared a dish. There were covered bowls of rice for each of us, small bowls of miso soup to be sipped during the meal, and main courses ranging from noodles, barbecued meats, and casseroles of fish or meat and bean curd to dumplings, pancakes, and noodle soups.

As serious meat-eaters, Eli and I craved bulgogi, barbecued beef beloved by Koreans. Barbecue, a specialty of Keum Ho, was a do-it-yourself affair. Marinated pieces of beef, pork, chicken, or tripe were brought to the table along with a pile of bright green leaf lettuce. The waiter turned on the built-in gas-powered grill, and the noisy overhead ventilators leapt to life. We began by laying a few moist morsels on the grill, turning each one until minimally done, and then wrapping it in lettuce. Since bulgogi was about meat, we used lettuce sparingly. Tripe, when we ordered it, was especially savory, an unexpected grilling surprise.

I couldn't resist japchae, a delicate, slightly sweet cellophane noodle dish with julienned vegetables. "What, japchae again?" Eli would say, challenging my courage and curiosity. The challenge was good-natured. Eli knew my habit of falling into comfortable choices. He knew me, and I was lucky that he did. I didn't mind being twitted. In fact, I counted on Eli, in this and many other respects, to push me further than I would have pushed myself.

Chung, the round-faced chef and co-owner, always came by to greet us. "Everything okay?" he would ask, offering a handshake to compensate for his limited English. "Delicious," Eli would say, especially if he had ordered his favorite, kalbi tan, a zesty stew of short ribs made with only a touch of red pepper and garlic. "Great, just fine, thanks," I would say. A more complex response would have been confusing. It would also have compromised our status as those nice, tall Americans who love eating Korean.

On one visit to Keum Ho, a new waiter talked us into a special tofu and beef casserole, which turned out to be more peppery than either he or the menu promised. When Chung stopped by, he nodded at our daring choice and sent over a complimentary order of mandoo, Korean dumplings. "Lovely," Eli said to the waiter, "please thank the chef for us." We devoured the dumplings and saved (everyone's) face by taking the casserole home—to our own garbage can. Was it a fiery kimchi in the tofu and beef casserole that made it "special," we wondered?

I fretted about my kimchi problem. Since kimchi is "the real thing," the heart and soul of Korean cuisine, how could I fail to embrace it without feeling ungenerous—or provincial? Sometimes I told myself that serious eating involves discrimination. But I worried over how to disentangle my food preferences from other systems of culturally biased judgments, and how I might get beyond the confines of acculturation to something like a neutral palate.

Is Korean food more like Chinese or Japanese, friends used to ask when we suggested yet another Korean restaurant or described 1990 as "the year we ate Korean." "Is an apple more like a peach or a plum?" I liked to answer. Still, the resemblances between Korean, Chinese, and Japanese cuisines are more striking than the differences. Rice and soy products are essential to all three. Food preparation, in response to historic shortages of fuel, generally involves slicing, chopping and/or mincing a variety of ingredients so that they are suitable for rapid cooking—and for being eaten with chopsticks.

Nevertheless, when I pass a Korean restaurant at mealtime, my nose knows that the establishment is neither Chinese nor Japanese. The potent combination of garlic, sesame oil, hot red pepper, ginger, soy sauce, and green onions exploding through closed doors and windows is unmistakably, unforgettably Korean.

Soojee and her coworkers recommended the Hana Hana, a family restaurant on the top floor of a mini-mall in Fort Lee. Shoppers, who came to the mall to rent Korean videos or to buy antiques or children's clothes "in Korean," often finished their errands with the Hana Hana's famous seafood pancakes. On our first visit, I gave short shrift to the restaurant's long menu, some sixty items described in English and Korean, and ordered a salad of jellyfish in mustard sauce. "You're kidding," Eli said. "When I order jellyfish in Chinatown, you complain about the lack of taste; you talk about the slimy creatures that swam with us in Grenada and the nasty red marks they left on your thighs." "Yes, jellyfish," I told the waiter, pleased with my perverse choice.

"Real Korean dish," the waiter smiled approvingly. "Good for being sick."

With my first taste of the crunchy, shredded jellyfish, I felt the mustard blast through my nasal passages like Drāno. My eyes filled, my nose ran, and I coughed miserably. Water helped. Afterward, Eli laughed and I laughed and we turned in relief to the bland, slippery sea cucumber in brown sauce that had been his choice. Between bites of the sea cucumber, I picked gingerly at the jellyfish, breathing in the mustard before each tiny bite. We took home the leftovers, but not to save face. The next day for lunch, I added a half-cup of shredded celery and carrots and a tablespoon of mayonnaise to the mixture. "Will our waiter curse me for corrupting his food?" I asked Eli, "or will he just shrug?" "The waiter has forgotten us," Eli assured me. "But if the waiter's fifteen-year-old daughter were to add mayonnaise to the jellyfish, she'd be asking for trouble."

Leonia, Cliffside Park, and Fort Lee, New Jersey, 1991–1999

Eli died in August 1991, shortly after I had abandoned Soojee in Fort Lee for a more convenient nail salon in Leonia. I remember asking Joy, my bright-eyed new manicurist, about the paucity of Korean cookbooks in English. We were just getting to know each other. Joy looked at me strangely. Cookbooks were the last thing on her mind. Like Soojee, she was too busy working six long days a week (to support herself and her husband while he pursued an MBA) even to think about labor-intensive Korean cooking.

To the dismay of her mother-in-law, Joy told me, she bought kimchi in jars, Korean vegetables in cans, and noodle soup in packages at a local Korean market. In America, she said gravely, "women don't spend days in kitchen," and she had no intention of doing so. She did not want to be a Korean-style housewife, she confessed, knowing that I was a women's studies professor and would understand her rebellion. "I like work," she said, "not shopping and cooking and staying in house with kids and in-laws."

Often, when Joy took my long fingers into her small, competent hands, I delivered mini-lectures on multicultural families, the best and the worst of American education, and the changing lives of women. It was hard not to be the teacher I was—or the feminist researcher wanting to probe Joy's life history and examine how it differed from my own.

The day I told Joy about my students' journal-writing assignments, Christine, at the next nail station, rolled her manicurist's chair six inches closer and joined the conversation. "English is my passion," she announced. "I would like to be a translator or interpreter." A halo of springy black curls framed Christine's radiant face. Like Joy, she studied education and English at a college in Seoul. Feeling stymied because she did not want to teach, she "ran away from home—and Korea—at age twenty-one." That was in 1982, seven years before Joy's journey to the United States. Lonely in New York, Christine soon married a good-looking man she barely knew with a welcoming Italian American family.

Christine and I had our best talks in the waxing room, where she presided over my mostly naked body. While I assumed the position of the psychoanalytic patient, Christine did most of the talking. "Books nurture me," she said. "They lead me to myself." Edith Wharton and Jane Austen, with their seductive accounts of the marriage plot (and trap), were among her favorites. Recently she had discovered Simone de Beauvoir. America, Christine told me during another round of waxing, "is my magical place, a gift I gave myself in order to be a work in progress, unfinished."

When Joy and Christine opened a larger salon in nearby Cliffside Park, I followed them there. My weekly appointments were like an unexpected soup or surprise dessert. I could never predict what detail about my life or theirs would shape the conversation. "My women students don't want to be dependent on a husband's support or fidelity," I remember telling Joy. "They believe that feminism is about equal opportunity and having a career." I asked Joy and Christine whether the shop gave them a sense of autonomy. "To feel secure, I have to earn my living," Christine said. In fact, both women valued their moneymaking skills. They were also proud of their progress, moving up from salaried manicurists to shop owners. But neither woman confused owning a small business with having a career.

When her daughter was born in 1995 and her son less than two years later, Joy embraced motherhood as the great challenge of her adulthood. The children justified her migration, she said. Now that she had children of her own, she felt less selfish about abandoning family members in Korea for a more liberated life in the United States. Joy reduced her workweek to three days. Christine, also ripe for a change, began studying Korean-style massage. In a jiffy the partners agreed to sell Magic Nails to one of their employees.

In the summer of 1998, when I invite Christine to my house for a catch-up lunch, she arrives with her portable massage table. At forty, Christine has the slender shape of a seventeen-year-old, but she knows how to marshal her strength. I get a magical hour on the table, release from bodily tensions. Christine gets a modest chicken salad, dressed up with green grapes, almonds, and dried cranberries, and sliced mango for dessert. It's a diet-friendly, minimalist meal, the kind I make for myself. Remembering several abundant Korean lunches we've had together, I worry that my lean cuisine may be too lean for Christine's physically demanding routines. "It's hardly an even exchange," I lament. Christine brushes aside my apology. "Doing massage gives me energy," she says. "Massage is part of my yin and yang, part of my discovery of myself as Korean and American." After lunch, Christine holds forth about the encouragement she finds in Gloria Steinem's recent writing on the struggle for self-esteem. "Knowing Steinem," she says, "I know myself better."

"Why aren't Americans interested in Korea?" Joy asks me one day in autumn 1999. Joy, Christine, and I are lunching at Dae Bak, a Korean-owned "Japanese" restaurant in Fort Lee that serves Korean food to Korean customers. The Japanese part of the menu, at the front, is meant to bring in occasional Anglos. Sushi is a feature of this restaurant. Korean sushi chefs, trained in a U.S., Korean-owned sushi school, take pride in their presentation arts. The three of us have ordered hwe dub bab, described on the menu as "small bits of sashimi, lettuce, turnips, garlic, green pepper, and sesame oil, on a bed of white rice and served with a spicy red pepper sauce." The colorful seafood salad, in an enormous bowl with plenty of vertical heft, is a great favorite of mine. Koreans add generous doses of sauce, squirted from a plastic bottle, onto the salad and mix the ingredients thoroughly with a long-handled spoon. Even though I know it's bad form, I prefer to drizzle the dressing over the top and nibble a mixture of raw fish and greens. Rice is a carb I can do without.

Joy's question, with its uncharacteristic edge, hangs in the air. I have just returned from a Chinese American feminist conference in Beijing and nine days in central Asia. "You travel everywhere," she continues. "China, Japan, Nepal, Mexico, and many places in Africa. Why not Korea?" Suddenly we are in complicated waters. The immigrant from Asia who began her U.S. sojourn seeking to minimize cultural differences now wants those differences attended to. Joy wants Korea to appear on my map of the world. "Perhaps I will visit one day," I respond carefully. Joy and I fall silent after that, closeted in our separate speculations.

Joy's question comes at a curious time. I'm in the process of proposing a paper for a panel on the new Asian immigration. It will describe Joy, Christine, and their middle-class coworkers at Magic Nails. After almost a decade of playing accidental ethnographer, I'm eager to write about the salon and my friends. Christine and Joy's presence in my life—like an extended family, but without burdensome family dynamics—invites exploration. My children live far away; Christine's and Joy's parents live far away. The three of us are tied by affection and the accidents of geography. Propinquity is a powerful force, the impetus for my fascination with Korea-in-America. "Most of the time, professional opportunities account for my traveling," I tell Joy. "So far, no one has invited me to Korea."

Seoul, Republic of Korea, 2002

"Stay at Hotel Riviera after conference," my Korean American travel agent insists. "On classy South Side of Seoul," she says, "near shopping. Very busy. Many restaurants. Just like LA." Do I look like a woman who is going to Seoul to shop? Or is this a compliment? Could it be that the travel agent sees me in my narrow black pants, black sweater, and blazer as a Ralph Lauren woman rather than a frumpy academic?

This conference, in October 2002, is my chance to take Joy and Christine to Seoul with me—not literally, but in a literary guise. The Korean Society for Feminist Scholarship in English Literature has accepted my proposal to speak at the group's second annual international meeting. The topic of my paper is personal narrative as a mode of self-exploration and a means of connecting storytellers and listeners. As the subtitle states, it's about "Years of Talk at Magic Nails in Little Seoul, New Jersey."

Three days of meetings pass in a flash. My Korean hosts organize lavish meals, an afternoon of shopping for crafts in the specialty shops of Insa-dong, and an evening of spectacular traditional drumming and folk dancing. In between these events, we follow from a bound text as colleagues race through presentations that are always longer than the allotted twenty minutes. The whirlwind wipes me out. I look forward to the quiet of my own company at the Hotel Riviera.

Like every good hotel on the new South Side of Seoul, the Riviera is technologically au courant. When the bellboy hits the switch, the computer on my dressing table, in front of an enormous mirror, emits electronic greetings. After four nights in a university-run hotel, I'm grateful to be back online, reconnected. Little Seoul and Seoul have never seemed closer. But they are not necessarily similar. The hotel lobby teases me with its transnational, late-modern, nonspecific look. My Little Seoul, a meandering, multi-mile string of low-rise buildings and blocky Korean signage, seems more "Korean" to me than this slick watering hole and its posh urban surround. Ironies abound. I'm at a hotel with an iconic French name where the dining room menu is printed in Japanese and German as well as English and Korean and the hotel staff members speak better English than the Korean American shopkeepers in Little Seoul.

When I ask the doorman for directions to COEX, the new Korean World Trade Center, he promptly signals for a cab. "No," I say, "it's only a few blocks away." Tourists aren't supposed to walk in this gridlocked city of twelve million people, especially those staying at the LA-like Riviera. But fifteen minutes of crisp air, with the Han River visible across eight lanes of traffic, is just what this tourist wants.

COEX, like all major malls, is designed to mystify the occasional shopper. You have to be a regular to navigate this nonrectilinear underground of clothing and gift stores, fast-food joints, coffee bars, and banks. An unregenerate shopper (the travel agent was right), I take advantage of this free morning to meander and browse. My destination, the Kimchi Field Museum, remains open until 5:00 p.m.

I'm not in the mall twenty minutes before I've got food on the brain. Maybe it's the spatial maze that's making me hungry—or a lifetime of identifying shopping with snacking. This morning, ignoring the Riviera's big breakfast buffet (fish and sushi, cold meats, cheeses, breads, noodles, steamed buns, stir-fried vegetable dishes, and kimchi), I ordered yogurt with fresh fruit. The yogurt, presented in a frosted pink dessert dish with a sprig of mint and a red tea rose (tasting like the best New York Jewish sour cream), provided enough energy for my walk to COEX, but not for the emotional demands of this site.

The slight queasiness in my stomach says a definitive "no" to a couple of inexpensive quick-lunch counters and a darkened, upscale restaurant with an engraved, oversized menu on a stand at the door. Three young women in jeans are sipping coffee at La Patisserie when I claim a stool at the counter. On display are brioche, fruit pastries, triangular mini–layer cakes covered with dark chocolate, and a variety of bagels: plain, blueberry, garlic, and tarragon. I'm laughing at myself as I bite into the tarragon bagel, knowing I will hate it—and I do. The texture of the bagel (at $1.25) is cakelike, and the tarragon tastes stale. But the coffee is almost as smooth as Starbucks.

The Kimchi Field Museum is empty of tourists when I arrive. A narrative in the red-carpeted entrance explains that the museum is devoted "to the culture of kimchi as one of the best-known Korean foods." I look forward to being fed without eating, to feeling sated from kimchi while saving room for sushi or a sandwich. I look forward to postcards of kimchi in saturated colors, irresistible, making their way across the Pacific to friends on both coasts.

Indeed, the museum is a visual feast: a series of intimate, red-carpeted, beautifully designed spaces featuring the history, production, and diversity of kimchi. Among the multimedia displays are enlarged historical documents, a life-size installation showing the making and storing of kimchi, dioramas, plastic replicas, photographs, and cartoons and a video for kids. Everything is explained, in Korean and English, crisply and clearly.

My favorite installation is a group of dark wood cabinets with tightly fitted doors, built into a wall, housing garlic, red pepper, ginger, and sesame. I open each door and peer into the unlit spaces, where the seasonings and spices give off their fresh-smelling, distinctive perfume. In the home of ginger I close my eyes and imagine a luxurious bath. Thinking of a ginger soap I once bought in Hawaii, I feel refreshed. How ingenious these cabinets are. The odors that are essential to the story of kimchi do not overwhelm the Kimchi Field Museum.

When I get to the tasting room, I wonder whether the museum is odor free because this room is deserted. Tastings, a guide tells me, are usually held only for schoolchildren or adults on tour groups. Still, what's a kimchi museum without the real thing? On a counter directly in front of the tasting room, I notice two tiny plates with tidbits of radish kimchi under clear plastic domes. I grab a toothpick and lift one of the domes.

In the museum library, I browse through magazines, children's books, scholarly publications, and beautifully illustrated cookbooks, all but one in Korean. The young curator in blue jeans offers to e-mail me visuals of the installation for a newspaper article I tell her I'm writing. "People in New York and New Jersey who know kimchi will be interested in your museum," I explain. "Korean food is discussed on the food pages of the *New York Times*," I add. Do I detect my parochial perspective at work? Am I trying to impress this young woman with the attention my country's press pays to Korean immigrants in the United States and their foods? Not exactly. I've been well fed, and I wish to give something back. The curator is a cultural anthropologist and food specialist. My anecdotal data on the global impact of kimchi addresses one of the themes of her collection. As a Korean and a professional, she is pleased to be on our American map of world eating—just as Joy is pleased, for similar and different reasons, that I'm now in her homeland.

I spot Kyoung Hue, Christine's sister, as soon as I emerge from the hotel elevator. Perhaps I should say, since we haven't met before, that I spot a woman in student gear—jeans, crewneck sweater, red ski jacket, and a backpack slung over her right shoulder—and approach her with confidence. Like Christine, she has an open, eager face and seems easy in her body. Kyoung Hue tried on her nicest clothes before meeting me, she confesses in an e-mail message some months later, but ended up picking the most boring ones. Christine certainly would have dressed for dinner. Still, Kyoung Hue's impulse to be natural, to be herself, reminds me powerfully of her sister.

Fifteen years younger than Christine, Kyoung Hue grew up in a more prosperous and sophisticated Korea. From 1998 to 2001 she lived with Christine in New Jersey, working and studying English. From time to time she saw Ryan, her Canadian boyfriend, whom she originally met in Korea. Now she shares an apartment with him in Seoul and is finishing her undergraduate degree in English.

I've chosen the Riviera's fancy restaurant for our meal, mostly because it's my last night in Korea. Shiny black tables, minimalist white china, and very bright lights are softened by Korean jazz on the sound system. I would have preferred earth tones and tablecloths. We order lightly: beers, shumai, salmon with ginger and bean sprouts, and a noodle dish. Four miniscule and uninteresting kimchis are set before us. With the second sip of beer, we're joking about Christine's devotion to journal writing. "If I call her at 9:00 a.m.," I say, "she'll be scribbling away, exploring the newest balance between her Korean and American self."

There's no ice to break. "My sister is different yet same," Kyoung Hue says. "She fought my parents for herself. I don't fight hard to be free. My parents let me go. They like my Canadian boyfriend." Kyoung Hue doesn't have to escape from Korea to define herself. "In the States," she says, "I thought I'm a very conservative, bull-headed Asian. When I came back, friends kept telling me I am not me. Changed too much. They are right. The new culture made me flexible."

For the time being, Kyoung Hue plans to remain in Seoul with Ryan, who has been teaching English. Perhaps they'll start a tutoring business in Korea, where opportunities for both of them are better than in North America. Kyoung Hue mentions that she had invited Ryan to join us for dinner, but he was busy. "I was expecting him to fill up blanks in conversation," she says. "But we don't need help."

We have a second round of beers. "I'm sorry the meal is quite ordinary," I say. "One expects more from such a slick, upscale restaurant." My lament, automatic under such circumstances, sounds silly the moment I utter it. Slick rarely translates into good. Had I chosen a less upscale place, we might have been served a better meal. But I doubt that it would have improved our connection. "We have made rich side dishes with talk," Kyoung Hue responds.

Little Seoul, New Jersey, 2004

I linger among the pomegranates and Asian pears at Han Ah Reum, a huge Korean supermarket and mall about fifteen minutes from my house. I imagine the crisp, white slices of pear sprinkled with ruby pomegranate seeds on a bed of arugula, topped off by walnuts—an ideal summer salad. But these aren't the items that lure me to Han Ah Reum. Asian pears and pomegranates are available at Julio's, my local fruit and vegetable boutique. Korean-owned Julio's, however, caters to well-heeled, orthodox Jews whose chatter about preparations for Shabbat plays havoc with my complacent secular identity. If only I could have Mozart with my fruits and vegetables instead of residual guilt. At Han Ah Reum, the indecipherable sounds of Korean allow me to be present in the present.

In the fruit department I ready myself for the real task at hand: a slow tour of the kimchis and other in-house-produced vegetable, fish, and seafood products. Just as tennis players need a warm-up to find their rhythm, I need this transition time to think garlic, sesame, ginger, and hot red pepper. Walking past the fish department, I notice a forty-something woman shopper checking the liveliness of blue crabs in a bin. She pokes at them roughly with long tongs, picking up one after another. With her jaw clenched, she bangs on their shells and pushes them around like hockey pucks. I wonder what arcane—or ordinary—knowledge of the species she possesses. I wonder how she treats her house pets. I wonder whether she's in a rage about her daughter's hair color or pierced belly button. When the woman finally dumps two crabs into a plastic sack, I breathe a sigh of relief and move on.

Beyond the fish department are the freshly made kimchis. I confront a dozen powerfully pungent red, brown, and dull green items, all gooey and full of heat: oyster kimchi, salted pollack roe kimchi, salted cod-gut kimchi, sesame leaf kimchi, chili pepper leaf kimchi, radish leaf kimchi, pickled baby shrimp, and pickled anchovies. Once upon a time, I regarded these exotic comestibles with awe. But this afternoon, my gut resists the invitation to adventure.

The moment for extending my kimchi repertoire, as my Buddhist son would say, is not auspicious. I've come to Han Ah Reum without a mission, hoping to find inspiration in research. On this hot summer day, only salads speak to me. Han Ah Reum overwhelms my modest needs. Perhaps at one of my local Korean shops, where food isn't mixed in with cameras and comforters and pricey woks (all artlessly displayed), I might have bought a cool daikon kimchi or my favorite, a mild, cooked spinach salad. Maybe the woman behind the counter would have encouraged me to buy seaweed snacks with salt and sugar, and I would have returned home amused.

It's normal, I know, to find strange foods disgusting. It's normal to be repulsed by the ugly head of a monkfish, a mushy order of eggplant, a salad that is drowning in dressing, or an aged parmesan cheese that smells suspiciously like vomit. Repulsion illuminates attraction. Disgust deserves an honest reckoning.

How do I explain the onset of this insistent inner voice saying "Not me, not my taste"? Has my comfort zone narrowed without warning? Am I responding like an old lady who says "No, I won't wear purple any more" because it doesn't work with her newest hair color?

Certainly I've been ambivalent about the characteristic tastes of kimchi, especially the astronomical endowment of garlic and hot red pepper, from my first anxious bites fifteen years ago. The wake-up taste of fermented cabbage, which I sometimes crave, is bitter and intense. That strong smell will forever be strange to me even as I cheerfully dig into the small dishes on the lunch table—or into an order of kimchi pancakes or dumplings with kimchi. Unlike most of my friends, I cook with very little garlic. In Italian restaurants, after enjoying sautéed broccoli rabe, I lament the choice; the taste of garlic lingers in my mouth despite chewing gum, strong coffee, and peppermint toothpaste. In Mexico, I prefer admiring powerful poblano chiles in the market to ingesting them at dinner.

Nevertheless, my kimchi flirtation continues. I keep coming back for more— even as I suspect that this lover is not for me. Kimchi challenges me: to distinguish myself from the monoculturalists; to break out of the confines of a parochial Euro-American palate; to do better than "tolerate" the huge cultural difference between how I ordinarily choose to eat and how Koreans eat.

"These days I eat 80 percent Korean, 20 percent American," Joy tells me over the phone after my return from Han Ah Reum. She says this in response to my lament that after all these years Korean food remains unfamiliar and mystifying to me. We know each other well enough that I want to speak truly. I want to confess that at Han Ah Reum my responses to kimchi bordered on repulsion.

I want to tell Joy about my early days of shopping with Eli for meat during our stay in Tunis: bloody heads of cows hung in front of the stalls, signifying freshly killed beef. How could I rejoice in the fresh kill in the face of blood still dripping and with tripes hanging out, oozing? It was early fall, and the weather was still quite hot; I remember protecting my nose against the pungent livestock smells and clamping my mouth shut. Meat was displayed on ice—we saw no refrigerators. So we didn't buy. For weeks we didn't buy meat—until we began shopping at the Marché Central, where we noticed working refrigerators.

"I've been eating Korean food about as long as you've been eating American," I tell Joy. "Since 1989." How long does it take for one to accept as "normal" a very strange cuisine? Does such a cuisine ever become "normal"? Much as I do not tire of good Chinese food, I don't want steamed buns or gruel-like soups for breakfast. At a certain point, I do not want any more wok-cooked vegetables, and I do not want my chicken or pork in a brown sauce. At a certain point, I yearn for meats simply grilled or broiled or pan fried: foods that are not too rich or spicy or heavily sauced. This realization surprises me; these sound suspiciously like the foods of my youth: the boring lamb chops and steaks and the unadorned vegetables, foods I've spent a lifetime attempting to improve upon. Is there a lesson here? Perhaps the diet of childhood, like a first language, is too deeply imprinted to be willfully sloughed off. Perhaps it's easier to add on kimchi, as women my age long ago added pants to our wardrobes, than to deny the fomative impact of family foodways.

On the phone with Christine, as we plan our next lunch together, I introduce the notion of disgust. I describe my last visit to Han Ah Reum, where the authentic Korean "raw materials" for stews, sauces, kimchis, and dipping verged on repugnant. I tell Christine that it's more important than ever to eat Korean foods with Koreans. I need their help in exploring my kimchi problem.

Pangane, a restaurant in Fairview, New Jersey, where we agree to meet, "might not have a sign in English," Christine warns. "But you'll see an old-fashioned wooden door and an ethnic façade—like the entrance to a temple." The interior of Pangane is spacious and plain, half of it given over to low, traditional tables set for groups of eight. Joy, Christine, and I are seated at a Western-style table for six, with no other diners nearby. The limited menu, printed in Korean on white paper placemats, lists three lunch specials (at $7.95 to $8.95) and a handful of pricier dinner items. Christine and I both order the goat stew; Joy chooses Cornish hen stuffed with rice and dates in its own broth.

Six small vegetable dishes appear, including a conventional cabbage kimchi and a crunchy, bland winter cabbage kimchi served in a water-based liquid. We nibble unenthusiastically. Our main courses arrive in sizzling black crock pots. Dok bae gi, stewed goat with vegetables, Christine says, used to be made with dog in Korea. Koreans valued dog for the great energy it was said to give. A very spicy red dipping sauce with scallions and sesame seeds accompanies the goat stew. Roasted salt mixed with a bit of pepper is served with the Cornish hen.

The pale Cornish hen reminds me of my grandmother's underseasoned, dreadful-looking boiled chicken. "I would never order a dish like yours," I tell Joy, explaining my associations. However, after my first taste of the goat (with bitter greens from radish tops) and a bit of the intolerably hot sauce, I welcome a small portion of Jewish-Korean comfort food.

The stewed goat (which I try not to prejudice by thinking about dog) isn't as unpleasantly fatty as versions I've eaten in the Caribbean. The hot sauce, I decide, is a problem; ditto the bitter greens. In fact, Joy's salt and pepper combo works beautifully with bits of goat. Relaxing into the goat soup, I enjoy a dense, intense meat broth, like beef but a touch gamier.

Christine celebrates the goat dish as authentic. "Like my mother's cooking," she adds, "Not from Seoul." Joy agrees that our dishes are country fare, not modernized for hip urban consumers. "All the customers in the restaurant"—there are maybe fifteen others—"are in their forties and fifties or older," Christine observes. "This is food for our generation," she adds, "not for those techie Koreans who have cameras with cell phones and messaging built in." Having figured out how to enjoy the goat stew, I dig in.

Driving home along Main Street through Fort Lee, I note for the umpteenth time a photo shop, Korean owned, called Shalom Photo. I assume that Koreans bought the place from Israelis—or something like that. Still, why would Koreans add their logo, in Korean, to the name "Shalom"? What does this mean—that two constituencies are better than one? That the Israeli has remained a junior or silent partner?

The sign echoes other unlikely ethnic mixes, including the Indo-Pak combination one sees in Jersey City. A Korean-Jewish blended photo shop, however, pushes the unlikely to new heights. I suppose Koreans, with their entrepreneurial talents, have been compared often enough to Jews. Perhaps the sign at the photo shop is signaling more than just a history of ownership.

The word *shalom* means peace; the greeting implies welcome, as in "Shabbat Shalom," welcome to the Sabbath. Are the Jews welcoming the Koreans? Are Koreans identifying with Jews? Is there profit to be made from this name?

What about my own sense of welcome—and its relevance for eating? For many reasons, I welcome Koreans to my neighborhood, which was never very Jewish but once was white. Their reputation as hardworking, ambitious, educated, upwardly mobile immigrants with tidy habits serves them well. They improve their houses, beautify our streets with their flower gardens, and raise standards in the public schools by demanding disciplined study and high achievement from their kids. Clever and efficient businesspeople, Koreans in my community run first-rate dry cleaners, greengroceries, nail salons, and convenience stores. Their politeness and sense of service put native-born business owners and employees to shame.

Koreans are slow to integrate because of language limitations and because they have their own welcoming and supportive communities. Relationships require work. Food, chosen with the other's comfort in mind, is the bridge; language is the barrier.

What do we hope for from neighbors who are strangers? Most of all, that their presence and institutions enhance our American crazy salad. This was the lure of kimchi pride. Suddenly, in the late 1980s, Eli and I found our neighborhood infused with novelty and strangeness. We found that we could "add on." The Korean restaurants that Eli and I began frequenting in 1989 and 1990 enlivened our daily routines; they added zip to our midday lunch and broadened our options for moderately priced dinners out.

"Adding on" is the pluralist model, the mosaic. In Hawaii, where the Asian-Anglo mix is different and more long-standing, kimchi is more integrated. It's on the plate lunch and among the cafeteria offerings.

I can add on just fine. It's easy, almost too easy. What I have trouble with is integrating, making Korean food my own.

Maybe this integration is too much to ask, and it may be unnecessary. After all, I don't consider eastern European food my own, or Chinese or Mexican or even Portuguese. However, none of these are as challenging to the palate as Korean food—and none are so palpably with me, on the streets where I live.

Here in my neighborhood, where an amazing variety of Korean foods is readily available, I have a rare opportunity. It's tempting to return time and again to these shops. Parking is available, the shops are spotlessly clean, and the salespeople, even when they can't say much in English, are generally friendly. Informants who are friends offer to shop with me and answer my questions. Korean cookbooks (now commonplace in English) help me make sense of what I am seeing, ordering, and eating. Labeling in English is becoming more ordinary.

I can experiment freely in different settings almost without risk. When I gamble on foods that are not to my taste, I shrug and throw them out. Given the relatively high standard of hygiene in Korean restaurants and shops, I don't worry about the body's revenge. There's a plethora of choices, no pressure to eat some weird dish or go hungry. I'm in control of the options.

Han Ah Reum is putting on its Sunday show. A thirty-foot-long kimchi table is set out with a dozen (mostly) red mixtures, many featuring fish or seafood, and many of the gooey-looking variety. Behind the table two tall, pretty young women fill plastic containers for customers and two older women package freshly made whole cabbage kimchis. Most of the items for tasting are labeled in English and Korean. I make my way down the table, tasting every other dish. The first, an aggressively salted "salty pollack," is bright red and slippery. I spear it with a toothpick. The dried and reconstituted pollack has an easy, chewy texture, a bit like fresh squid. But the flavor of the pollack eludes me; I taste only salt, garlic, red pepper, and sesame oil. The same is true of the salted squid, the bellflower and cucumber, and the spicy mixed skate wing and vegetable.

I ask one of the young women behind the counter about the "seasoned Perrila leaf"—flat and dark green when cooked, with a resemblance to the sesame leaf. Shaking her head, she lets me know that it is a mystery to her too. The bitterness of the Perrila leaf and the intense salt and fermentation catch me by surprise. At home, I would have rushed to the bathroom to spit it out. Is there a water fountain nearby? (Of course not.) What to do? I propel my almost-empty cart around the nibbling shoppers and their frolicking kids toward the puffed rice cake machine where nine-inch rice cakes explode out of the old-fashioned contraption throughout the day. Samples are usually available in a basket nearby, and I grab the biggest one. My mouth calms down. The bitter-salt taste recedes.

I circle back toward the prepared foods, noticing five-pound plastic bags of ground hot red pepper and five-pound jars of cleaned garlic cloves. Amazing! At two small tables, beef, pork, chicken, and squid are marinating in a spicy barbecue sauce. After the intensely seasoned kimchis, the cooked beef I sample seems delightfully mild. An Anglo man in his thirties standing next to me urges me to try the pork. "It's perfect," he says, "especially with these." He waves a container of kimchi-style cucumbers in my direction. "Yeah," I say, "I love them, too." I do.

In my shopping cart is an Asian pear, ideal for a salad, along with some mesclun greens, cherry tomatoes, and New York strip steaks. I don't anguish over today's kimchi road not taken. For a long time I have assumed mistakenly that my fascination with Korean food should lead to embracing it all. Nonsense! Choice is part of living. In the supermarket I systematically boycott sugary cereals and soft breads, canned vegetables, frozen dinners, processed cheeses, chocolate bars, layer cakes, soda, and instant coffee. I deny myself ice cream for months and then give in to Ben and Jerry's newest chunky innovation. I rarely buy fish, but dark-meat mackerel sings to me. Cilantro is a sometime passion. Clearly, I have preferences, aversions, and inconsistencies wherever I eat, in whatever tradition.

In truth, I don't need a Pathmark supermarket in my life, but I'd hate to lose Han Ah Reum. Let a thousand kimchis bloom. I'll pick and choose and promote my favorites to friends. I'll wrap the containers holding strong-smelling foods in extra plastic and find room for them in my refrigerator. But not today.

Part 3

A GLOBAL APPETITE

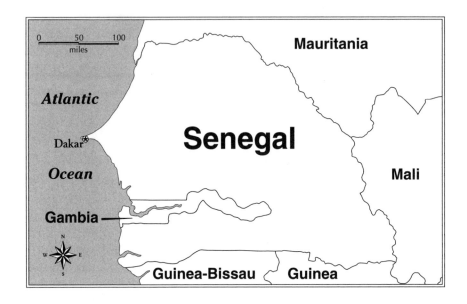

THE REAL SENEGAL

On the Outskirts of Dakar, Senegal, 1976

At the luxurious Hotel Ngor, on the Senegalese coast facing the Atlantic, Eli and I begin lunch each day with a perfect mango. The gleaming orange flesh, carved into a crown of cubes and triangles, is sweet, firm, and silky smooth in the mouth. Each bite releases in us a flood of French superlatives: *étonnant, parfait, merveilleux, incroyable, extra.*

Chedli, our regular waiter, beams in response to this extravagant but heartfelt praise. It's for him, too, he feels. After all, the incomparable mangoes are fruits of his earth. Planted and tended by brothers and cousins, they pass through his hands to our table—his altar—like proud offerings. We eat as if blessed, and Chedli also counts his blessings. Serving us is easy, he says; *vous me comprenez, vous aimez mon pays,* you understand me, you like my country. He wants us to know that hassles and verbal abuse are more common than compliments, especially from hotel clients who do not speak French.

At breakfast the previous morning, we had intervened in a small war between a group of African American tourists calling out to waiters in English and the waiters pointedly ignoring them. Our American compatriots would like their orange juice and coffee, Eli explained in French to the headwaiter, using the polite (and correct) subjunctive to mollify him. My waiters don't like being treated so rudely, the headwaiter replied, smiling at us. It's a misunderstanding, I said, as I watched the hurt turn to anger on the face of a social worker from Atlanta. These Americans are so eager to know your country. *C'est dommage, vraiment,* it's too bad, really. They just don't have the words, *la langue,* to make themselves clear.

Chedli's inflections and rhythms in French are different from Eli's and mine, and we often ask him to repeat a word or phrase. French, the official language of Senegal, is Chedli's third language, the one he uses only with foreigners. He is a modest man, not loquacious, but amiable and open. We ask about his family and volunteer information about our New York origins, our children and professions. The talk is simple, larded with politesse and platitudes on both sides. Yet we settle comfortably into the routine, inventing bonds, as eager tourists and affable hotel workers often do.

th day at the Ngor, Chedli takes us by surprise. He invites us to
use the following afternoon to meet his two wives and children and
. We are moved and delighted by the gesture; we tell Chedli we will
consu... late books and let him know in a few hours.

I visualize the scene at Chedli's. After a wicked taxi ride, bumping along dusty roads, we approach a cluster of mud huts with thatched roofs. Tropical sun invades the taxi, and I feel my uncovered arms beginning to cook. Flies buzz in the stillness. Chedli's family is waiting for us, perhaps beneath the lone mango tree in a browned-out courtyard. As we emerge from the cab, neighbors gather in front of Chedli's house, grinning and chattering. The children have slightly swollen bellies and beautiful white teeth. No one except Chedli speaks French. We are offered places of honor in the courtyard: two squat, hand-carved stools. *La maison est très chaude*, the house is very hot, Chedli explains, inviting us to peek into their dark, one-room hut with a dirt floor and no real window. Cold drinks and unfamiliar foods are pressed upon us with great ceremony, and we are unable to refuse. Eli distributes cigarettes to the adults and chewing gum to the children. We both smile until our jaws ache.

In Chedli's family compound, beyond the confines of the Hotel Ngor, the "real" Senegal awaits us. But the bitter truth is this: I am a false adventurer, squeamish about insects and repulsed, each time we venture forth from our air-conditioned retreat, by overpowering smells of sweat and sewage. A week before, during an American studies conference in the Ivory Coast at a five-star hotel with interior waterways and an ice-skating rink in winter, a stomach virus laid Eli up for three days. Now I am afraid of the drinking water, the crockery, and the food of poverty.

Eli and I thank Chedli profusely for his invitation. We send warm greetings to his wives and best wishes from our children to his. I reach for Eli's hand before explaining that we must be in Dakar the following afternoon for a last visit to the National Museum before returning to New York.

THE POLITICS OF COUSCOUS

Tunis and Suburbs, Tunisia, 1978–1979

We have rented a white house with sky-blue shutters on a rocky outcropping facing the Mediterranean. It is a serene retreat, twenty minutes by car from the Tunisian capital and my job at the University of Tunis. I open the shutters each morning to catch the rising sun and the sounds of the advancing tide. From our living room, french doors lead onto a red-tiled terrace, where I sun and doze and fret over unfinished lectures. The broad, sweeping beach, empty from October through April, is two flights of stairs below. On mild days, I watch our neighbor Françoise adjust the angle of her well-toned body as she zips across the horizon on a yellow windsurf.

When friends drop by on weekend afternoons, Eli and I load a tray with tiny black olives, salted almonds, and glasses of local red wine and head for the fresh sea breezes. Two carved stone benches, mimicking the ruins of nearby Carthage, are our coffee table. We flex our lips, preparing to do battle in French. Tunisia was a French colony until 1960, and the imperial imprint remains in street signs, wine drinking, touristic amenities, the university curriculum, and *la langue française*, which dominates international exchanges among non-Arabic speakers.

Some evenings we walk barefoot along the water's edge to La Poissonaire for platters of baby squid sautéed with tomatoes, dry white wine, and a whiff of garlic. Often Françoise or Paul and Eveline, who live nearby but have no phone, will appear on the terrace to invite us to a little *cocktail* or a *diner* they are planning. *Joli, d'accord, certainment!* In this community, entertaining is a serious business; and beautiful food earns big dividends.

A Mediterranean climate and the remnants of imperial France have lured us to a place that neither our mothers nor our children can locate without the help of an atlas. Tunisia, friends in the State Department assure us, is a gentle Arab country of eight million people, about the size of New York State, wedged between Libya to the east and Algeria to the west. Paris is only an hour by plane from Tunis, and Sicily is a couple of hours by ferry.

Eli, on sabbatical, can forget about his students and give his full attention to painting. He has set up shop, with a small easel and paint table, in the midst of our light-filled living room. To accommodate his makeshift studio, we have moved

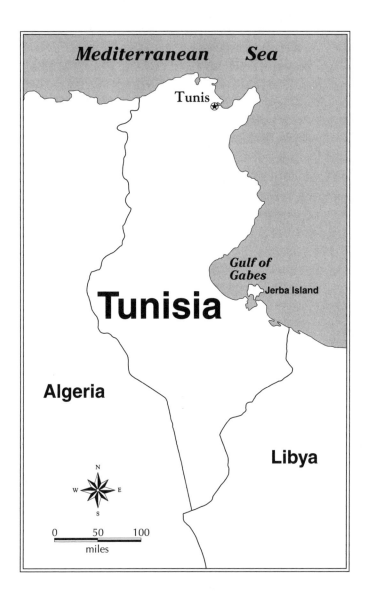

the dining table and chairs into a storage room. We eat our meals at the large white coffee table opposite a sofa with bright blue cushions and white wood trim.

Eli is busier than either of us anticipated. He chauffeurs me to school because the local driving is too aggressive for my laid-back American sensibilities. He calls plumbers to deal with stuffed toilets. Every two weeks, rain or shine, he supervises the ragtag oil delivery crew whose way of filling our tank is to aim their hoses at the tank's small opening from the house's upper terrace, showering the smelly stuff all over our main terrace and the stairs to the sea. In Tunisia, dealing with service people requires a confident French speaker and a strong male voice.

In between these chores, Eli devotes himself to painting Tunisians—courting, carrying wood, killing sheep, selling birds and jasmine, arranging marriages, posturing, peeing, and guarding parked cars. In the face of cultural rituals so different from our own, he lets his satiric imagination run rampant.

In my work, however, playfulness can only be at my own expense. Two mornings a week, as a Fulbright professor of American studies, I lecture in English to large groups of English majors on the topic "Pluralism and the American Experience." It's always a test of my adaptability and cool. The three hundred students, whose names and faces I confuse, depend almost entirely on my presentations and blackboard scratchings for their introduction to the United States. The books I ordered have not arrived. The American Studies Library, where I meet with my graduate students, is off limits to undergraduates, and the procedure for getting materials copied at the university is too arcane for a non-Arabic speaker.

In class, I invite discussion, a habit I sometimes regret. The radical students who pick up the gauntlet, men only, relish the opening. Repeatedly, they challenge my version of "America" as U.S. government propaganda or CIA disinformation. My views, they insist, reflect Israel's Zionist henchmen at the *New York Times*. This is heavy stuff, especially for a liberal-left Americanist who conflates their perspective with an Israel-obsessed, state-controlled press. How can I hope to open their minds and persuade them of my independence when they seem unable to get past what they see: a tall, casually dressed blond woman of about forty with good legs—a dubious authority.

Gammarth, the post office designation for our strip of beach and handsome villas, has no stores of its own. So Eli and I make the five-minute drive to the busy La Marsa market almost every day. We rarely see Americans here, and no English is spoken, only Arabic and French. Eli, with his uncannily precise Parisian accent and swarthy complexion, passes for French and gets respect. I get attention—not always a happy matter—for my Nordic looks. However, as soon as I order 100 grams of capers or green beans in serviceable, well-accented French, I'm welcomed into an amiable, ritualized world of marketplace banter.

Even on the hottest of days, Mustafa, the chicken man of La Marsa, wears several layers of soiled white garments, topped off by a red checked headdress. Tall, stooped, well past sixty, and usually unshaven, Mustafa has a natural grace. Even his formulaic greetings seem heartfelt. While most merchants use the ritual *"Asslamas"* (peace, or God be with you) followed by *"Ça va, Madame?"* to commence selling, Mustafa never pushes his chickens—or his customers, for that matter. Time is there to be passed as agreeably as possible. Allah will see to it that the chickens make their way from Mustafa's counter to his customers' kitchens.

In truth, I don't fancy Mustafa's well-recommended chickens, or anybody else's. The scrawny birds lie out in the open, unrefrigerated and unprotected from flies. Buying them makes me jittery. But eating them—sautéed, fried, or in soup, I encounter a delicate, sweet taste and a nonplastic texture. At home, industrialized food production has not only destroyed chickens but also our memory of chicken. In La Marsa, however, after exchanging good wishes with Mustafa and commiserating about the weather being too hot or too cold, I dole out my dinars for the pleasures of pretechnological *poulet*.

Mahmoud, the *brik* man, doesn't have a stall in the La Marsa market, just a bit of floor space, roughly three feet square, where he sits on a low stool with his large rattan basket in front of him. *Briks* are a distinctly Tunisian creation: a flat, round, thinly rolled piece of dough, around five inches in diameter, filled by home cooks and restaurant chefs with a tuna fish mixture and a raw egg, folded in half, carefully sealed, and quickly fried. A man of few words, Mahmoud, like Mustafa, does well without salesmanship. *Briks* are always in demand, and he is likely to be sold out by midmorning.

I am shy about making *briks*, reluctant to cross over and do the distinctly Tunisian thing. It is so easy to make a mistake, I tell myself: seal the packet badly, undercook the egg, or burn the *brik*. When Mounira comes to work for us, I watch closely as she fries our *briks* to a golden perfection. On her days off, I experiment and mess up. The talent for *brik* making is not in the genes, and it doesn't require extensive cultural experience. Anyone should be able to assemble a *brik*; it requires only a measure of eye-hand coordination—or is it confidence?— that eludes me in this strange setting.

Our blue-and-white kitchen at 87, rue Taieb Mehiri is larger than our kitchen in New Jersey. The refrigerator, with freezer space large enough only for ice trays, is a tad smaller than a standard American version, as is the four-burner stove. But the blue tile counters, ample white cupboards, and double stainless steel sink invite serious eating and entertaining. Of course, a dishwasher is unnecessary. The owners of the house, a French-educated engineer and his family, bring their maid to the beach when they come for the summer. They expect their tenants to do likewise. After our fashion, we do.

Mounira, our dark-skinned Tunisian housekeeper, is too well educated to be a maid. A graduate of the lycée in La Marsa, she is poised, well dressed, and a graceful French speaker. She is also something of a free spirit. At twenty-three, she enjoys the relative autonomy of household labor and the adventure of working for foreigners. Best of all is the chance to be creative in the kitchen. Mounira hones her culinary skills by reading cookbooks in Arabic and recipes in French-language women's magazines; also by watching the television, notebook in hand, while a Tunisian chef demonstrates, à la Julia Child, the classics of her national cuisine.

Tuesdays, Thursdays, and Saturdays, Mounira cleans and cooks for us. Lunch on Thursday is always special. I return from the university at 1:00 p.m., drained after four hours of laboring to be clear, entertaining, and amiable under fire. Smells of cinnamon, laurel, onions, and beef fill the house, signaling a tagine in the oven. Tunisian tagine, unlike its Moroccan cousin, is essentially a soufflé: beat eight eggs, the recipe reads, and in a frying pan sauté onions and add garlic, laurel, and ground beef. The beef and onion mixture is then baked with the eggs, to which flour, parsley, and cinnamon have been added. The top browns gently just as the eggs set, and voilà—the tagine is ready for the table.

No meal is complete without one of Mounira's artfully composed Tunisian salads. Whatever she finds in the refrigerator will work. She cubes tomatoes, onions, green peppers, and cucumbers; she adds some cooked potatoes or a hard-boiled egg, a half-cup of white beans, or a touch of lettuce. The dressing is always the same, a garlicky oil and vinegar and, for an extra touch of color, finely chopped parsley, tiny black olives, and carrot rounds. While I can make this salad at home in New Jersey, I can't replicate its freshness. I can't bring myself to do what was natural in Tunisia in the late 1970s: relish the local and seasonal, quality over variety, even items that don't appear picture-book perfect.

Although Tunisians are addicted to harissa, a hot red pepper sauce that is common in North Africa and the Middle East, Mounira blessedly is not. Nor, oddly enough, is she keen on couscous, the quintessential North African dish and the basic fare of generations of Tunisia's Arabs and Berbers. What a shame, I think, since couscous is the fare of the country and since our kitchen comes supplied with an aluminum *couscousière*: two large pots, one with a perforated bottom, which are set up in double boiler fashion. In the bottom pot, meat or chicken and vegetables such as chickpeas, okra, carrots, potatoes, and zucchini simmer together with seasonings, infusing the pale yellow grains of semolina that steam above. The cooked couscous grains are then served in heaping portions with a bit of the stew and a generous dollop of harissa.

With an inactive *couscousière* at home, we pay attention when the national dish is served elsewhere—at Fahti and Michelyne's, for example. In their quaint studio house, perched high above the sea at Sidi Bou Said, the evening begins predictably enough, with talk over drinks about the conflict for Tunisian artists between native craft traditions and European modernism. The debate is passionate but closely argued and nuanced. However, when our hosts interrupt the conversation to present a robust, aromatic lamb couscous, the company responds with patriotic adoration and sentimentality. Fahti, a painter married to a Canadian weaver, and his academic and journalist friends launch into elaborate narratives, partly for the enlightenment of their American guests. We would watch my mother, Fahti says, inspecting the couscous grains for twigs and dirt. Forever hungry, we would watch anxiously as she cut the potatoes and carrots into small cubes. She never smiled. She just kept working to keep seven of us fed and alive. My throat tightens. I steal a look at Eli, who is reaching for his handkerchief.

The stories that Fahti's friends tell are virtually the same: of poor, overburdened, heroic mothers with many mouths to feed, fending off hunger with couscous, and of eager, perpetually disappointed youngsters always confronting the same meager meal of a few spicy vegetables and a big pot of grain. The heat intensifies around the low table where we are seated. Beneath the calculated black humor, the Tunisians' fury festers. I'm suddenly fearful. Are we, who grew up well fed in a distant place, somehow responsible? What is our role in the release they seek? Perhaps it is simply to witness our companions' rage and bonding; to be mindful of our bounty as middle-class Americans.

I remember thinking, a few days after our dinner with Fahti and his friends, that such a despairing history should have turned Tunisians against couscous forever. But I misunderstood. The memory of privation, interpreted in the context of colonial exploitation, has made couscous into a battle cry and a badge of politically correct cuisine. The rituals of couscous are acts of Tunisian self-affirmation; they announce resistance to imperial France in general and French cuisine in particular. Fahti and his friends intentionally use harissa with a heavy hand—as a test of fortitude and a measure of manliness. Couscous is a stance as well as a diet.

Although more than twenty-five years have passed since those evenings with Fahti and Michelyne, I recall embracing the politics of couscous even as my palate remained fettered to France. Yes, I confess, eating out in Tunisia I unfailingly ordered *ris de veau, civet de lapin, cervelle avec beurre noir,* even *bifstek et pommes frits* rather than the national dish. Lately, however, my palate has made a great leap forward. At home in metropolitan New York, with hot cuisines moving into the mainstream and North African restaurants fine-tuning their fare to American tastes, I have been known to wax eloquent about couscous and consume it conspicuously.

From the rooftop of 4, rue Djamaa ez Zitouna, six stories above the darkening medina, I train Eli's binoculars on a Tunisian family in the throes of their Ramadan feast. They have taken to their terrace on this sultry June evening, hoping to catch a breeze while they eat and party, as is customary, at the end of another day of mandatory fasting. Their rickety wooden table is covered with food: round flat breads, little dishes of olives, a salad, grilled meat on skewers, couscous, and a bowl of apricots and peaches. Beverages include a pitcher of water, two bottles of red wine, and a liter-size bottle of Coke. Four children and three adults huddle around the table. Intent on the food, they eat silently while a velvet-voiced Egyptian pop singer croons on the cassette deck.

Our hosts and good friends, Umberto and Mariu, Italians who have lived their entire lives in Tunisia, are uncharacteristically irritable during Ramadan. Food shopping is particularly difficult because Tunisians, 98 percent of whom are Muslim, counter their acts of religious abnegation during this month with a manic greed: they buy in vast quantities, depleting the stores of eggs and chicken, beef, figs, and cheese. After giving Allah his due during the daylight hours, they generously reward themselves at nightfall.

At a deeper level, the Ramadan rituals of fasting and feasting, which seem to bind the Tunisian people as one family, are bitter reminders to Umberto and Mariu of their abiding outsidership and their vulnerability as Jews. All the more reason, perhaps, that the couple has made their handsome, meticulously cared-for house an emotional fortress. At Djamaa ez Zitouna, in the shadow of the oldest mosque in Tunis, they lavish their warmth and hospitality on a select few. We visit often and allow Umberto to pamper us with Johnny Walker Black Label; Mariu follows suit with tart homemade sorbets and honey-drenched filo pastries.

The first time we met I asked Mariu what kind of work she did. It is one of those feminist questions that often gets me into trouble in Tunisia: some of the most thoughtful women I encounter, often highly educated and ambitious, are married to diplomats and corporate executives who move every four years—a lifestyle ill suited to the two-career family. These women envy me my work, and I sympathize with their frustrations. Mariu is a different case altogether. "I'm at home," she announces in French—we always speak French—without the slightest indication that she might wish to be anyplace else. I stare at her, utterly confused. Here is an intense, articulate, and discerning woman of about forty-five with a head like Nefertiti's. "At home? You mean, you have young children?" I ask. "My son is dead," she answers. Her tone suggests ten weeks, but it's actually ten years since they buried their boy.

At home, Mariu devotes herself to the memory of her son, the care of her husband, the upkeep of their treasure-filled apartment, and the arts of Italian cuisine. A maid works in the house six hours each day, but Mariu trusts her mainly to mop the floors and wash the sheets. The real work of the household is hers alone.

Mariu consecrates herself as high priestess of her kitchen. If it can be made at home, she will make it: preserves and liqueurs, yogurt and mayonnaise, fruit pies according to the season. On the shelves of her pantry, process reigns: eau de fleur and rose water are slowly distilled; in two enormous jars, black and green olives are curing; and fine pasta waits to be cut or dried or filled. Only when it comes to bread—truly wonderful French baguettes baked several times a day all over the city—does Mariu allow basic foodstuffs to travel directly from Tunisian hands to her table.

Fear of contamination and disease obsesses her. Each morning she positions three impeccably white towels on three white hooks next to the sink: one for silver and utensils, one for plates, and one for pots. Mariu's purification rites, including the meticulous washing of each leaf of lettuce and the scrubbing of each tomato and carrot, even each orange and lemon, had not been enough to save her son from cancer; but perhaps they can still protect the living. Around these domestic rituals and a shared understanding of the links between suffering and Jewish victimization, we bond for life.

Mariu and Umberto's Jewishness, rather like Eli's and mine, is a passion apart from faith or observance. They speak no Hebrew, Yiddish, or Ladino, they never visit the synagogue or celebrate the holidays, but they are fiercely proud of the achievements and genius of Jews, both ancient and modern. Umberto remembers watching as his family's property was confiscated during World War II; he holds on to the sense of helplessness he felt as a ten-year-old, being elbowed off the narrow sidewalks of the medina by Tunisian toughs. While Umberto and Mariu identify themselves as Italians and are bearers of Italian passports, they never forget that Umberto's Jewish birth defines who in Tunis is to be trusted and who is not.

Living among Arabs in inflammatory times, our friends are compulsively vigilant, especially when it comes to Israel, which they cherish as a Jewish homeland, even though, should they need to leave Tunisia, they would surely take refuge in Italy or France. We learn from Umberto and Mariu to refer to Israel in code as *le pays de pamplemousse*, the land of grapefruits. Anxiously, we take in the venom that spews forth in the daily press against the Zionist demon and its American co-conspirators on Wall Street; we worry about the Arab states making good on their threats to Israel's security.

We are warned not to identify ourselves as Jews; nothing good can come of it. I even consider removing the "made in Israel" label from the suede jacket that lies on my desk when I lecture. Predictably, Tunisians claim not to be anti-Semitic, just anti-Zionist and certainly not racist. After many painful conversations about race with Mounira (whose father is southern African and black), we are not naive about equality under Allah. When students inquire about my origins during a unit on patterns of immigration to the United States, I mention Austria-Hungary during the Great Migration and count on my green eyes, blond hair, and German name to bar further inquiries. I "pass" easily but feel compromised.

The sky darkens at noon and the heavens roar on the day that a freshly slaughtered wild boar is dropped unceremoniously on the lawn of the U.S. embassy in Tunis. The boar, a gift from Tunisian villagers to the American ambassador, is a sign of Arab hospitality and a tribute to the power of his office. The ambassador, a charming, thirty-nine-year-old wunderkind, has been visiting outlying regions of the country. Everywhere he goes, feasts are organized in his honor and presents are bestowed upon him. In one village, his hosts hold forth on the splendors of the native boar and promise to send him one forthwith. Now the beast lies like a pariah, bloodied and ugly in the pouring rain. When the Muslim grounds crew at the embassy refuses to touch the unclean animal (pig is outlawed by the Koran), six U.S. marines drag it from the embassy's front lawn into hiding.

We learn of the boar two days later, as we are playing on the tennis court of the ambassador's residence. The ambassador's wife—trim, blond, thirty-something—is claiming the boar for *un grand diner.* "I'm thinking about a very boaring party," she jokes as we towel off between sets.

We catch the tension beneath her banter. To be the wife of an ambassador, even a hip, jeans-wearing ambassador, is hard on a modern American woman. There are the endless formalities and forced smiles, the tedious receptions where men do business and women discuss children and travel arrangements, the attention to protocol, and the difficulty of learning enough French to communicate with the household staff. However, something about the boar speaks to the rebel-imp in the ambassador's wife. I sneak a look at Eli, knowing that he has registered this domestic drama and will review it with me as soon as we are on our way home.

The boar is intended for Christians to feast upon. Under the watchful eye of the embassy's chef, the beast is eviscerated, cleaned, and sectioned. In chunks, it marinates for two weeks in olive oil, red wine, thyme, parsley, black pepper, and onions. Then, on the appointed Saturday evening in June, some three dozen Americans, an equal number of western Europeans, and a handful of favored Tunisians convene on the great lawn of the ambassador's residence overlooking the jade-green sea at Sidi Bou Said.

We are all impeccably tanned, coiffed, and groomed: the men in beige linen suits and pale seersucker, the women in crushed white, airy chiffon, and stark summer black. Formally attired waiters pass around platters of plump shrimp with chili sauce and warm *paté en croute*; they fill and refill our glasses of full-bodied French cabernet and white burgundy. All around us, the talk is of vacations in France and Italy—where you can really eat.

I stand at the far end of the pool with Lilly, the adroit wife of an American diplomat, who is watching the movements of the ambassador. We are discussing the problem of getting our "artifacts," purchased from an itinerant peddler who is supplied by grave robbers, out of the country. Suddenly, I am light-headed from too many glasses of red wine consumed too quickly. A glance at my watch indicates that it is barely 8:00 p.m.

Finally, the chef and his sous chefs take their places behind two mammoth silver serving dishes positioned on metal racks above warmers. They lift the silver

covers, releasing a fuselage of lustily perfumed pork. Then, with appropriate grav-
ity, they load our plates with the pork, rice, green beans, and salad. Surrounding
the great serving table, our party rejoices in the kill. We praise the bounty of Tunisia, the generosity of Tunisians, and the brilliance of our Tunisian chef. We raise
glasses to our spirited hosts, little dreaming that before the autumn is over they
will be going their separate ways.

I hesitate for a minute, reluctant to break the spell with anything so ordinary
as a taste. I am light-headed and full from hors d'oeuvres. But my nose tells me all
I need to know: after nine months of remarkable eating, this is something else.
Extra, as the French say, meaning over the top. In this gated compound, under the
protection of the American flag, the star of our Last Tunisian Supper is a proud
creation of the diplomatically correct *cuisine française*.

THE BEST CHEESE IN THE WORLD

Coimbra, Portugal, 1987

Our neighbor Francisco, a portly man of sixty, hangs out weekends in the doorway of his street-front garage. Weather permitting, he soaks up the sun while gossiping with friends. When he spots Eli and me heading his way, arms laden with books, beer, and bread, he beckons us inside. The dim room resembles a hardware store. Metal shelves, brackets, tins of nails, and stacks of cardboard boxes cover the concrete floor. "From my factory in the north," he says in Portuguese, gesturing at the clutter. "We manufacture." I'm puzzled. Surely Francisco hasn't invited us into the garage to admire his industrial shelving. Adjusting to the light, I notice bushels of oranges, potatoes, and onions lined up along the rear wall. "From my farms," he adds. "I grow."

Like many Portuguese, Francisco continues to cultivate land in his ancestral village. He lets us know that there is nothing better for a city dweller than eating his own farm-grown produce. By way of demonstration, he sniffs an orange and passes it to Eli. Eli holds the orange to his nose, out of respect, for twenty long seconds. "*Muito bon*," he says, understating the compliment in the Portuguese fashion. Eager to get upstairs, I shuffle my packages and look meaningfully at my husband. But Eli is intrigued. He waits patiently for Francisco to make his pitch.

Patience, Eli knows from his measured, painstaking approach to painting, is first cousin to cunning; both are investments in secrets to be discovered. Eli will prowl a beach, alert for tiny treasures in the sand, while I march ahead, face toward the sun. I am impatient by nature. I shoot off my mouth, often for the pleasure attached to a speedy formulation. A fast starter, I'm likely to weary of a problem just as Eli is warming up. This afternoon, in Francisco's garage, there's no urgency to be elsewhere. Go easy, Eli urges me with an attentive look; something curious is brewing.

At home in New Jersey, we both feel the pressure to be off and doing. Abroad, we slow down; we relish our freedom from routine obligations to family, friends, colleagues, and housekeeping. Creative disruption, I call it: in this case, six months in Portugal, courtesy of another teaching Fulbright (at Coimbra University) and a preretirement sabbatical for Eli.

In January 1987 we set up housekeeping on the outskirts of Coimbra, a historic university town two hours north of Lisbon. Now, halfway through our stay, we can chitchat in minimal Portuguese. Drawing on our French, my Spanish, and Eli's Italian, we take in much more than we can produce. Since my colleagues in the Department of Anglo-American Studies, who are also our friends, speak fluent English, we practice our Portuguese each day with waiters and shopkeepers.

In Portugal, we had decided, I would not cook. We would leave the burdens of shopping, preparing, serving, and washing up to restaurant wage earners. Liberation for the working woman! Eating out—either lunch or dinner, depending on my teaching schedule—has skewed our language skills toward food. The word *laranja* hovers in the air. I wonder whether our neighbor is pushing oranges. And if so, how many will he expect us to buy?

Francisco inspects his potatoes and then his onions. Do we like cheese, he wants to know—good Portuguese cheese, *queijo da serra*? From the *Serra da Estrela*, Mountain of the Star, he has brought a few rounds of "the best cheese in the world." The very best, he insists. From sheep. Like butter. Like Brie, but better. Made entirely by hand. Are we interested? He places in my hands a tough-skinned, light-mud-colored round of cheese. It is about nine inches in diameter and heavy, more than two pounds. The cylindrical rim is swathed with a crude, linenlike bandage that functions as flood control for the soft, runny center.

Perhaps Francisco has read horoscopes this morning, and he's been promised fair-weather dealings with friends and neighbors. Of course we like cheese. We give a good cheese the right temperature, decent bread, and a proper glass of wine. In fact, we've been a bit cheese-starved in Portugal—insufficiently adventurous in the markets and poorly rewarded for our occasional, haphazard purchases.

The moment, like Francisco's *queijo*, is ripe. We nod. He weighs the uncut round on an old-fashioned balance scale: one and a half liters, about three pounds. Gently he fingers the cheese, as if it were the cheek of a small grandchild. It yields properly to the pressure of his thumb and forefinger. The price, he announces, is four thousand escudos. Wow! Four thousand escudos in 1987 is a serious budget item: about $30, or three dinners for two.

I imagine the meals that this precious *queijo* might buy. Among my favorites is a Sunday lunch of *leitão* (suckling pig) with green salad and *vinho verde* at one of Mealhada's fancy suckling pig palaces. At least twenty-five restaurants, all with signs announcing *leitão*, line the commercial strip that skirts the nearby town of Mealhada. Their menus are identical. However, quality is especially important in eating suckling pig: only slow, careful cooking will eliminate the thick layer of fat between the crisp skin and the moist, tender pork. At Pedro dos Leitãos, one of the best pig palaces, families with wizened great-grandmothers and well-behaved toddlers gather at round tables for eight or ten. When the glistening hunks of meat arrive, their chatter ceases. Like the Portuguese around us, we eat deliberately, savoring each bite. We lick our fingers with delight and wipe our lips with heavy white napkins. An ordinary Sunday turns into a quasi-mystical culinary holy day. The two of us can dine, in pig heaven, for two thousand escudos.

Budget eating, if one knows the right spot, provides a different sort of entertainment. Several colleagues recommended the boisterous hole-in-the-wall where 'Ze Manel (Jose Manuel) presides over vats of steaming pork bones. Entering the tiny restaurant, we are assaulted by a heady perfume of red wine and garlic, in which the bones have been steeped. The counter in front of the chef is laden with clear-eyed fish, rough breads, and seasonal fruits. Oddly shaped sausages and hams hang like mobiles from the darkened ceiling—still life for a sixteenth-century Flemish painting.

We sit at a tiny Formica table, almost in the laps of our neighbors. We're so close that we have to resist casting our eyes too lovingly on their tripe with white beans and *bacalhau* (salt cod) with boiled potatoes. Sometimes the regulars at a nearby table offer us the red wine they've brought from home instead of the red *vinho da casa*. Your red is unfit even for pigs, they shout to 'Ze Manel, who bows and waves in response. Lunches for two at 'Ze Manel's cost a mere five hundred escudos.

I turn back to Francisco and his *queijo*, determined to enjoy this game to the fullest. Buying cheese is a very particular commodity transaction. While it involves looking, touching, and smelling, there's also the requisite commentary—about sweetness and sharpness, firmness and smoothness, spices and herbs; commentary also about the animal of origin, the cheese's provenance, and the ranking within its generic family. Otherwise, cheese shopping is like picking lottery numbers: a conjunction of hunch and pseudoscience.

"*E perfeito,*" it's beautiful, Francisco says, sparing us the language of connoisseurship. As the three of us know, Eli and I are easy marks. We owe Francisco for helping us deal with a stalled car two weeks earlier. How could a couple of comfortable Americans, who avow their passion for Portuguese food, refuse a neighbor who has done them a favor? Eli digs into his wallet, figuring the cost of car support into the weight of the cheese, and we head upstairs to test the treasure.

Our rented flat, on a street of small, new apartment houses, has a well-equipped but underutilized kitchen. Not a single pork roast or chicken has made it into the oven. Even if cooking were on the agenda, nothing in my repertoire matches the succulence and deep seasoning of chickens we buy from the chicken-only rotisserie just a mile down the road. However, we keep the refrigerator well stocked with eggs, bacon, hard sausages, yogurt, greens and tomatoes, good butter, beer, and white wine. A real breakfast together has always been our ritual. The other at-home meal—an omelet or salad or dressed-up packaged soup—merits a well-set table and a pause in the day.

In our Coimbra flat, the dining room table has pride of place. We have positioned it in front of the picture window overlooking fields with beat-up barns and fat cows grazing. In the distance, a high-rise suburb is under construction. Seated at the round oak table, we contemplate the drama of Portugal's future pressing in on its past. The quaint medieval city, with its narrow, winding, cobblestone streets, seems immune to modernization. The famous university is a hub, holding on to its graduates and luring small-town residents in search of work and entertainment. According to our friends, apartments in the high rises will be sold before the buildings are finished.

Facing outward may be irresistible, but it is also necessary. The living room, dominated by two clunky, studded-leather chairs and a huge TV, is an eyesore. Sometimes, when I curl up with a book, I yearn for our comfortable velour sofa at home and our indestructible coffee table, which accommodates spilled drinks as well as stocking feet. Looking at the cheap reproductions of sentimental nineteenth-century paintings, I miss the bold, anguished forms of Eli's Tunisian peasant women, with piles of wood on their backs, trudging through a bleak landscape.

At the table, with our backs to the living room, we feel most at home. We munch on tiny black olives and salted nuts. We drink pleasant, inexpensive Portuguese wine. We listen to Mozart on the cassette player. Eli reports on his obsessive writing project: the shattered remains of a life-sized Last Supper by sixteenth-century sculptor Phillipe Hodart, which is housed in the local museum. I mull over the touching narratives of family migration (involving Angola, Mozambique, France, Brazil, and Canada) that my Portuguese students have written in preparation for reading Maxine Hong Kingston's *The Woman Warrior*. Eli urges me to write an essay about the migration project, but I resist, preferring to spend my free time playing tennis with him. We plan outings, to Porto, Portugal's second city, where the tripe is said to be outstanding, and to Tomar, to see the famous citadel built by the Knights Templar beginning in the twelfth century, and the synagogue (now a museum) built in the fifteenth century. Living without a telephone, we feel unharassed and productive.

Now, as Eli cuts a slender wedge of the *queijo da serra*, a smooth, ivory flow escapes from the round and spills onto one side of the plate. How lucky that we've just brought fresh *pao*, Portugal's dense peasant bread, from the bakery. *Pao* is a perfect host for Francisco's *queijo*. The cheese, neither sharp nor bland but exquisitely mellow as promised, glides onto the bread. It caresses my tongue.

I fill two wineglasses with a lusty Dão and pass one to Eli. "To the cheese of angels," he says. "May the sheep of the *serra* continue to flourish." "To the Queen of Portuguese cheeses," I respond. "May the shepherds be supported in their devotion to the sheep and in the labor of their hands."

Time stops. The clunky chairs evaporate. I have all that I need.

A VIEW FROM THE FORTRESS POLANA

Maputo, Mozambique, 1993

The breakfast buffet at the Hotel Polana is thirty running feet of elegant imports: decadent patés and seductive herring, vegetable salads and classic French cheeses, fruit pastries and croissants, fried eggs, sausages, and, for the cholesterol conscious, granola and yogurt. Self-indulgent on my first working day in Maputo, the capital of Mozambique, I sample almost everything and reject the compunction to clean my plate. Still, my pleasures give me pause. Mozambique in 1993 is one of the most woebegone countries in Africa. On the UN's quality-of-life chart, it ranks close to the bottom. How can I reconcile this five-star extravaganza with the poverty and fragile peace beyond the Polana's protective walls?

Muito obrigado, I say to the formally dressed waiter who serves me coffee from a pewter pot and steamed milk from a matching pewter server. His gaze is grave, almost paternal. Do I sense a concern, perhaps extended to all solitary diners, about how I am coping alone? Gratitude wells up in me, to the waiter, but also to the U.S. government for cushioning my visit with this lavish breakfast. In stressful situations, comfort counts, especially the comfort of favorite foods, beautifully presented. What comforts does the waiter enjoy, I wonder. How many mouths can he feed for the price of my breakfast? What kind of food does his meager salary (perhaps a dollar a day) provide? I imagine my Mozambican colleagues—university teachers of American studies with whom I'll be consulting—finishing their morning porridge or toast and tea. What ever would they think of my gluttony and wastefulness?

After breakfast I visit the American embassy for a routine briefing with the security officer. "When you leave the hotel," he instructs me, "do not carry a pocketbook and do not wear jewelry; and be sure not to walk alone after dark. In the hotel, if anyone asks you too many questions or behaves suspiciously, notify me immediately." I nod, more amused than disturbed by the possibility that the "fortress" Polana might actually be a den of post–Cold War conspirators.

Back at the hotel, Dr. M, the chair of social sciences at the Instituto Superior Pedagogica (ISP), is waiting to drive me to campus. I will be working with members of his faculty for the next three and a half weeks, developing a college-level

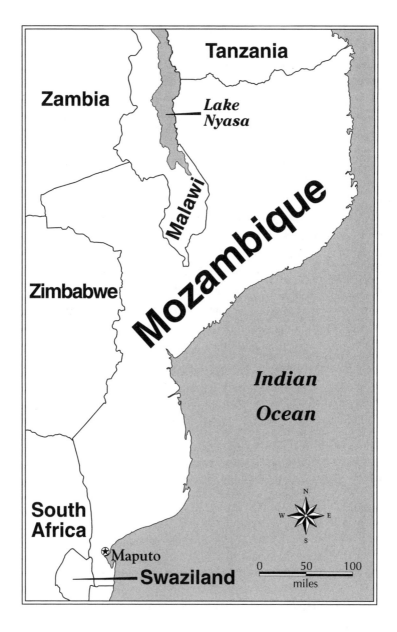

curriculum in American studies for future secondary school teachers. We chat about my flight connections to Mozambique and the pleasant weather. It's July, winter in Maputo, the best time of year for a visit, Dr. M assures me. Then he switches from English to Portuguese for more serious talk—about the American embassy's support for his program and my consultation. Language, it is clear, will complicate our relationship. While Dr. M speaks perfectly adequate English, he prefers Portuguese, the official language of Mozambique. I understand some Portuguese, thanks to the Fulbright that took me to Portugal, but my fluency is limited to ordering from a menu. Nevertheless, I embrace the linguistic disadvantage. It's what academic specialists abroad should do, I tell myself: demonstrate flexibility and, above all, refuse the imperialism of English. Thus, the basic pattern is established: Dr. M usually speaks Portuguese to me, I speak English to him, and we hope for the best.

The best, I suspect from the start, is not to be. The sunny office I have been given boasts a new Mac. But it is without a single book or magazine, without a university catalogue, telephone directory, sheet of paper, ballpoint pen, floppy disc, or printer. With the computer, even though getting online is a problem, a freshly painted Instituto gropes toward the future. After almost five hundred years as an ill-tended Portuguese colony (independence was declared in 1975) and sixteen horrendous years of civil war, illiteracy in Mozambique is a tragic 86 percent. The country's history underscores the mission of a teacher-training institution like ISP. Its priorities—obtaining more resources, better information, and higher standards for staff and students—are all part of the rationale for my consultation.

As we stroll through the jerry-built facility, deserted during the semester break, I am reminded of summer camps run by settlement houses where I worked in the 1950s: no-frills buildings with a strong whiff of disinfectant masking the odor of latrines. The late morning sun beats down on the back of my neck. Sweat marks form around the open collar of my host's white shirt. After consulting his watch—we've been talking for approximately one hour—Dr. M proposes that I enjoy a three-day weekend before we resume activities. He has been instructed not to overwork me, he explains, as he drives me back to the fortress Polana.

The Polana's enormous swimming pool is deserted at 11:30 a.m. I settle into a chaise, adjust the straps on my bikini, and order a *cerveja* (beer). In my orange tote bag are materials for a working afternoon: Portuguese language tapes, a Walkman, a Portuguese grammar, number-8 sunblock, and two collections of essays on the United States. Gradually, the lunchtime pool regulars claim their chairs: a thirty-something British expert on railroad engines, a strawberry-blond Irish woman with a six-year-old son whose husband works for a Swedish telecommunications company, and an attractive French-speaking man in his fifties with a preoccupied academic air. He's Belgian and a specialist in the administration of ports, he tells me—the fancy title for controlling corruption.

Over grilled chicken sandwiches, served on linen-covered trays with over-sized white linen napkins, my male companions complain about how tough it is to get things done (their way) in war-torn Mozambique. Remembering my bright, dysfunctional office, I smile knowingly. Of course I know nothing except that I have time on my hands and only six hours of scheduled meetings for the week to come.

When long shadows descend at 4:30 p.m., I move my books and materials from poolside to bedside. I check out the listings on CNN and BBC, the contents of the minibar (stocked, from champagne to nuts), and the room-service menu. Salad greens, the menu announces, are washed in purified water. Perhaps I'll have a Nicoise with a beer when I turn on Wimbledon for the evening's entertainment. There are two desks at my disposal, lamps and wall lights all in working order, and an inviting queen-size bed. It's almost like being at home.

But I haven't come all the way to Mozambique—six hours from Newark, New Jersey, to Lisbon and then another ten hours to Maputo—in order to hole up "at home." However, I am an American woman who has been warned about venturing too far from the fortress. Even though there has been a cease-fire for almost two years (since October 1991, between FRELIMO, the government forces, and South African–backed RENAMO), the ravages of war are palpable. Out of Mozambique's fifteen million people, three million have left their villages in search of food and safety in the capital and a handful of smaller cities. Maputo is crowded with homeless refugees, people with no work, no place to wash, and not enough to eat.

When I do venture out on a free morning, past the chattering merchants who set up their souks on the other side of the Polana's brick wall, I am surprised by the silence of the city. On the main street, the Avenida Julius Nyrere, there are few cars, no buses, and only an occasional truck. A woman sitting on the sidewalk just a few blocks from the Polana presides over a stash of seven oranges. The woman next to her, without shoes, has five. Will the sale of these oranges consti-tute a passable working day for these women? Will the small change they earn be used to buy flour or bread? Will it pay off a debt or keep a daughter from barter-ing her body? A young boy approaches me with a single cassette tape to sell. An-other has a handful of glass buttons. I have been told that there are bookstores, but I see no books for sale, no records or newspapers along the avenue. Postcards are as uncommon as tourists.

Eager for access to the real Mozambique, I phone Ciro P., a painter whose name I've been given by an American friend, and invite him for a drink at the hotel. Ciro is Portuguese, a short, pale man married to a voluptuous, dark brown Mozambican. His chest swells when he shows me her photo; she is his steadiness, he says, and Mozambique, his adopted country, is the brilliant canvas on which he works. When I tell Ciro that my husband was an artist who used African sculptural forms in his own work, he rattles off names of the best galleries in town and artists I must meet. He takes me to his studio to show me his recent work: lush yet airy blue-green acrylics, paintings exploding with energy and joy.

We take a bus to the dusty outskirts of Maputo in search of an art school for children run by Ciro's friend, Miguel. The school is modest, Ciro warns me, operated on a shoestring. Art supplies in Maputo are both scarce and terribly expensive. He tells me that $25,000 worth of paints, a gift from a U.S. organization, have been rotting at the port for a year because the government insists on an import tax and no one has the necessary cash.

Miguel, a large man with a full salt-and-pepper beard, welcomes Ciro and me with bear hugs. The school, located in the main room of his house, is free, he tells us. I'm investing in our kids, he says in Portuguese, investing in the future. Miguel removes two chipped white cups from the cupboard above the propane stove, where a Turkish coffee pot sits, and pours espressos for Ciro and me. The children's watercolors brighten the dark walls: abstract paintings with subtle colors and a strong sense of design—a remarkable display. Miguel pours three whiskeys into tiny glasses, saying that my visit is a special occasion. He asks me to select a watercolor as a souvenir, to show friends in New York what a young Mozambican artist can do.

One evening Ciro invites me to the Poets' Club, where we join a group of six at a battered wooden table under the stars. Platters of fried shrimp served with peppery ketchup and pitchers of beer appear without ceremony. Mozambican jazz booms over the speaker system. As more friends arrive there's much embracing and vigorous backslapping. Everyone teases and expects to be teased. Speaking in Portuguese and English, Ciro's friends draw me into a conversation about the obligations of artists to their people and nation. I tell them in Spanish that I envy their community. My husband, Eli, would have felt at home in the Poets' Club, I say. I don't say that, alone in Mozambique, I'm missing my friends and my own community.

My academic colleagues, most of them male, are more guarded with me than the crowd at the Poets' Club. At the Poets' Club, I'm the friend of a friend and the widow of a painter. However, at ISP, I am their "first-world" consultant, the so-called specialist, whose Portuguese is poor. I'm sure that my gender is a barrier, as well as my height (I'm taller than all of them), my white skin, my salary, and my room at the Polana (where dollars or South African rand are needed to buy a drink or a meal).

ISP faculty members tell me candidly that, more than American studies, their students need Mozambican studies. They need to know their own history and culture. Officials at the U.S. embassy have assisted several of these faculty members with research and travel grants, and now it's payback time; yes, they will give more attention to the United States in their curriculum.

I speak Spanish with the Cuban-educated political scientist, who confesses that I am the first (North) American with whom he has ever had a conversation. I speak French with the Paris-trained anthropologist about the urban ethnography he does with student researchers. I listen to complaints from the senior American historian about the unavailability of scholarly books and his dependence on the library at the American Cultural Center for materials on contemporary American society. Mixing English and Portuguese, I tell a twenty-three-year-old geographer that he will need to improve his English if he is to do an MA in the United States. Only the historian shows me a syllabus, a document featuring the names of U.S. presidents, wars, treaties, and acts of Congress that reminds me of the table of contents in high school history texts from the 1950s.

With Dr. M away for the second week and no meetings scheduled, I spend time with colleagues from the American embassy and with other hotel guests who are also at loose ends. We venture out, in their cars, to Maputo's modest continental restaurants. After we have parked and tipped the self-appointed car attendant, we dash rapidly from the car to the restaurant without allowing a hungry young drifter, under the cover of darkness, to grab someone's wallet or the car keys.

Jean-Pierre, my Belgian hotel companion, has been in wilder places, he assures me as we take our seats at an outdoor seafood restaurant and jazz hall. When the beer arrives, we plunge into intimate talk: about my husband's death from cancer, our travels in Francophone Africa, and the lack of excitement in his marriage. The grilled shrimp are fat and garlicky. I lick my fingers as Jean-Pierre leans toward me with an admiring comment about Saul Bellow's Jewish intellectuals. For a moment, I lose my bearings—or maybe I regain them. In this turn of the conversation, the categories of foreign consultant and white female tourist in southern Africa recede. I relax into myself.

When Jean-Pierre returns to Belgium, I turn my attention to shopping. At the stalls outside the front door of the Polana, hip young merchants make small talk in English and French as well as Portuguese. The masks, small stools, wooden bowls, fabric hangings, carved and painted animals—most of them too crude or too slick for my taste—are neatly displayed. These guys know how to flatter a customer. They make eye contact and praise my French; they boast about the authenticity of their pieces. When I finger a nicely finished carved giraffe, I'm told that it's a special piece, quite old. I ask if the carver is the merchant's cousin and get a hurt look in return. I'm an amateur at this game of killing time, but I see that the merchants are grim beneath their bright patter. On a morning when I fail to buy, one fellow complains that he hasn't made a sale in two days. Another tells me that his father is ill and there's no money for medicine. I'm hungry, a third dealer says, and my two young children are hungry, too.

Late on Friday afternoon, at the end of my unprogrammed week at ISP, I am gossiping with the Polana's amiable doorman when three young women wander in, hoping to cash travelers' checks. Well put together in their jeans and sandals, they are bright-eyed, black, and beautiful. One sports a Big Apple T-shirt. I fantasize a *New York Times* tucked away in her bulky straw bag. In less than five minutes the four of us are drinking iced coffee in the courtyard café, rhapsodizing about New York as The Place to study and live. Two regal-looking women with the cheekbones and leggy look of *Vogue* supermodels are sisters from Swaziland, graduates of Barnard (my alma mater) and NYU. Their companion, from Jamaica, with the Big Apple on her chest and a matching ebullience, is also a Barnard alum.

When I mention that I've been teaching women's studies since the mid-1970s, the conversation surges forward. Feminism has shaped their choices and mine. It has freed us to compete and achieve, and to think critically about power and privilege. It's clear to the four of us, as we sip iced coffee, that feminism enlarges our interest in one another, our appreciation of differences; it provides a common vocabulary that bridges those differences. I tell the young women that I have brought photos of my students' female forebears, along with the stories of their difficult lives, here to Mozambique—as an illustration of feminist pedagogy and also the diversity of American society. They tell me about the thrill of encountering feminists Charlotte Perkins Gilman, Gloria Anzaldúa, and bell hooks in their women's studies courses, about their degrees in economics and their fast-track jobs in the corporate sector. Now, however, all three are giving up the comforts of New York to work on planning and public policy in their own troubled countries. In their place, I wonder, would I choose to go home? Are they likely to make a difference? It takes time to make a difference, I remind myself, and the luck of good timing, too.

I invite the three to Sunday brunch to continue the conversation. The buffet is my bait; I tell them that the setting is like the Plaza in New York, only more relaxed. They are delighted to come, they insist, for the conversation as well as the omelets and croissants. As we linger over miniature French pastries and a third cup of coffee, the Jamaican woman returns to the subject of going home. The first test, she says, frowning, is whether she will be tough enough for her sexist culture; the second is whether she will be able to tolerate family members' telling her how to run her life. Feminism gave her some tools, she adds, but how far will they take her?

Decorating the lecture hall at the American Cultural Center are photographs and narratives from my university's Generations of Women collection—images of women from many cultures and social classes whose life stories are dominated by struggle. The occasion is a forum, hosted by the center, entitled Mozambican and U.S. Perspectives on Feminism. About a dozen people are in the audience, including women lawyers, the nation's only female judge, two community organizers, an academic, and two men who have just returned from a study tour in the United States.

Dr. Z, one of a tiny number of women historians in Mozambique, opens the session with an overview of the status of Mozambican women. Her Portuguese is rapid, but I catch her drift: Since independence, women have made significant strides as citizens whose rights are protected by law. However, the daily realities of women's lives are grim poverty, illiteracy, hunger, economic exploitation, and domestic violence.

When it's my turn, I offer a case study of feminism in the university curriculum. Speaking in Spanish (which Portuguese speakers understand), I describe the Generations of Women exhibit—enlarged photographs of my students' female forebears—as an effort to make ordinary women visible and every woman's story important. I explain that the exhibit calls attention to differences among women while underscoring the common bonds created by patriarchy, biology, and gender.

The lawyers and activists in the audience look at me despairingly. I am talking feminist pedagogy, but they are hungry for feminist politics. They want strategies for empowerment. What can American feminism teach them about achieving women's basic rights to food, clothing, shelter, freedom from battery, self-respect, and participation in national decision making?

These are tough questions. The major thrusts of American feminism over the past twenty-five years have involved gender equality (especially in education and the workplace) and reproductive freedom, goals inseparable from the values of an individualistic, advanced industrial society. Mozambique is rural, communal, historically exploited, and "underdeveloped." I breathe deeply and reckon with my confusions. Surely American feminism has something to offer these women, even though it grows out of a different context. My Spanish is faltering now. I take the easy way out, suggesting that Mozambican women might have more to learn from Kenyan, Indian, and Brazilian feminists than from women's movements in the United States.

Several faculty members who attend my seminars at ISP are interested in writing a history of modern Mozambique. They are both fascinated and troubled by the notion I have advanced that the everyday lives of ordinary people, properly explicated, constitute a nation's story. They challenge my emphasis on diversity. What is it, they ask, that makes America a nation, that holds the country together? I am delighted to talk with them about the common bonds of law and civil society, ideology and technology.

One of my research interests is the subject of a seminar I've scheduled: American Foodways and the Study of Everyday Life. I hope that the food talk will provide the Mozambican social scientists in our group with a model for self-study as well as a handle on contemporary America. I explain that the ideology of multiculturalism encourages immigrants to maintain their food traditions and take pride in hyphenated identities. By way of illustration, I show slides of an Italian food market where the immigrant founder's college-educated grandson makes mozzarella by hand, in the old-fashioned way, six days a week. Another set of slides focuses on a family of Palestinian restaurateurs who cook with olive oil shipped to New Jersey from their own olive trees in Jerusalem. Images of Isumi, a Korean-Japanese restaurant, focus on the Japanese-born sushi chef and his Korean wife, who prepares bibimbop and barbecue in the kitchen. As the photos make clear, some of the customers in these (and many other) ethnic food establishments are "insiders," ethnics upholding family traditions. However, the photos also reveal shoppers and eaters who are "outsiders," Americans of other backgrounds who relish the chance to pick and choose in America's culinary salad bowl.

The Mozambicans are befuddled. They are not following my English. Nor are they grasping the differences between Italian broccoli rabe, Korean bulgogi, and Middle Eastern baba ghanoush. Later, I realize why. First, although Maputo has a population of over a million, it is not a global village. Imported foods arrive in Mozambique, but only at places like the Hotel Polana. Western-style *supermercados*—supermarkets—have not yet come to the city proper. In addition, there are no billboards advertising brand-name foods or food chains. Moreover, educated people with modest incomes do not all have television. In short, Mozambicans are out of the loop of globalized marketing and the globalization of culinary diversity.

Second, if diversity is the bewildering text of my slide talk, "plenty" may be the offending subtext. The poor Americans in my photos are shown devouring burgers and greasy fries; from the perspective of a devastated developing country, they are well fed. It occurs to me too late that the abundance and variety of foods in the slides, the decadent sensuousness of surfeit, may feel more like an affront to this audience than a lesson.

Nine of us gather around tables that have been pushed together in the darkened dining room of the Hotel Andalucia. On my last day in Maputo, I have been invited for morning tea by a group of women faculty and staff at ISP to talk about women's issues in the university. It is 10:30 a.m., but the Andalucia is still asleep. I watch a lackadaisical waiter make a point of ignoring us, and I wonder if this is standard treatment for women guests—or for women unaccompanied by men.

Speaking in Spanish, I offer our stateside consciousness-raising model as a way of getting started. The theme is our experiences as professional women; the procedure is for each of us to speak personally about conflicts we face and our ways of dealing with them. One young woman shakes her head shyly when I indicate that it's her turn to speak. In a barely audible voice she explains that women in her country aren't in the habit of exposing private matters in public, especially in the presence of a stranger. An unsmiling psychologist with hair in a very short Afro and a deeply creased forehead jumps in. "I don't know which is worse," she says in Portuguese—"the hypocrisy at home or the constant sexism at work. My husband supports my career," she explains, "but he is afraid of my independence. He's glad that I have a title and salary but furious when I'm late to dinner because of meetings. He never offers to pick up our son from school or his soccer match and never helps the boy with his homework. That's your job, he tells me. My male colleagues are worse than my husband," she continues. "They're nasty and snide. They don't like to think of me as a member of their department. They say that a woman who is ambitious is not feminine. I'm as smart as they are, but I won't get a travel grant until every man in the department has gotten one first."

The psychologist has been twisting a necklace of small brown seeds as she speaks. Now she gives a small gasp and covers her mouth with both hands. The women on either side of her move closer, murmuring softly.

Suddenly, several women are talking at once. There is fight in their voices, defiance. The excitement is palpable, perhaps even to the waiter, who has been roused from his torpor by the command of the woman to my right, a history instructor at ISP and the only woman who participated in my seminars. He brings us strong tea and weak coffee, platters of sliced white bread with American cheese, and gray, fatty ham. I cannot tell whether the dismal appearance of the food is disappointing to my hosts, who are obviously preoccupied—or only to me. Have they gotten good value for their hard earned *meticais*? I haven't a clue.

The real value here is where it belongs: in the flood of gritty revelations and communal warmth. Looking around the table at eight women whom I may never see again, I'm certain that there is value in this feminist ritual—exploring our experiences and breaking bread together—which carries us, if only for a brief time, across barriers of culture, race, language, and economics.

Food and drink make a difference. As we pass platters and pour tea, we feel connected and nurtured. Our protective shells soften. What might have happened at ISP, I wonder, if my colleagues and I had gathered for a meal or relaxed over beers? What kind of anxiety—female self-consciousness, perhaps—prevented me from inviting the American studies group for drinks at the Polana? It's hard to know. Better to rejoice in the women's tea. My consultation has not been entirely in vain. I'm ready to check out of the fortress.

DAL BHAT AT PHARPING

Kathmandu Valley, Nepal, 1997

The fruit trees ringing the house at Pharping produce apricots, peaches, cherries, and pears—amazing pears, my son Adam boasts. The air is sweet and fresh; it's the opposite of the killer exhaust and rotting garbage that clog our nostrils in Kathmandu. "We should all go up for an overnight," Adam says, "and let Sangita feed us dinner. That way you'll understand why Laura and I bought the place—how peaceful we feel there."

Running a business in Kathmandu doesn't allow Adam much peace. He worries about the competition—all those other solar energy businesses that have sprung up since he and his partner started Lotus Energy in 1993—and the baksheesh-dependent government that requires courting as well as payoffs. Then, too, there are doors that suddenly open, full of risk that is another name for opportunity. Thus, when the call comes from Indonesia, five days after my arrival in Nepal, announcing that one of Suharto's grandsons has a matter he would like to discuss with Adam, my son calls his travel agent and is off in a jiffy.

"We'll go anyway," Laura announces, releasing her crinkly, sun-flecked brown hair from a makeshift bun. Like Adam, Laura is an adventurer. Living the daunting, occasionally glamorous, expat life in Nepal is a choice she embraces. "We'll leave the kids with the *didi*"—the housekeeper—"and enjoy the excursion alone."

"Alone" in Nepal is a relative term. Laura and I drive forty-five minutes from Kathmandu into the terraced green hills and north to Pharping. Turning off the main road, we bounce along rutted paths. Slightly built men, each carrying sixty pounds of firewood, like free-form sculptures tied to their backs, make space for our 1969 VW to pass. Where the path ends we unload the car and trudge along narrow footpaths about a quarter of a mile until the house comes into view: a brown two-story wood building, with a thirty-foot-long front porch, shaded from the late afternoon sun.

Two young men who are lounging on the porch jump up to help with the bags. They are neighbors, sons of the farmer whom Adam employs as a watchman. "Namaste," we say, pressing our hands together in the traditional Hindu greeting, followed by a mix of hellos and smiles. Laura has very little Nepali, I

have none, and the young men's English is exhausted by greetings and thank-yous. Three of their younger siblings join us on the porch, smiling, shy, and silent. Then Sangita, the mother of the clan, a vigorous, handsome woman in her fifties, appears to welcome us. We exchange namastes and smiles that stand in for ritual greetings and good wishes.

Our arrival is an event for Sangita and the household. Because Adam and Laura's house has no kitchen or running water, she will provide dinner for us later in the day. The arrangement is twenty-five (Nepalese) rupees per person per meal, or about forty cents (at the 1997 rate of exchange). It's a good economic arrangement for the family, who live close to the dollar-a-day level characteristic of Nepal. And it's a fabulous deal for us: no fussing with prepared food from the city and no campfire heroics. Better still, we get the Real Thing: a simple, rural meal served to us in a farmhouse less than one hundred feet away.

The shadows are deepening at 7:00 p.m. as we enter Sangita's house through the barn, where two cows and a dozen-odd chickens reside. We climb the narrow slat stairs past small bedrooms on the first floor, up to the second. The kitchen and dining area is an open space about twelve by fourteen feet, with a dirt floor. There is a fire at the cooking end. Three round straw mats, about twelve inches in diameter, have been laid out for the two of us and a Buddhist monk who is doing a retreat at Adam and Laura's house. We settle ourselves on the mats and wait to be served.

The ordinary Nepalese meal is dal bhat: lentils and rice served with vegetables and chutneys or pickles. One of Sangita's sons hands us tin plates, which are divided into three unequal wedges: the largest for rice, the middle for vegetables or meat, and the smallest for condiments. Sangita's husband fetches a big pot of rice from the fire and serves each of us with a large tin spoon. Another son delivers small bowls of soupy brown lentils, which are to be poured over the rice. He returns with a green, squashlike vegetable and chutney. Then the husband passes around cucumber pickle.

The slightly sweet smell of curried lentils is seductive. I pour some lentils over the rice and with the fingers of my right hand mix the rice and lentils with a bit of the vegetable. I add a little chutney, which has been served on its own tiny tin plate, to the mixture and swirl in a taste of cucumber pickle. Making a ball-like shape with my fingers, I bend over my plate, hoping to contain the spillage as I eat. I'm as quick as any American to devour grapes, pizza, french fries, grilled shrimp, even chicken legs and baby lamp chops with my fingers. Dal bhat, however, is another matter. The pale pink polished nails on my right hand are turning the color of sunflowers: my yellow badge of courage. This story from Nepal will certainly entertain my Korean manicurists in New Jersey.

My stomach rumbles. I look over at Laura, wondering how little I can eat without appearing rude. Now it's not my discolored nails that I'm worrying about but rather the relation between intake and output. Laura and I will be sleeping on the second floor of the house. The outhouse, which boasts one of the establishment's two electric lights, is a rickety flight of stairs down and thirty feet of foliage away from the house. There is no way to explain to our hosts that eating less is the path of wisdom. I probably wouldn't explain if I could.

The dirt floor is hard on my backside and harder still on my back. Laura, thanks to years of Buddhist practice, seems perfectly at home on the floor. She sits straight and eats heartily, as does the monk at her side. I squirm and watch through the window as the sun disappears behind the hills. No pain, no gain, the Buddhists teach. True enough. I imagine that I am not my body. I imagine that I am home in Leonia. In my own bed. Asleep until morning.

SCHLOSS LEOPOLDSKRON

Salzburg, Austria, 1995

Ahmed stares at the photo of Fatima Abbasi. The young professor from the West Bank studies the beautiful woman with coal-black eyes and a direct, unsmiling gaze. She stands at a table in her kitchen, stuffing grape leaves with a mixture of bulgur, ground lamb, onions, and currants. The narrative on the wall next to the photo explains that Mrs. Abbasi and her family came to the United States from Jerusalem via Jordan in the late 1970s. The dolmas she is making, with olive oil from her family's groves outside of Jerusalem, are destined for Ali Baba, the family's Middle Eastern restaurant in Hoboken, New Jersey. What is Ahmed thinking—does he imagine Fatima Abbasi as an exile or an immigrant, or both? I remember a comment she made when this photo was taken. "I live in New Jersey," she said, "but my heart isn't here."

Ahmed's face shows the first hint of a five o'clock shadow. His expression gives away nothing—except, perhaps, the habit of keeping his emotions under control. Perhaps Mrs. Abbasi reminds him of his mother or his wife; or the extended family of Palestinians scattered around the world. Her experience of diaspora belongs to his history. Seeing the two of them together is a small revelation: American diversity, the boast of the photos on the wall, is built on the losses and tragedies of others.

I'm on the verge of interrupting Ahmed's communion with his countrywoman, but I hold back. In my eagerness to make contact, I'm likely to be too breezy or too intimate. Besides, there's plenty of time. This is the first full day of the workshop he is attending with twenty-four other foreign scholars entitled The Literature of Ethnicity in the United States. We will be together at the Salzburg Seminar for another twelve days.

An hour before, I opened the program with a lecture, "The One and the Many: The Current Debate on Unity in American Life." Now, standing at the back of the lecture hall, I watch the group of fellows (as the participants are called) react to the exhibit Eat! Eat! Food as Family and Cultural History. They move, like a slow chorus line, from one picture to the next, reading the narratives with care. Three older scholars from Uzbekistan and Kazakhstan, speaking Russian, appear

to be comparing translations of the texts on the wall. Their American English, gleaned from the novels of Hawthorne, Hemingway, and Dos Passos, is not likely to include words like "wasabi," "hominy grits," "graffiti chic," and "Styrofoam."

Many of the fellows are puzzled. As teachers of English and American literature, they fail to grasp the link between ethnic eating in America and ethnic American writing. It's for this very reason that I've brought the pictures with me to Austria. In graphic terms, the photos pose some of the same questions that emerge from considering the literary canon: Who are Americans? What unites a people? How does American diversity create discourse as well as discord? The exhibit is an extraliterary way of exploring ethnicity and culture.

The seminar's participants come from twenty different countries in Europe, Asia, North Africa, and the Middle East. Many tell me later that they had hoped to find their own national group on the wall. Why, they ask, are there three photos of Italian people and products and none of Spaniards, Poles, Portuguese, Czechs, Moroccans, or Austrians? Instances of crossing ethnic lines—a Greek-owned pizzeria and a black woman selecting Levy's Jewish rye bread—provoke a Polish professor to wonder why we have focused on exceptional cases. A Sri Lankan scholar offers a piercing critique. Aren't these ethnic foods just capitalist window dressing? he asks—ways of diverting attention from the exploitative power of multinational companies and industrial agriculture? The real losers, he adds, are small farmers in countries like his own.

I had another, sly motive for bringing the exhibit to Austria: to introduce a contemporary American presence into this aristocratic, old-world conference site. Schloss Leopoldskron, the eighteenth-century baroque palace that houses the Salzburg Seminar, boasts sweeping marble staircases and manicured gardens. It is a place of great privilege in a country that is chary of outsiders. The subjects of Eat! Eat! are working-class people, making or selling humble foods from a dozen culinary traditions to consumers like themselves. These "outsiders," who may still feel unwelcome in America, are changing my nation's definition of itself.

I josh with my faculty colleagues, Paul Lauter and Kris Versluys, about the place of the food exhibit in the seminar. It's an appetizer, I say, preceding the overstuffed literary main course. American literature as it is taught in many of the countries represented in our workshop is the domain of "dead white males." Paul, Kris, and I have two weeks in which to introduce texts by African Americans, Latinos and Latinas, Native Americans, Asian, Jewish, Italian, and Irish Americans, and women of all backgrounds. Inclusion, Paul, Kris, and I insist, is a complex, asymmetrical process. On the one hand, newcomers on the fringe struggle to be acknowledged. On the other hand, the so-called cultural mainstream resists, bends, adapts, and offers up new forms of resistance. New voices aren't just add-ons, we argue. They create new paradigms; they change the mix.

At the Salzburg Seminar, participants attend to the mix that is American culture through readings, lectures, and discussions. But they also learn by mixing with one another: during meals, at coffee breaks, and evenings in the *bierstube*, the beer hall. We dine leisurely in the Marble Hall, an august space with interior balconies, gilt mirrors, and carved ceilings thirty feet high. Enormous eighteenth-century portraits of royalty loom overhead. The Austro-Hungarian Empire is long gone, but it lives on in these imposing subjects. Are these images of privilege an unspoken affront to the seminar's democratic endeavors? Perhaps that history is less important than the present arrangement of power, invisible on the walls: the global dominance of imperial America. How ironic to be flexing our polyglot American, intellectual muscle in this aristocratic old-world setting.

Breakfast and lunch buffets and family-style dinners speak to more than the body's needs. Abundant food handsomely presented offers solace and the promise of community. An Austrian chef has modified the cuisine of central Europe to accommodate the dietary requirements of Muslims, Hindus, religious Jews, vegetarians, and weight watchers. Spinach strudel with cheese, chicken "oriental style," cauliflower soufflé, turkey kebabs with curry sauce, and a U.S.-style salad bar are among his gestures of inclusion.

Each morning, after pouring the first cup of steaming coffee from the breakfast buffet, I wonder where my table companions' talk will lead us. Mornings we're often in low gear, recovering from the previous night's reveling and too many free beers. Mornings, especially if I'm sitting with women, are time for personal talk about parents, children, and making a career. A female colleague from the Middle East tells me about the stigma that attaches to her divorce and the pressures she feels to live like a conventional Muslim woman. As a teacher, she encourages her female students to think for themselves and assert themselves. An Austrian woman whose work is on Chicana literature complains about the senior members of her department. They can't imagine why she has taken this strange ethnic "turn." "I'm surrounded by reactionaries," she says, "by white men without any respect for women or people of color."

At midmorning, after a lecture in the Meirhof, the Schloss's conference center, we return to the main building. In the salon, a large, dignified room with french doors leading to a flagstone terrace and the lake, our coffee break awaits: three buffet tables laden with small pastries, fruit, juices, coffee, tea, and bottled water. Those who didn't make it to breakfast can still get their calories and caffeine. While I don't need the calories, I crave this break—and a copycat version in midafternoon. The one-minute stroll between buildings eases the tension behind my eyes. A coffee and two cookies recharge the system. After the heated discussions following the morning lecture, talk in the salon is muted. No one is on stage. No one is maneuvering to claim the floor. A Tunisian fellow, a freethinking intellectual who had been my graduate student fifteen years earlier, describes the religious fervor now common among his colleagues. How does he cope, I want to know. "It's not easy," he says. "We are at home a lot." I join Ahmed, who is standing alone sipping a coffee. When I mention that he looks distracted, he tells me he is worried about his family's safety. I'm about to press him for details when a Moroccan fellow interrupts with a question about the morning lecture.

Attending the seminar is a big perk for all of us, faculty as well as fellows. The richer the perk, the more professionally validated we feel. Nevertheless, it's tempting to snipe at the hand that feeds us: to attack our American patron (a USAID grant supports this program) for using the seminar to co-opt criticism and buy friendship. The underside of the perk, for some fellows, is feeling like a very poor relative; they lack cash for shopping, phone calls home, or small personal indulgences. At the seminar, we try to level the playing field with our jeans and sweaters and the use of first names in defiance of ever-greater inequality between nations. It's not the task of our literary project to change the world. But the world's inequities do intrude on the seminar's business.

For the nine Arab Muslim fellows at the seminar, some of the world's inequities are reflected in our principal text, the *Heath Anthology of American Literature*, of which Paul Lauter is the general editor. The pathbreaking *Heath*, first published in 1990, integrates an astonishing range of literary voices and documents into a new literary canon. But the Arab Muslim fellows ask: Where are the Arab American writers? And why is so much attention in the seminar lavished on Jewish American writers? Paul is a Jew. I am a Jew. Kris, whose specialty is American-Jewish writing, must surely also be a Jew (he isn't). The power of Jews, they suggest, spreads from Wall Street to Hollywood to Harvard. Who speaks for the Palestinians?

Ahmed says very little. Of course he's angry with Americans and the American-Jewish lobby for our support of Israel. World Zionism is to blame for chasing his people from their villages, leaving them to fester in camps, and denying them the dignity of a state. I don't want to argue or make excuses for either Israel or the United States. I want to take refuge in the long history of multiple wrongs and failures of trust. I want to say that both sides have responsibilities. I want to admit my own uncertainties. Mostly I want to remove a stone or two from the wall that divides Ahmed and me.

In such painful situations, I am a coward. Still, for my own sake as much as Ahmed's, I push the process along. I ask him about his teaching and the problems of his university. He tells me about the psychic damage inflicted by the occupation and the scarcity of materials and funds. "Everything is a struggle," he says.

At 3:15 every afternoon we break for coffee, sweets, and fruit. Sometimes, after a quick hit of caffeine, I escape to my sun-filled suite on the third floor of the Schloss. In the study, gauzy curtains flutter in the breeze. I smell pine and mountain laurel. From the window, I admire the trees turning gold and russet and the snow-topped Alps in the distance.

Two days before the final banquet, peering down at the reflecting lake, I catch sight of a group of Japanese tourists, video cameras in hand, strolling along the opposite shore. The Schloss was immortalized in *The Sound of Music* as the putative home of the Von Trapp Family Singers. It's a popular destination groups from all over the world. Now I wonder foolishly whether the Japanese group's guide, after giving the requisite *Sound of Music* spiel, tells the "real" story. Does he explain that in 1938 the Nazis confiscated the Leopoldskron estate, then owned by theatrical producer Max Reinhart, because it was "Jewish property"? I was two years old that year, a blond, green-eyed toddler in New York. The flight of my four grandparents from Austria-Hungary some forty years earlier launched the American branch of our family.

On the next-to-last night of the seminar, I give a reading from my food memoir-in-progress. "It's the onset of Yom Kippur, the Day of Atonement," I say by way of introduction, "the holiest day on the Jewish calendar. Jews all over the world are fasting, and I've just dined on grilled brook trout, asparagus, and chocolate mousse. As a secular person, I don't ask forgiveness for failing to honor the holiday. I'm wry about all holiday rituals," I add, "Passover, Thanksgiving, even Ramadan."

I read from "Yom Kippurs at Yum Luk," about my teenage rebellions: sneaking out of the synagogue to feast on egg foo yung made with slivers of forbidden pork. I read about protecting my children from required attendance at my mother's Passover seder. I read about the lovely convolutions of my son's Jewish-Buddhist wedding. Watching the expressionless faces of the Muslims in the audience, I worry that I am claiming too much time for the Jews. Then I read an account of Ramadan in Tunisia, a story of an intimate family meal framed by greedy shopping at the beginning of the holiday and wild partying once each day's fast is finished. I try not to imagine what Ahmed is thinking.

The applause at the end is friendly but not enthusiastic. I probably should have given the tensions a rest. I could have turned the evening over to the fellows for a program of their own. Identity politics aside, I've had my share of performance time.

"You were brave," Saline, a woman from Morocco, tells me as we leave together, "to reveal so much about your life and your family." My eyes fill. They often do in moments of honest exchange. I am more sentimental than I care to admit, but not always predictably so. I didn't cry when my husband died in our bed. I don't cry at funerals or automobile accidents. It's hope that makes me emotional—hope that I can make contact when it counts: with a student in trouble or a difficult colleague, or my son when he feels he's been judged harshly or misunderstood. It's hope as represented by the founding of the United Nations, the discovery of the Salk vaccine, *Roe v. Wade*, the Velvet Revolution, and the election of Nelson Mandela. Saline's kind words give me hope. I relax a bit, not daring to wish for more.

Before the final banquet, we gather for drinks and hors d'oeuvres in the mirrored Venetian Room. Soft lights from sconces, candles, and an exquisite chandelier add to the glamour of the setting. I spot Ahmed, in a white shirt open at the collar, dark gray slacks, and a dark tweed jacket, standing alone. Ahmed, a good Muslim, doesn't drink. I'm drinking quickly, for courage. Whatever he might think, I tell Ahmed as rock music blares from the speakers, my memoir is not a celebration of how I was formed—my Jewish background—but an exploration of how I have chosen to be. I'm on my third glass of wine, rapidly losing focus. "How complicated we all are," I say. "It's easier to understand fictional characters than to understand one another."

I stand very close to Ahmed, with my hand on his arm. "I want Palestinians to have a state," I say, not for the first time. I utter the words slowly, with my eyes on his. Then I add, "But I also want Israel to be recognized by the Arab world." Over the speaker system drums roll, moving toward a crescendo. Neither of us moves. I think I detect a change in Ahmed's breathing, as if more air has entered his lungs. There is nothing else to be said. I feel my tears coming. He gives me a rare half smile.

At 4:00 in the morning, I pace between the bedroom and the study of my suite. My body feels the burden of too many midmorning cookies and midafternoon petit fours, of chocolate mousses at dinner and drinking in the *bierstube* until midnight. The abundance of the Schloss provides fuel, solace, and nurture. I take what is offered, more than I need, in the interests of social recycling. With so much lavished upon me, I want to behave generously. The effort shows on my waistline.

My head spins in confusion. The harder I struggle to understand others, the less I understand myself. Conflict is the norm for healthy people, but too much conflict is disabling. This community of scholars at the seminar is collegial and endearing but too diverse to be cozy. Almost all of us have worked hard to balance ego and self-restraint. My own package of conflicts is out in the open. First there is the professional Americanist who is most comfortable as a critic of America, except when foreigners are unfairly critical. Then there is the secular Jew and uneasy Zionist who rejects family traditions while embracing the ideology of multiculturalism. Finally, and less visibly, there is the feminist teacher and solo traveler who misses her dead husband's hands caressing her shoulders and back.

I contemplate a hot bath or a double scotch. Suddenly I am impatient to be home. Paradoxically, the very things I look for in travel—the epiphanies, the enlarged purview, and the rush of adrenaline in the rituals of farewell—are taking their inevitable toll.

Back home in Leonia, I receive a letter from Ahmed, dated December 18, 1995. He has inserted a postcard which, he writes, "is somehow related to ethnic food." The postcard shows Samaritans, a Jewish minority among Palestinians, engaged in the ritual sacrifice of a Passover lamb. Wearing red fezzes, white cotton pants, and shirts without collars, they are preparing a freshly slaughtered animal for barbecue over an olive-wood fire. One man is reading from a leather-bound prayer book; others are praying. The description on the back of the card is in Hebrew, English, and French.

Ahmed's letter begins with the seasonal "Merry Christmas." He writes about signs of hope for Palestinians and for the future of the West Bank: "Nablus is free. People are thrilled to see their own police in the streets and celebrations are everywhere. . . . As you may notice the stamps are Palestinian." He goes on to say that the Salzburg Seminar, where we met, was a unique educational and cultural experience. He asks me to write to him frequently.

I mull over Ahmed's choice of postcard. The subject is the Jews' Passover ritual. But is there a subtext here? Is the message that ritual slaughter, to maintain a tradition, requires the sacrifice and suffering of innocents? Muslims have these same traditions, but this card from Ahmed is about Jews. Is the reference to Jews as murderers? We are such subtle creatures. But sometimes we act from simple motives. I am confident that this "crossover" card, showing Jews who look like Muslims, is a gesture of friendship. I also believe that the card speaks to our common traditions as killers in God's name.

CHAPULINES, MOLE, AND FOUR POZOLES

Oaxaca, Mexico, 1996

On a blisteringly hot afternoon in Oaxaca, my friend Nancy and I stroll north from the Zocalo in search of a restaurant called Las Quince Letras. The guidebook warns that Las Quince Letras is easy to miss: we're to look for a plain purple entryway and a sign saying "*restaurante*." We fail to spot it on the first pass, peering foolishly at rows of unmarked doorways for the address, Abasolo 300. The street is deserted, soundless. We feel disoriented. Behind the ubiquitous closed shutters, are local residents eating their *comida* in silence? Or, having finished the midday meal, are they grabbing a siesta before the second half of a long working day? Although we have been in Mexico for almost two weeks and feel no jet lag, our clocks still don't run on local time.

It's shortly after 3:00 p.m. when *el restaurante* snaps into view. "*Gracias a dios,*" I catch myself thinking, a phrase I never use in English, but one that falls naturally from my lips in Spanish. The proprietor of Las Quince Letras greets us with polite restraint. But when I ask quickly *si podemos comer*, hoping that it is not too late, he flashes a smile and waves us in. We follow him through a cool, darkened room into a plant-filled courtyard where lunch will be served—to us, and to us alone.

Although Las Quince Letras has been touted as "an outstanding small restaurant," more than just another *comida* is riding on this visit. I have come for the house specialty, *botana oaxaqueña*—an array of twelve appetizers, including raw vegetables, chorizos, chicarrones (fried pork skin), tacos, guacamole, quesadilla, and my nervous passion, *chapulines*.

Chapulines, fried grasshoppers, are distinctly Oaxacan. At daybreak during the summer months, the small bugs are harvested in cornfields with fine nets, killed in a bath of scalding water, fried in lard, seasoned, and carried to market. They are sold from straw baskets on the main streets of the city by dozens of women and girls, who nibble as they walk, hand to basket to mouth. The bright red, crunchy snack—to be munched like peanuts or *pepitas*, pumpkin seeds—is seasoned with garlic, chili powder, and lime juice. *Chapulines* are nippy and, for Oaxacans, addictive.

On my first trip to Oaxaca, in 1966, the mere mention of *chapulines* unsettled my stomach. Tasting them was out of the question. I feel differently now, more attuned to the vagaries of human consumption and more avid for oddball edibles. My stomach is different too: educated, over the past three decades, in New York's ethnic eateries and in exotic venues from Rio to Cairo and Kyoto to Kathmandu, to appreciate strong tastes and weird textures. I've also learned, on trips like this, to cushion my digestive system with a morning cocktail of Pepto-Bismol and to keep a stash of Gelusil in my Sportsac along with Band-Aids, bug spray, and sunblock.

In the cool of the courtyard, Nancy and I wolf down warm tortillas and guzzle Coronas. When the *botanos* are spread out before us, I fixate on the dish of bright red *chapulines* catching the afternoon light. They glow. Our table, with its red, blue, and green striped cloth, gaily painted crockery, and yellow zinnias, also glows. The owner, Señor Alberto, stands by, alert to our needs. His wife, Susana, the cook, grins encouragingly at us from the doorway of the kitchen. Three pre-teen children sprawl on the floor near her, drawing contentedly. My tourist anxieties fall away. This tranquil domestic setting offers more protection to two *gringas* than a squadron of police: protection from beggars and sellers of trinkets and lottery tickets, from the din of traffic and dirt on the streets, from an overactive imagination of disease.

I turn off the movie in my head of female vendors fondling *chapulines* with their well-licked fingers and reach for "our" *chapulines*. I sprinkle a few on a bit of tortilla slavered with guacamole and take a cautious bite. The bland tortilla, the smooth-cool guacamole, the wake-up call of citrus and spice, and the airy crunch of *chapulines* make music in my mouth—not Mozart or hard rock but jazz riffs, full of sudden twists and surprises. From there on in, it's my hand to the dish to my mouth, again and again and again. Nancy, a fearless traveler who has driven across Asia with a fifteen-month-old child in a VW van, watches in amazement as I devour the grasshoppers. She leaves the treat untouched.

Chapulines enchant me because they are of Oaxaca, for Oaxacans: exotic, categorically Other, incorruptible, beyond the reach of global markets. Or are they? Several years ago, in Zabar's on the Upper West Side of Manhattan, I spotted chocolate-covered grasshoppers, six ounces in a slick package costing more than some Oaxaca market women earn in a week. I remember fancying the "candy" as a reminder of a food frontier I could not cross. Now that I had crossed over, I considered buying the chocolate version to amuse my grandchildren when I spin out my tale of *gringa* triumph. But no. As good Buddhists—brought up not to kill insects—the little kids would be horrified that I was so proud of being so cruel.

Teotitlán del Valle, Mexico, 1996

Most tourists go to Teotitlán del Valle, a famous Zapotec weaving village about forty minutes from Oaxaca, to shop for rugs. Nancy is eager to see weaving in situ; she wants to engage with the weavers, make a connection, bargain hard, and buy when the terms are right. While I'm a willing accomplice in this ritual encounter between first-world buyers and third-world sellers, I have my own consumer's agenda; my destination is Tlamanalli, a restaurant hyped by food connoisseurs as *the* place for "authentic," expertly prepared, and beautifully served Oaxacan cuisine.

When our taxi turns off the main road from Oaxaca at a sign announcing "Teotitlán del Valle/Centro," I am bewildered. I remember my original pilgrimage here in the mid-1960s, when the red clay of the unpaved road clung to my feet and left a fine dusting on my khaki skirt and bare shoulders. I also remember drinking two Cokes and two orange sodas to counter hunger pangs because no eatery seemed welcoming or clean enough for a *gringa* tourist.

In 1996, the road is still red clay, but now there is a new community center, a sprawling modern school, and perhaps a dozen large brick houses, "compounds" with center courtyards, some with fancy showrooms at the front for conducting business with corporate clients. Bloomingdale's and Pier 1 have opened global markets to the weaving establishments of Teotitlan del Valle; their demand for rugs, cushion covers, and wall hangings is so great that a few successful families now employ large numbers of poorer villagers, who were once independent weavers.

Tlamanalli, the restaurant, named for the Zapotec god of food, occupies a handsome, newly built brick building about a block from the center of town. The only identifier is a small bronze plaque near the door, a plaque so discreet as to be almost invisible. Passing through a twenty-foot vaulted doorway, Nancy and I enter a vast, bright, barnlike space. Tall trees and lush, semitropical plantings divide the restaurant proper from a gallery, where carpets woven by the renowned Mendoza brothers are displayed. The finest of the brothers' rugs, on permanent display at an art boutique in Oaxaca, sell for $10,000 to $70,000.

Abigail Mendoza, the owner of Tlamanalli, is a sister of the weavers; her indispensable collaborators in cooking and serving are her five sisters. When we visit, four of them are in the restaurant, all short, smooth-skinned women with waist-length, shiny black hair braided with colored wool. They wear long, brightly printed cotton dresses covered with white aprons. The sisters' traditional Zapotec appearance contrasts sharply with the low-keyed, modern style of the furnishings: blond wooden chairs, blond square tables, pale pink tablecloths, and smart, tiny vases filled with home-grown roses—a look popularized by Martha Stewart, the Gap, and Pottery Barn.

The menu lists about a dozen Oaxacan specialties, all freshly prepared in the open kitchen at the rear. We observe Marcelina, on her knees, bending over a *molcajete*, a black basalt mortar, making guacamole. With a pestle in hand, she mixes the avocado, bits of chopped onion, tomato, chiles, and other seasonings. A few feet away, Maria Luisa, also on her knees, grinds corn for *masa* (to thicken the soup) on a grinding stone, also made of black basalt, with a *muller*.

Our waitress, Rosaria, demure yet dignified, presents us with a complementary *mezcalito*, a small shot of mescal that is the traditional Oaxacan "opener." A few minutes later she brings toasted blue-corn tortillas and a smooth guacamole served with red salsa. Rosaria tells us that the corn for these tortillas was ground this very morning by her sister Adelina. As we speak, Adelina kneels in the rear, grinding nuts that are used in all the moles on the menu.

We order the *sopa de flores de calabaza*, a delicate, mildly perfumed soup made with golden squash blossoms and purslane (a celerylike vegetable), thickened with *masa harina* (freshly ground corn), and served with a perfect, triangular, golden-fried quesadilla (a taco with slightly sweet white cheese). The soup is beautiful to behold, silky-smooth and delicate in the mouth. Perfect—just as three English-language restaurant reviewers have promised, in articles framed and carefully displayed on the restaurant's long wall. And *suficiente*, enough. Our North American requirements for a midday meal in midsummer are more than satisfied. However, we are committed to continuing: with *mole negro*, black mole, the most celebrated and possibly the most complicated of Oaxaca's seven moles.

Mole comes from the Nahuatl word meaning "concoction," a sauce or stew containing chiles, nuts and seeds, spices and herbs, tomatoes and meats. *Mole negro* at Tlamanalli is a rich, succulent, nuanced, black-brown sauce covering a piece of braised chicken, which has probably been finished in the sauce. It is served on a large white plate accompanied only by a small portion of white rice dotted with cubes of carrot and zucchini. Simple looking, but impossible for the inexperienced mole eater to analyze or adequately appreciate.

Like most gringos, I mistakenly attribute the elegant black-brown color to chocolate. Chocolate is used in the recipe, along with peanuts, almonds, walnuts, sesame seeds, green and sometimes red tomatoes, onions, garlic, tortillas and dried bread, banana or plantain, many spices, and four or five different kinds of chiles. All of these elements are painstakingly worked into four purées and then blended into a single concoction. But the secret of the color, I subsequently discover, comes from toasting the seeds of the chiles (including black *chilhuacles*) until they are burned to a distinctive charcoal black.

Attacking my *mole negro* with an amateur's abandon, I wonder, certainly not for the first or last time, about the relationship between knowing how a dish is made, appreciating its nuances, and assessing its quality. I may know what I like, but surely what I like is conditioned by what I know. In eating, as in loving, ignorance is only momentarily bliss. Alas, even as I struggle to do justice to the multi-layered sauce and subtle chicken, the odds for a discerning response are poor. I am already too full from the guacamole, the brilliant *sopa*, and the picture-perfect quesadilla.

But something else is also at work, interfering with my attention to the *mole negro*. The restaurant as a site distracts me. On the one hand there is the apparent authenticity of the Zapotec kitchen and cuisine: the impressive, labor-intensive display of chopping and scraping, soaking and toasting, roasting and frying, mixing, blending, and puréeing, all by hand, by women on their knees, close to the earth. On the other hand, there is the creation that is Tlamanalli: a shrewdly conceptualized, appealing, and pricey mecca for tourists accustomed to mixing commerce and the arts of collecting with serious, high-end eating.

Tlamanalli sits both inside and outside the Zapotec past. Time stops in the preparation of food, but there's nothing old-fashioned about the Mendoza family's understanding of the power of tourism to enrich their coffers while eroding their traditions. The preindustrial and the postmodern meet in Tlamanalli: for Abigail Mendoza and her sisters, there is the restaurant business as cultural preservation; and for first-world travelers, there is the "experience" of a seemingly timeless, exotic cuisine in a well-lit, living museum.

Guanajuato, Mexico, 1996

Manolo, the Mexican guitarist at Shisuke's birthday party, leans toward me, his bedroom eyes fixed on my blond head, and pontificates: "Mexican music celebrates the woman, *ay, si, la mujer, su belleza*, her eyes, her hair, her skin, her face." I paste a smile on my face. Then, catching the look of unconcealed disgust on Nancy's face, I wish I hadn't. Macho treacle goes down hard at the tail end of the twentieth century—in spite of everything I've been told about the serenade ritual as a demonstration of "*la cortesía mexicana*." In a moment of confused consciousness, I blame myself for giving Manolo the opening. I initiated the conversation with him, *en español*, to be charming and to pass the time while waiting for the festivities to begin.

Reaching for a beer, I remind myself that Nancy and I are guests of the Instituto Dinámico in Guanajuato, where Shisuke, a corporate manager from Japan turned Spanish student, is being feted. The Instituto, a new, American-owned language school, occupies the second floor of a dilapidated building with a graceful center courtyard. Its freshly painted rooms, white with a snappy folkloric blue and yellow trim, merit an A for *ambiente*. However, the collection of card tables and unmatched folding chairs in the office and classrooms, the handmade signs, the sparse library holdings, and the phone on the floor all announce that the school is—to put it generously—a work in progress.

Shisuke's party is our second huge meal of the day at the Instituto. It's also our second pozole, one of the richest and heaviest (and sometimes spiciest) of Mexican stews, made of hominy and pork and garnished with fresh vegetables and tortillas. For those of us given to eating salads in summer or a piece of grilled salmon with a splash of lemon, *pozole* is more than a challenge; it's a threat. My irritation with Manolo, it occurs to me, my unseemly humorlessness, may be related to how uncomfortable I'm feeling from the excesses of the midday *comida*.

The first pozole colors the day. The event leading up to it is billed as a cooking demonstration. Beginning at 9:30 in the morning, Rosalinda, a local chef, is teaching students and staff to make *pozole rojo*, the hominy and pork stew flavored with intense red chiles. Our friends Jim and Jennie from Portland, Oregon, who are studying Spanish at the school, have invited us to come along and watch. They are making a video of the demonstration as a favor to Rosalinda and Mercedes, the school's director.

The kitchen of the Instituto has no ambience but considerable authenticity. It is a small, dark, corridor-shaped space, barely large enough for Rosalinda and Shisuke, who has been enlisted as sous chef, dishwasher, and errand runner. Rosalinda presides over a two-burner propane stove stacked on top of a makeshift counter; Shisuke peels, cuts, and chops on a rickety card table, the kitchen's only workspace. Crowding the stove is the sink, a chipped, narrow, porcelain relic that provides cold water only.

Jim, Jennie, Nancy, and I hover in the doorway of the kitchen. We kibitz quietly, jostling one another for a view of the action. Mercedes, her secretary, and her male assistant drift around behind us, torn between the demands of the chef and the chores of the day. Rosalinda, worlds removed from Julia Child, is a no-nonsense cook: no jokes, no smiles, no entertaining anecdotes, no camaraderie with the video crew, and no thank-yous to Shisuke, whose eyes tear from onions for almost an hour.

But Rosalinda knows pozole. Like a surgeon in an operating room, she barks instructions to her underlings while announcing each procedure clearly in Spanish. For almost three hours we stand by as boiled kernels of corn, the hominy, simmer slowly in water to which pieces of pork shoulder, garlic, and salt have been added. We stand by as the chiles are grilled until they blister, then soaked, drained, puréed by hand, and strained through a sieve into the soup. We stand by as the garnishes of lettuce, radishes, onions, and lime are cut into slices and wedges and tortillas are crisp-fried.

There's no glamour here, only knowledge of the craft, gritty labor, and attention to detail. By the time lunch is served, in cheap red clay bowls, we are weary but well informed. I eat carefully, alert to my body's messages. The heat and spice of *pozole rojo* will be bad for my digestion; the Coronas I drink to cool the mouth and throat will be bad for my head. Even before I finish my portion of pozole, I long for Gelusil and an unlimited siesta. I swear that I'll put nothing in my mouth for the rest of the day.

My wish is not to be. In travel, even more than at home, debts must be acknowledged and honored. Mercedes, who welcomed Nancy and me to the cooking demonstration and incorporated us into the little family of the Instituto, requests our presence at a party for Shisuke. We cannot refuse the invitation; nor can we resist the pressure to eat. The evening's *pozole blanco*, made without red chiles, which Mercedes has prepared during the late afternoon, is unexpectedly delicate and delicious. *Muy sabroso*, delicious, I tell Mercedes, hoping she won't notice that I've barely touched my dish. In fact, she doesn't. Mercedes's attention is focused on Shisuke, the shy guest of honor, and on Manolo, who seems happier drinking beer than singing for his supper. I'm grateful for Manolo's indolence, since his guitar playing is as bad as his conversation. Still, when the hat is passed at the end of the evening, I contribute generously. The food has been free, unforgettable—and *sabrosa*. The bounty, in pesos, is his.

New York, 1996

Three months later, on a chilly fall day in New York, I study the menu at Gabriela's while waiting for Alice to appear. A Mexican restaurant with a folkloric-funky decor, Gabriela's is popular with Upper West Side artists and intellectuals. The food, cooked by Gabriela Hernandez and her relatives from Jalisco and served by her husband, Miguel, is straightforward and lusty—authentic in its resistance to New York hybridities and New York chic. Portions are huge, and the price is better than right.

It's 2:00 in the afternoon, a fine hour for *comida mexicana*, especially if one relishes the illusion of a restaurant of one's own. Alice, who arrives as I'm sipping a Corona, waits for my enthusiasms to announce themselves. I order Yucatan-style barbecued chicken, a local favorite, flavored with intense ancho chiles, garlic, and oregano. For Alice, I insist that only pozole will do. Her hominy and pork stew is presented in an enormous earth-colored soup bowl, accompanied by raw vegetables and *tostados* (little fried tortillas). Steam from the bowl rises like a great mushroom cloud, releasing an awesome chile-garlic aroma. I immediately regret ordering the chicken.

Alice, for her part, would have welcomed the chicken. She plans to write later in the afternoon and has begun agonizing over the impact of pozole on scholarship. I sympathize, releasing her from the obligation to earn an A for adventurous eating. After all, when Alice and I get together, having a meal is only an excuse for swapping stories about work, travel, and family. And so we do at Gabriela's, for almost two hours, slipping out of our grating New York rhythms into the softness of Mexican time. Then, as the late autumn sun drops beneath the high-rise canyons on Amsterdam Avenue, we ask for *la cuenta*, the reckoning.

A tourist's learning curve is slow, I remind myself. There are such deep and elaborate constructions of the self to confront, so many actual and imagined barriers to overcome. A few weeks in a foreign place, and I've barely nicked the outermost rings of the onion. But I'm lucky. At home in metropolitan New York, thanks to migration and global economics, my traveling continues. The next time at Gabriela's, I'll order a pozole of my own.

Patzcuaro and Tzurumutaro, Mexico, 2000

Lupe, the housekeeper at Casa Don Miguel, is feeling low this Thursday morning. So is her perpetually cheery four-year-old daughter, Alejandra. When I ask Alejandra how she is, she responds with a well-trained *muy bien gracias. No es verdad*, Lupe gently admonishes Alejandra; tell *la señora* that you are sad, *que estas triste.* Alejandra is sad, Lupe explains, because she loved her *abuelito*, who has gone from this life. Thus I learn of the death of Lupe's father-in-law, Eduardo Luna.

Lupe wants all of us at the Casa to come to her house in Tzurumutaro that evening. The family will gather, and there will be prayers and food. She presses me to say yes and I nod warmly, with more eagerness than I feel. Ordinarily, Lupe's style is soft and accommodating; her ready smile is a disarming survival strategy. Today, behind the pleading in her eyes, I detect the stubbornness that sees her through.

It's Lupe's wanting that interests me. Why should my presence matter? Even though we chat at the house, and I often make a small fuss about some new outfit of Alejandra's, I am a stranger, a tourist passing through. Would my coming lend importance to her role in the family? Does she want me there for her husband's benefit? For her mother-in-law's? Or is it simply that on such occasions mourners yearn for a large crowd, signaling respect for the deceased and respect for the family?

A stranger's presence, especially a stranger from El Norte for whom one works, carries weight. Still, during most of my waking hours in Mexico, I'm too preoccupied with my marginality to gauge my importance. Lupe knows better. The living she and her family eke out is what marginality means. With the money and freedom to spend a month in Patzcuaro, I have the power that counts.

I find Esperanza, Lupe's aunt and our cook, cutting flowers in the rear garden and ask about funeral protocol. A trim woman in her mid-forties, Esperanza has a cooler temperament than her thirty-year-old niece. She never smiles for form's sake. She doesn't tell gringos what she thinks we want to hear. Now, as I ask her advice, the opportunity to speak candidly excites her, pushes her beyond her cultivated diffidence. Esperanza seems surprised that her niece expects me to visit the house this evening. There will be a rosary, beginning after 9:00 p.m., when people are home from work, she says. It will be hard, that late at night, to get a cab back to Patzcuaro. Just come to the funeral on Friday, she tells me. I'm relieved to be off the hook. Another Casa resident is leaving for the States this evening, and I had been looking forward to farewell margaritas at our favorite restaurant on the Plaza Grande.

On Friday, after an early lunch, Brian, a young poet at the Casa, Esperanza, and I leave Patzcuaro together. We take the fifteen-minute bus ride to the edge of Tzurumutaro, an indigenous Purepecha village of one thousand people. The town's main square, with the church at one end, looks dusty and poor. We enter the church as the funeral mass is in progress. All around us little children are sitting quietly with their mothers. They kneel, stand, and cross themselves without prompting. Two small boys roam the aisles, and a third stretches out on the wood floor. Just as the priest reminds the mourners that the departed Eduardo Luna has been called to his final resting place where his sins will be forgiven, an infant begins to shriek. The priest continues his ritual unperturbed.

When the service ends, there is a round of handshaking. My neighbors say *la paz*, and I shake hands and repeat the greeting, *la paz, la paz, la paz*. Male relatives carry the coffin out of the church and lead the funeral procession through the square, along unpaved village streets, across the highway, and into the cemetery. Earlier in the day these men dug the grave into which Eduardo Luna will soon be lowered. Brian and I walk with Esperanza near the end of the procession. Almost everyone is carrying freshly cut gladiolas, marigolds, or daisies. Having left the matter of flowers for the last minute, I am carrying a half dozen red silk roses, purchased minutes before we left for Tzurumutaro.

The mourners, perhaps a hundred people in all, gather around the freshly dug grave. As the casket is lowered, a middle-aged woman collapses in the arms of female relatives and is helped away from the site. Standing in front of me, three carefully groomed young women in tight jeans and close-fitting tee shirts wail *abuelito, abuelito.* The widow wanders among the company, unattended by family members. A shrunken old woman with a wrinkled face, she is teary but composed. Now the mourners begin to refill the grave. One by one they gather up handfuls of earth, which they kiss and let loose over the casket.

As family, friends, and neighbors fill the grave, Lupe and her two sons kneel nearby, pulling the petals off hundreds of marigolds. They load the petals into black plastic bags and carry the bags to the gravesite, where a neat mound of earth now covers the casket. Two men spread the marigold petals over the mound; a third collects the mourners' flowers and lays them on top of the petals.

There is no formal end to the ritual. Gradually the mourners drift away. Esperanza, Brian, and I extend condolences to Lupe, who immediately invites us back to the house for pozole. Esperanza begs off, saying that her son is home alone. Brian and I also beg off, citing our prefuneral *comida*, which has left no room for another big meal. If not today, Lupe insists, then we must come in nine days, when the period of mourning is officially over. There will be another gathering at the house, another rosary followed by another pozole. We must come, Lupe reiterates. *Claro que si*, we respond. Certainly we will be there.

Fifty people, about half of them children and most of the adults female, turn out for the final rosary in honor of Eduardo Luna. On the porch of the Luna house, at the far end, an altar has been set up. A monumental metal cross, surrounded by white flowers in copper vases, looms over the embroidered cloth that rests on the altar. On the ground in front of the altar, white flower petals form another large cross, some five feet long and two feet wide. Two lines of plastic chairs form a narrow aisle leading to the altar. In the dirt yard beyond the porch several wooden planks are laid across cement blocks to form benches.

Brian and I arrive by cab shortly before the designated hour of 5:00 p.m. At Lupe's insistence, we've brought along my cousin Caryl, who joined me at the Casa earlier in the week. The three of us, like visiting dignitaries, are asked to take seats close to the altar. Several older women, wrapped in striped rebozos, join us on the porch. Women of the middle generation, wearing the faded pastel Purepecha apron but no shawls, fill the benches in the yard. Most of the children sit with their mothers. They do not chatter or fidget or whine. A few of the youngest chase one another around the courtyard, knowing somehow not to shout as they run. Four mangy-looking dogs wander in and out. Esperanza, who sits opposite us on the porch, delivers a deliberate kick each time one of the animals brushes her ankles.

As the light fails, we can still make out the open kitchen on the far side of the courtyard. There are four vats on the stove, Lupe tells us, with enough mild white and spicy red pozole for a small army. Ten women have worked most of the day, soaking the corn (or hominy), as is traditional, in lye, boiling it slowly so that the kernels absorb the liquid, and then adding the pork, which cooks for four hours. Finally, there are the trimmings to prepare: chopped onion, chopped cabbage, slices of avocado, and chunks of lime along with oregano and dried red pepper.

A big crowd, I think to myself, as I sit and stand through the long, repetitive ceremony. A lay preacher, a vigorous woman in her sixties, leads the service. Mourners of all ages join in, singing and chanting with emotion. Halfway through the service Luna's brother distributes candles and gladiolas to all of us as we move toward the altar. He lights the first candle, and the light is passed from person to person, first along the length of the porch and then to those in the yard. Holding my candle, I think about my husband, for whom I have never lighted one. Tears run down the left side of my face.

After the service, we are served rum and Coke and white pozole in paper bowls. My appetite fails me. While I haven't grieved for the unknown Señor Luna, I have felt his family's loss and reexperienced my own. I would like to pass on the pozole, but I know my responsibilities as a guest. I eat—much more than is comfortable. However, when the red pozole arrives immediately after the white, I turn it down. Gratefully I accept more rum and some hot tea, followed by the traditional *mezcalito*. With the booze brightening my mood, I assure the two elderly women to my right that I adore pozole, that *el pozole blanco de esta casa es tan delicioso* and I'll remember it always, always.

It appears that I am to be rewarded for my enthusiasm. No sooner have I uttered the last *delicioso* than Lupe appears with two plastic containers of pozole for me to take home. Neither my enthusiasm nor my status as a stranger accounts for this "reward," merely custom. All of the women sitting near me are presented with plastic containers—or, in some cases, plastic buckets. I can't help wondering about the traffic in these plastic items. Do members of other households who expect to take home leftovers bring their own? Is there an informal pooling of plastic containers, available to any family in mourning? Will Lupe retrieve the ones we are taking to the Casa once they are emptied? Around such details cultures are organized.

It was not a good turnout, Esperanza tells me the next morning. For our family, she says, attendance is usually much better. I let her comments hang for a moment, uncertain about how to proceed. In my mind I am still replaying the funeral as ritual, but Esperanza is leading me in another direction. If we were speaking English, I would probably say, "Tell me more." The Spanish equivalent, however, seems both too direct and too vague. Instead I ask the age of Señor Luna's widow. Only seventy, Esperanza responds. She looks older; she has had many cares. The departed Eduardo Luna was a bad drunk. He beat his wife, Esperanza adds, and other family members, too. His son, Lupe's husband, is one of those apples that doesn't fall far from the tree. *Otro borrocho*, almost dead himself a few months ago of cirrhosis of the liver, and still he loves his wine. People in the village know these drunks, Esperanza continues, and the damage they do. They don't deserve respect. Mexican men are like that—good for nothing.

GEORGIA ON MY MIND

Tbilisi, Republic of Georgia, 2002

Arriving at London Heathrow from Newark, I check the boards for my British Air flight to Tbilisi, the capital of the Republic of Georgia. Terminal 1 for European connections, the signs announce, and Terminal 4 for Asian connections. The map in my head isn't helpful. It shows Georgia at the crossroads between Europe and Asia—wedged between the Caucasus Mountains and Russia to the north, the Black Sea to the west, and Turkey, Armenia, and Azerbaijan to the south. A sympathetic clerk directs me to Terminal 4, where I queue up behind a group of chatty diplomats and NGO staffers. In French and English they trade complaints about power outages in Tbilisi, along with homeless refugees, corrupt politicians, and closed museums.

No announcement is made about our flight, and no light flashes at Gate 17 as we board. When I question two French speakers about these irregularities, they shrug. For Eurasia, *c'est normal*, they say. The smart traveler, I remind myself, accepts confusion as a given.

On this trip, I am fortunate in having my confusions tended to. My hosts for the two-week visit, sponsored by the U.S. embassy in Tbilisi, are Georgian colleagues in the field of American studies. Lika, Vaso, and Nana greet me with hugs at midnight when my flight arrives. In battered Russian cars, they chauffeur me to meetings and lectures and show me around their gritty, once glorious city. Best of all, they and their colleagues spoil me with sturgeon and caviar for lunch and sumptuous evening bacchanals.

Although Georgia is an economically distressed and floundering postcommunist state, my colleagues believe in its democratic future. Their professional work, as teachers and scholars of American history and culture, links them to the U.S. model of a free society.

Café Manhattan is decked out with wraparound murals of the New York skyline. The Twin Towers shimmer in the evening sky. "I Happen to Like New York" plays

on the sound system. My colleague Nina, a professor of English, and her husband, Boris, have chosen this spot for our after-dinner drinks. I feel them watching my face, eager for reactions. I don't know whether to laugh or weep. It's April 2002, seven months after 9/11. New Yorkers, even those of us who now live in New Jersey, are still vibrating from the jihadist attacks. We speak in depressed tones and sleep badly. The iconic New York of the mural and song is in deep disrepair, along with our national psyche. My paper for the Georgian Association of American Studies conference in Tbilisi, two days hence, is a meditation on these troubles. I'll be probing connections between the Twin Towers and Big Macs, between U.S. economic power, popular culture, military penetration, and arrogant, unilateral overreach.

From the Georgian side, the picture is different. Mindful of seventy years of Soviet oppression, Boris and Nina, like so many Georgians, welcome Uncle Sam's interest in their small, vulnerable nation. With McDonald's golden arches not yet a blight on their landscape, they appreciate the United States as Georgia's largest foreign investor and largest donor of aid (about $90 million in 2002). They nod sagely when I mention the pipeline that is to run through their country, carrying oil westward from Kazakhstan, as a motive for U.S. support.

Café Manhattan has its own special meanings for Boris and Nina. In the 1980s Boris had a job with an international bank in New York. He adored the city and adapted his English to its slangy rhythms. After work each day, he returned to his apartment in suburban Cliffside Park, New Jersey, a town just six miles south of my home in Leonia. When Nina visited her husband, she and Boris often ate at Kervan Kebab, my favorite neighborhood Turkish restaurant. Could we ever have crossed paths there, I wonder? Could we have been seated at adjacent tables, eating the same shepherd's salad, taramasalata, and shish kebab? I tell Boris and Nina that the Turkish owners of Kervan Kebab have recently added Georgian wines to their wine list in response to requests from Georgian immigrants.

We've been discussing Georgian wines since dinner at the Café Toucan. "We are wine drinkers and wine lovers," Nina says, "not like the Russians. Georgian wines are as central to our culture as French wines are to French culture—and as good." Partisanship about Georgian wines runs high among all the people I meet in Georgia. They speak about their local vineyards in superlatives. Five hundred varieties of grapes are grown. Wine, they tell me, has been cultivated in Georgia since the fourth century BC, and *glovino*, the Georgian word for wine, existed before the words *vino* and *vin*.

I confess to being a dedicated but fussy wine drinker, preferring light, dry whites. No problem, Boris assures me. The white Prince of Imereti that arrived at our dinner table earlier in the evening at the Toucan was perfect: like a lean California sauvignon blanc. We raised our glasses. "To friendship," Boris said. "To American studies," Nina added. "To Georgia," I said. Since Georgians always drink with food, our appetizers arrived promptly: an eggplant salad, a salad of green beans with walnuts (walnuts are everywhere, I've been told), and *khachapuri*, the famous Georgian cheese bread, egg-enriched filling in a golden, yeasty dough, served in wedges. "You won't find this in Manhattan," Boris said, referring not to the *khachapuri* but the satisfying Prince of Imereti. "Our best wines don't travel."

Nor is the Prince of Imereti available at the Café Manhattan, where our conversation has taken a somber turn. "Change comes slowly in Georgia," Boris remarks, referring to President Shevardnadze's failure to rein in corruption in the public sector. "Change feels like the norm in New York," I say, "and too much of it is either regressive or dangerously out of control."

The gentrified neighborhood surrounding Café Manhattan is an emblem of change in Tbilisi. Restaurants and bars line the narrow cobblestone streets, reminding me of Greenwich Village in the 1950s. Smartly dressed young people queue up for tables, happy to have money in their pockets.

My hotel, the Primavera, also belongs to the emerging story of postcommunist Georgia. A joint venture between Georgian and U.S. investors, the new hotel comes equipped with a gym, skylit pool, and rooftop restaurant. It is engineered according to U.S. standards, my colleague Vaso assures me when I ask to move from a much smaller hotel that is far from Tbilisi State University. Vaso, a historian and president of the newly established American Studies Association of Georgia, spent several years in Washington DC, working for the Georgian embassy. Preferring teaching to diplomacy, he is proud of his country's progress since independence and passionate about bringing the best of American capitalism, democracy, and higher education to Georgia.

A large man with a broad Slavic face and blond hair, Vaso mixes can-do optimism with a politician's canny know-how. He has persuaded the U.S. embassy to help support the establishment of an American Studies Centre at Tbilisi State University. His wife and daughter have taught him to be a feminist, Vaso says winningly. I hold on to Vaso's assertions about the positive impact of American technology on Georgian tourism on the night my king-size bed lurches three inches to the right and then slips back into place. During the earthquake that night, even the half glass of beer on my night table remains upright. Primavera, springtime, is not the season for dying. How clever of the hotel owners, I can't help thinking, to give the place a tourist-friendly name associated with new beginnings.

"I'm the most energetic and talkative person I know," my colleague Nana tells me. She's not exactly boasting, just describing herself with characteristic self-confidence. With lustrous black hair, clear pale skin, high cheekbones, and a big smile, Nana is a striking-looking woman. A bold-patterned silk scarf flung over a neutral sweater is her signature look: bright and upbeat. Nana's passions, like her energy, are seemingly without limit: they encompass art and music, books and teaching, her two talented sons, friendship and food—especially Georgian food—and Georgia itself. Nana relishes words, both Georgian and English, and moves seamlessly between her native language and her professional language.

At the American studies conference, she sits next to me, simultaneously translating from Georgian into English. When I give my paper, "The Fog, the Big Mac, the Twin Towers, and the Flag: Perspectives on September 11," she stands beside me. In animated tones well matched to mine, Nana translates sequentially into Georgian. Seated in the front row during my talk are four professors of English, Nina among them. Occasionally, one of these colleagues interrupts Nana's translation with a better phrase, which Nana gratefully acknowledges. That's trust,

I think to myself, admiring the collaborative give-and-take among colleagues who are friends.

Whenever I ask Nana how she is, her response is the same. "Fine. I'm always fine. I can't afford to be otherwise." Nana's husband is working somewhere in central Asia while Nana supports herself and her two sons, both university students. "I do everything," she says. "I clean, I shop, I sew, I cook and keep the house in shape. I'm saving for a car," she adds, "because my sons will need one. No one helps me," she says without anger. To make ends meet and have something extra as well, Nana works all the time: at the university, with private pupils, doing translations—six and a half days out of seven. It's her friends who get her through, Nana tells me. She's with them several evenings a week, sharing a little food, drinking wine, smoking, and talking late into the night.

One evening, Nana's close friend Tati, a publisher of children's books, makes a dinner party in my honor. Ten of us gather around a small square wooden table that's the right size for four. Soon the platters, which Tati and three friends have spent hours preparing, are brought out of the kitchen with a flourish. There are salads of tomatoes and cucumber with parsley, dill, and walnuts; salads of eggplant and walnuts; freshly baked breads, *khachapuri*, chicken in a sauce thickened with walnuts, and all sorts of sturgeon—smoked and sliced, baked, and in a casserole. More dishes than I can remember.

As is traditional at Georgian dinner parties, a man serves as *tamada* or toastmaster. The honor this evening goes to Giorgi, a book designer who works with Tati. As soon as the food is presented, the toasts begin. The first round is to new friends (in my honor) and old friends. After Giorgi's toast, Nana says, "Friends are our comfort and joy. They turn our tears to laughter." "New friends are like windows," I respond. "They open the stuffy spaces we inhabit to unexpected breezes; they let the light penetrate dark corners. For these gifts I am grateful to all of you."

The toasts continue: to our children and our parents, to our food, our hostess, our work, to the land we love, to Georgia. The flow of tributes becomes increasingly affectionate. Men and women are equally sentimental, eager to expound on their love for one another and for Georgia. In the United States, presidents and politicians speak this way, but not my friends. We're more self-protective, more accustomed to irony. Critique is our business. If we celebrate America, we do so knowing that our advantages come at the expense of others—those who clean our houses, collect our garbage, and fight our wars. Nana and her friends, deprived of the burdens of affluence and empire, relish each hour they have electricity in their homes. They pamper their ten-year-old cars. They rely on one another. They know what counts.

I lay awake in my king-size bed on the top floor of the Hotel Primavera obsessing about public bathrooms. In the course of an ordinary day in Georgia, when I heed nature's call I'm likely to be directed to a latrine that is dirty and smelly, without lightbulbs or toilet paper. Since my bladder has become more nervous with age, I automatically calculate what I can eat or drink when I am not at my hotel or someone's home—or in the university rector's office, with its clean, private bathroom. (More than one cup of coffee is risky; a beer is impossible.)

The question of sanitation is culturally fraught. Our facilities in the United States and in the West generally are a function of economic development, not superior morality. Georgian women faculty and students make do year after year. The inconvenience I experience, as a visitor here for just a short time, is unimportant. Still, it nags at me. Now, when people ask me, "When will you return to Georgia?" I imagine blurting out: "When university authorities show enough respect for students and teachers to provide them with decent bathrooms."

One afternoon, my obsession gets the upper hand. At the University for Foreign Languages and Cultures, about fifty students and faculty members squeeze into a conference room to hear me give a talk, "How We Live Now" in multicultural America. My presentation includes a series of anecdotes about diversity. I describe the challenges facing the elementary school in my suburban town, where forty different languages are spoken. I explore the choices confronting my friend Liz, who left her black lesbian lover to marry her Chinese American boyfriend and then left him to resume her lesbian life. I mull over the verbal assaults I've absorbed from my limousine driver, a well-read, right-wing Italian American man who rails at feminism, welfare cheats, affirmative action, and my privileged life as a college professor. It's a wry personal narrative about the inequities, opportunities, and contradictions of contemporary American culture.

During the discussion period, a student asks when I will return to Georgia. "When will I return?" I say, repeating her query while contemplating the dour expressions of the faculty members in the room, mostly middle-aged women like myself. These shockingly underpaid professors (they earn $27 a month) who teach without supplies, professional journals, copying machines, computers, or a university bookstore will not be charmed by American candor about dirty bathrooms. To speak of such matters would be unmannerly, as if I were blaming them for their society's poverty and dysfunction.

Suddenly, the need to assert my candid American feminist self overcomes me. I want to speak as I would at home, provocatively, as if oblivious to cultural differences between the United States and Georgia. Just as the session ends, I confess my fastidious response to sidestepping puddles of urine in public bathrooms. There's no time for further discussion. I'm informed that a driver is waiting to take me to my next appointment.

Lika, a historian, refers to Georgia as a "southern culture" burdened by notions of honor, pride, and the need to save face. The macho men whom such a culture produces are difficult for women to deal with as rational peers. Of course, these men don't believe that women are their peers, she adds, even though women have had equal rights since the Soviet era and even though men rely on women's strength.

A founding member of Women for a Changed Society, Lika invites me to a dinner meeting at the home of Ia, the group's president. At the door, Ia greets us in a flowing crimson caftan. A regal-looking woman with black hair pulled tightly into an elegant bun, Ia is aglow with pride of place. Her apartment is freshly papered, in white with touches of silver, and her large sofa and overstuffed chairs have been reupholstered in a rich blue brocade. Given the shabby exterior of her building and most residential structures in Tbilisi, interiors, not addresses, are what count.

The two women helping out in the kitchen, Ia tells us, are refugees, her neighbors in a village in Abkhasia, where she has another home. They are in Tbilisi now, along with thousands of others, fleeing the ethnic war for independence from Georgia. Ia assists them with occasional work, food, and a place to stay in an emergency. "They're my neighbors," she comments, "so of course they come to me."

In the living room, which also serves as a dining room, we join twelve professional women, most of them between forty and fifty-five years of age. They are stylishly dressed, well coiffed, and carefully made up. Six of the women are biologists, two are university teachers, one is a librarian, and three are midlevel managers. Lika introduces me as an American professor of women's sudies and a feminist. The scientists, struggling with English, want me to know that Georgian women are well represented in the sciences (and that most doctors, a poorly paid profession, are female). The culture of science, they add with a mixture of resignation and rage, is dominated by men, and men control funds for research. Science has taken a beating since the end of communism, Lina, a neurologist, says. "We are devastated," she continues, "but we manage better than our male colleagues. They drink, become depressed. We take whatever job will put food on the table—nursery school teaching, nursing, cooking, too."

Ia's Abkhasian helpers, wearing simple cotton dresses and aprons, set out cold vegetable salads, bread, cheese, olives, sliced smoked salmon, and smoked sturgeon. Some twenty-odd dishes and platters cover the embroidered white tablecloth. As we begin helping ourselves, more platters are wedged into the remaining space: *khachapuri* (folded over rather than flat, in the form of an enormous Danish pastry), a crab salad, baked sturgeon, and a shredded chicken salad with walnuts.

At the table, most of the women eat very little and drink lightly; most of them chain-smoke. At regular intervals ashtrays are removed, emptied, and replaced. So much beautiful food sits untouched. Are they too tense to eat, I wonder, too burdened to drink freely—or simply worried about drinking and driving. While nobody speaks about weight problems, I wonder about the impact of a diet rich in carbohydrates on these women, who run the gamut from skinny to plump. Perhaps eating isn't the center of this gathering after all.

The abundant feast plays second fiddle to conversation. Sharing their struggles at work and at home, the women at Ia's table build community and support. Support, it appears, is less fraught than change. Certainly, these women want a more effective, forward-looking, and less corrupt government; and they believe that women working together can accomplish more than male leaders, politicians, and bureaucrats. However, they are uncomfortable about being aggressive. The men they work under and the men they live with need to be cajoled into changing their ways of thinking and acting. Around the table there is agreement about the importance of covert tactics: gentle manipulation, subtle suggestions, offering ideas that men can not only accept but claim as their own.

Is this smart pragmatism, I wonder, or defeatism? In terms of material conditions, the rapid changes of the postcommunist era have been disastrous for most Georgians, and especially for professionals. I think again about the uneaten salads and the platters of smoked fish; about the three enormous deep-dish custard fruit desserts (each of which could easily serve fifteen) languishing on the table. Are the uncertain costs of women's assertiveness and more social change too heavy for festive eating? So often, food is the fix we want. But not this evening among these women. If this were a gathering of U.S. feminists, I might be tempted to interpret their not eating as a politics of resistance: a determination to maintain some critical edge rather than comfort oneself, as convention would have it, with food and drink. I haven't been in Georgia long enough to know the meanings of this group's behavior.

When the round of ritual toasts begins, the first is "To women." The second is to the hostess for the feast she has orchestrated. The third is to mutual support. As a guest and an outsider, I am moved by these women's feelings of solidarity. Having other professional women as a sounding board mutes their frustrations. It strengthens their will to sustain themselves in the face of oppressive traditions, unpleasant bosses, and demanding husbands. Whatever their disappointments, they are professionals. Other women in Georgia are much worse off, they know.

I know that my friends and I are so much better off than these Georgian women. Yet we habitually complain. We want utopia now. As the toasting continues, I'm eager to express my admiration. "May American women learn from the example of the Georgian women," I say. "May we learn to remain optimistic in the face of hardship, learn resilience and good-natured perseverance, learn not to be overcritical and perpetually unsatisfied." My eyes fill. The depth of my feeling surprises me. And so do my words. I mean every one of them.

Vakhtang, the vice rector of a proud regional university in central Georgia, has chosen a riverside restaurant for our party of eight. After two days of lectures (about the meanings of 9/11 and U.S. multiculturalism) and intense meetings with faculty about American studies curriculum, I'm ready to party. So are Nata, the U.S. embassy's cultural assistant and my talented translator, and our driver, Merin. I can tell from the jocular tone of my academic colleagues, all close friends of Vakhtang's, that partying is on everyone's agenda this evening.

It's a weekday night and off-season for outdoor eating. The spacious main dining room of the restaurant, meant to accommodate seventy or eighty, is empty when we arrive and, except for our table, remains so all evening. Any doubts I might have had about the relationship between popularity and quality, however, are dispelled as the platters of food pour out of the kitchen: the familiar vegetable salads first, followed by lightly fried trout, baked sturgeon, cold jellied pork, garlic fried chicken, peasant bread, and two versions of *khachapuri*. Waiters continue to bring out hot and cold dishes until the table is covered.

Vakhtang, seated at the head of the table, smiles warmly at me as he lifts his glass for the first toast. "To new friends," he says, "who bring new ideas into our lives, new points of view. They come from afar and make our world seem bigger and smaller, too." We all empty our glasses, and Vakhtang and his male colleagues immediately refill them. Other toasts pick up on the importance of American studies to Georgia and the generosity of the American embassy in supporting this work. The cycle of ritual toasts continues around the table. Merin, our driver, toasts to his children, "who bring wisdom as well as joy to my life and ask questions that change my thinking." He's a trained lawyer, as it turns out, who makes a better living as a chauffeur for the U.S. embassy than he could as an attorney.

No glass remains empty for long. More toasts are offered: to new relationships, new programs, and peace. The Georgians' heartfelt style overwhelms my characteristically wry one when I raise my glass to "hospitality that is even more generous than the guidebooks guaranteed and warmth that transforms colleagues into friends."

With a Georgian love song blaring over the speaker system, Vakhtang invites me to dance. Alone on the floor, we do a slow two-step while others at our table watch, or try not to watch, or imagine scenarios that have no basis in fact. I feel Vakhtang's firm lead, his smooth face close to mine. We're both mellow with vino. And into veritas. "You're a master at handling people," I tell him, "with velvet gloves." Indeed, Vakhtang's charm camouflages his political savvy; it softens people to do his bidding. Without missing a beat, he compliments me on my lectures—and my looks.

Toasting in Georgia is social cement. I envy my new friends the cohesion it announces and the disappointments it cushions. I love when men become tender about their parents and children. They let tears well up. They invite strangers into an intimate circle of affection. Toasting, Georgian women and men seduce me with their unbridled affection. I want to stay in touch. I want to repay their extraordinary hospitality and kindness. Two weeks after returning home, I arrange to edit a special issue of an international journal on the topic of American studies in Georgia. It will be my gift to these generous friends. At my computer, as I bang out e-mail messages inviting colleagues to contribute to the issue, I drink wine and wax sentimental. We exchange spirited, tender letters. I stock up on walnuts and re-create salads of eggplant and green beans. At a local Turkish bread shop, I buy something that resembles *khachapuri* but isn't. I have Georgia on my mind. Later, when my friends' essay proposals are slow to arrive, I rethink my proposed publishing venture. It is premature, an instance of wine over reason: American studies is too new in Georgia for this kind of project. Perhaps in a few years, the Georgians will launch a volume of their own and ask me for a contribution. If they do, I'll write it as a toast to them.

CHEESECAKE

Johannesburg, South Africa, 2005

"Abueng has done us a great favor," my nephew Eric announces. He pauses to fill four glasses with South African sauvignon blanc. His parents and I are relaxing on the terrace of the Johannesburg house that Eric, his wife, and his daughter have rented for the year. Wine is a huge industry in South Africa, and our white is crisp and delicate. "I'd be happy drinking this at home," I say, thinking more about the politics of consumption than the particular grape. Until 1994, when elections and a new constitution ushered in democratic South Africa, we boycotted the wines of apartheid and the apartheid state. Now that the system of racial oppression has ended, Eric, an anthropologist, is thrilled to be spending his sabbatical year here. We all lift our glasses. "To South Africa," we toast.

Abueng, a geographer, is Eric's officemate at the University of the Witswatersrand. She has arranged to take us all to Alexandra Township to meet an elderly couple who were part of the struggle against apartheid. They have invited us for midmorning tea.

The next day, we take off from the university with Abueng, bearing a large cream-cheese cake adorned with strawberries, blueberries, sliced kiwi, and grapes. Eric had a moment of uncertainty before buying the cake, he confessed. He worried that it might seem overbearing—too much like an advertisement for ourselves. But then he yielded to his original impulse: to thank our hosts with a fabulous dessert. "Good decision," I say, thinking that the cake may also be a sly message to me. Consider this, I imagine my nephew chuckling. Here we are, bringing a cheesecake, with its New York Jewish roots, to a British-inflected tea at a black South African household.

After twenty minutes on the highway heading north, we approach the town everyone refers to as Alex. Tin-roofed shacks line the littered streets. We drive slowly, searching for landmarks. Two young women strutting along the street shoot hostile glances in our direction. In my imagination they are hissing, "Tour-

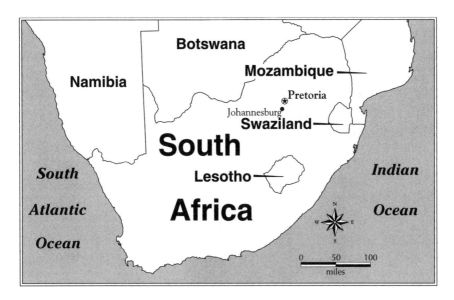

ists, go home! The animals you've come to see are in the game parks." They have a point. I am a tourist here, on the lookout for wildlife.

The windows of our car are rolled up, and the doors are locked. It's common-sense practice for both locals and tourists when they drive through communities known for high rates of unemployment and crime. (The United States is no exception.) I tell myself that it's reasonable to feel afraid. It's also reasonable to feel guilty: to acknowledge that my gaze is not disinterested. On high tourist alert, I "see" what I'm looking for. There, on the corner, a guy in a red T-shirt and shades is giving our car a calculating look. And I wonder, has one of the young women signaled him, perhaps with a quick flick of her elbow, to target the vehicle for profit or sport?

I'm relieved when we turn into Michael and Rachel's compound: a small cement yard boasting one tree, a simple, four-room brick house, and two other one-room structures. A half dozen squawking chickens are there to greet us along with Michael and Rachel. "Welcome to the ghetto!" Michael exclaims, as he opens his arms to Abueng. Then, after the briefest hesitation, he greets the rest of us with the same generous embrace.

Rachel's back is bent with arthritis. A plum-colored scarf wrapped around her head calls attention to her lively brown eyes. She wears a blue and white printed blouse buttoned all the way to the neck and a long, dark blue denim skirt. As she leads the way into the house, Rachel's step is surprisingly spry. One electric bulb, no more than 75 watts, lights the combined living and dining room.

Michael, tall, lean, and dignified, reminds me immediately of Nelson Mandela, South Africa's first democratically elected president. He wears a slightly yellowed white shirt, buttoned at the neck, and new-looking blue jeans. Our host gestures toward two red vinyl sofas and two matching chairs, all covered with plastic. The sofas are positioned opposite one another, less than two feet apart. When I lean forward to speak to Rachel on the other couch, my ample knees rub against her frail ones.

Our hosts—both in their mid-eighties, they want us to know—are eager to talk. Michael, with no formal schooling, credits Rachel as his teacher. She was trained in mission schools, she tells us, her speech clipped and precise. "I quit teaching sixty years ago," she adds, when the Bantu Education Act became law. "That curriculum treated Africans as if they were stupid and trained them for nothing. I would not teach that way, and so I became political."

Seizing this chance to put her story on record, Rachel describes the dangers of working as an agitator. At first, when the authorities hounded her at her former school, she acted coy and claimed to know nothing. For a while she successfully deflected their interest. But they caught up with her, and in the years that followed she was harassed, beaten, and finally imprisoned.

Michael holds forth with a politician's ease. He was close to both Walter Sisulu and Mandela from the beginning of the movement, he tells us. They were always at risk, always trying to stay a step ahead of the authorities. ANC (African National Congress) leaders had to be out front, where people could see them, he explains. They had an obligation not to be caught. "I slept in a different place each night," Michael says. "I had to be careful how I got word to Rachel. Imagine, I had to sneak into my own house to see my wife."

Rachel and Michael introduce Judy, who has been in the kitchen organizing our tea. Her open face reveals nothing. In her forties, she is their helper, like a daughter to them, they say. Judy brings out china cups and saucers with matching dessert plates; also hot water and tea bags, plain cookies, and the cheesecake. As we gather around the table, Judy asks that we pray together. "Our faith and our church are very important to all of us," she says, and Rachel nods in agreement.

The table, with a white linen cloth, is laid for eight, but there are only seven chairs. My sister-in-law Marsha and I share one without anyone noticing. My brother-in-law Cy asks Michael if he testified before the Truth and Reconciliation Commission. Michael shakes his head. "Some things are better not opened up," he says, without rancor. Now Cy looks meaningfully at Rachel. "I've forgiven them," she says. I want to ask about the relation between forgiving and forgetting.

How does she cope with memories of police banging on the door in the middle of the night or being beaten, bloodied, and dragged off to prison? The question feels too intimate for the occasion. I let it pass.

For the second time during our visit a young man in dreads, jeans, and a white T-shirt wanders through the room. No one introduces him to us. He is thin, in his twenties, with even features, a narrow face, and a lost look. When he appeared the first time, I thought that he might be a paid helper, doing chores. Michael subsequently refers to him as "my son," although grandson seems more likely. He's sick, Abueng tells me later, without further elaboration. I don't ask for details. We both know that South Africa has 4.5 million people who are HIV positive—the largest number of any country in the world.

Michael and Rachel's elastic family group includes Abueng, the scholar. Michael celebrates this "daughter" as a "girl" (at age fifty) "with a big passion for education." Abueng's research, which brought her to Michael and Rachel's door, focuses on the tangled history of black property ownership in the township. As longtime homeowners, Michael and Rachel are somewhat unusual in Alex. Their status, Abueng explains, does not guarantee popularity in a place where most people rent or squat or lean on relatives. The PhD in geography that Abueng is completing at the prestigious University of the Witswatersrand validates the aged freedom fighters' passion for education. In recent years they have urged local teachers to bring students to their house to use the books they have collected. The teachers aren't interested. But Abueng, the future professor, comes frequently.

The tea ritual anchors our visit. Sitting around the table together, caught up in our hosts' restrained accounts of suffering and courage, I feel much closer to them than I did on the bulky leather sofas and chairs. Before serving the cheesecake, Rachel hesitates for a moment. It's too elegant to violate with her knife. I know that moment, when a whole object takes on a mystical meaning. The uncut cake, rather than being a source of individual gratification, belongs to the communion of eaters. "I won't cut this right," she demurs, as we all urge her on. In fact, Rachel cuts with a practiced touch, all eight slices of uniform size and perfectly intact. The cheesecake, while airier than its New York equivalent, is wonderfully creamy, with a touch of vanilla, and not too sweet. The strawberries are juicy in the mouth, like strawberry wine. Sacramental. Before we rise from the table, Cy reaches toward Michael on his right and Rachel on his left. "I'd like us all to hold hands for a moment," he says," to mark this gathering and our friendship."

After tea, our hosts show us the rest of the property. We enter a darkened building across the courtyard from the house. "Over here," Rachel says, pointing to their treasure: six sets of ancient encyclopedias, including the *Britannica* circa 1949, are lined up on low benches against the rear wall. In the dim light, I'm on the verge of tears. Rachel has imagined eager fifteen-year-olds, sitting cross-legged on the bare floor, poring over accounts of proud African tribes and evil colonizers, World War II, the triumph over fascism, and the founding of the United Nations. She has imagined them cherishing the printed word. Reading, Eric and Cy comment, isn't what it used to be. Students avoid it like the plague—"even at Yale," Eric adds, "where they are showered with opportunities." But Rachel won't take comfort from our words. Reading is critical to her lifetime of struggle. What use is freedom for an ignorant populace?

"Here's where I earn my living," Michael says, unlocking his grocery store. The room, with a big window opening onto the street, smells fresh. Black metal shelves, filled with packages of Knorr soups, cans of beans and tomato herring, bottled water, powdered milk, ketchup, detergent, liquid soap, toothpaste, and bug spray line the walls. The shelves are dust-free. Not a single can or container is dented.

We take Michael's picture—standing tall among the sardines, soaps, and soups. We take pictures of the entire group, without the lost boy, and begin the recitation of farewells. "This visit means so much to us," Michael says. "It means a great deal to us, too," each of us responds as we exchange the final round of handshakes and hugs.

There's no midmorning tea on our schedule for the following day. And even if there were, it would probably disappoint. At 11:00 a.m., we are drinking lattes in Melville, a Johannesburg neighborhood of small ethnic restaurants and clever boutiques. Melville is a rarity in Johannesburg: an ungated enclave with a small-town look and global panache: a place where blacks, Asians, whites, and mixed-race people congregate to eat and stroll and buy crafts. From our sidewalk table we watch the young street vendors setting out their wares: droll-looking animals, mythological figures, cars, and motorbikes made of wire and beads. I have my eye on a fat turtle, about six inches in diameter.

Eric and his wife, Gul Rukh, dangle luncheon possibilities in front of us. There's Chili, an Indian restaurant, famous for "bunny chow," curry in a "nest" of a half loaf of white bread from which the crusts have been trimmed. There are Greek, Italian, French, and Brazilian bistros, and places with hip transnational menus like Soulsa, Service Station, and the Color Bar. Melville's witty entrepreneurs won't let us forget that South Africa is a country fractured by race and class.

Spiro's Café, where we are seated, is filling up with a lunch crowd. Young waiters move smoothly among the tables, bringing salads, pastas, Greek specialties in filo pastry, and eggs with bacon. A French-speaking woman two tables away is eating a slice of cheesecake. Full-color images of Rachel with her cake knife, the lost boy in his white T-shirt, and Michael in his grocery store parade before me, and I reach for my glasses. My aging eyes are playing tricks on me; so is my unconscious. The cheesecake I thought I saw is really a pale omelet in the shape of a wedge.

Is this how it will be, I wonder? Six months from now, when I'm eating out with a friend, will the sight of cheesecake still evoke the world of two aging freedom fighters? At what point will I no longer rush to describe, in meticulous detail, the morning that Abueng took us to Alex?

Part 4

---- ✄ ----

COOKING FOR A CHANGE

GRADUATION

Hillside, New Jersey, December 2003

The FoodBank's community room is festooned with red and yellow crepe paper streamers. On the wall behind the chairs of fifteen Food Service Training Academy graduates are their names in large black type. Blue balloons above each chair, with "Congratulations" and "Good Luck" in bold yellow script, thrust heavenward: ordinary markers of an extraordinary event.

The graduates look sharp in full whites and chefs' hats. Chef Robert and Chef Jimmy wear chefs' dress blacks. Tables at the back are set for a hot buffet lunch and desserts, including an oversized graduation cake decorated with roses. I look around nervously at the empty chairs. There are about twenty-five of us in the audience, mostly FoodBank workers from the warehouse and members of the administrative staff. As I drove down to the training academy that morning, I was thinking about Pearl, a student from Ghana with bright eyes and beautiful, buttery skin who had been in the United States for only nine months. I imagined her all alone, surrounded by the American students and their extended families. In fact, on this Friday morning, with a severe snowstorm predicted, most students are as alone at the ceremony as Pearl.

The academy gives lots of awards, Chef Robert explained, because the students who finish have truly achieved. Many of them are ex-cons, recovering addicts, and welfare clients—people with histories of hardship and failure. Indeed, the presentation of awards at graduation is a highlight of the event. Robert hands out certificates for teamwork, leadership, academics, and attendance; there are also awards for the comeback student and the outstanding student selected to be chef assistant, a paid staff position, for the next class.

After the awards ceremony, students make short speeches. One after the other, they thank the staff for believing in them. Will, the next chef assistant, weeps as he speaks. He refers to the program as "another start in life."

Chef Jimmy approaches the podium with a practiced performer's delight. "My friends tell me I'm a great chef," he begins. "I could be out there, at a fancy five-star restaurant, making piles of money. But this is my calling. I'm giving back.

191

Today is my payday." Jimmy's large frame expands with pride. The graduates give him a standing ovation, and the rest of us follow their lead. I reach for my tissues.

Chef Robert presides over the distribution of diplomas. The response, as each student's name is called, is loud, playful hooting and generous applause. As they make their way to the podium, graduates reach for the hands and arms of class-mates. Diplomas in hand, they hug each of the staff members. I see the scene before me as if in slow motion—the graduates clinging to one another's touch and warmth, hanging on to these precious moments.

I approach Pearl to offer congratulations. As we hug, she lets go with a flood of weeping. "It's been so hard," she says through her tears. "I never thought I would make it. So much is strange for me, the foods, the vocabulary, the kitchen. They all helped me so much," she says, wiping her eyes. I'm moved when she thanks me, again and again, for being with her, although she doesn't say that, when she feels so foreign and forlorn. She asks for my phone number, and I give her my card.

The main dishes of the graduation meal are laid out in large steam trays: fried chicken, lasagna, Spanish rice, stewed vegetables, and a Caesar salad with chicken made with iceberg lettuce. Guests followed by graduates fill up white Styrofoam boxes, which the commissary uses instead of plates. Even though this is only my fourth visit to the school, I feel too emotional to eat. But I let one of the student chefs serve me a huge portion of undressed Caesar salad that I splash with bottled Italian dressing. The lettuce is fresh and the chicken slices moist. Still, I'm grateful that this meal is not the reason I'm here.

I sit, drinking bitter coffee with Robert and Jimmy. Both seem giddy with exhaustion. The graduating class is their best to date, Robert and Jimmy tell me, the most cooperative as a group and the most professionally promising. A few of the graduates might actually become chefs, Robert and Jimmy agree. I'm giddy, too, for different reasons. "I'd like to come back," I tell them, "and follow a class through the fourteen-week program. I want to watch the process." In the grim, often hidden world of hunger—for food and self-worth—these two young chefs are testing their own recipe for the politics of change: change through teaching, through cooking, through competence in the kitchen. It's their gift, these young men with big hearts, to envision food service as empowerment. I envy their sense of mission.

INDUSTRY RULES AND ETHNOGRAPHIC ANGST

January 2004

"You have to be here," Chef Jimmy announces. "Every day. On time." His booming voice, like a drill sergeant's, fills the classroom. It's January 3, 2004, the beginning of another cycle of the Food Service Training Academy's free fourteen-week program. This is Jimmy's third year at the school, and the fourth year of the academy's existence. Out of seventy accepted applicants, only thirty-five have showed up for the first day. Women, about a third of the group, are clustered at the front of the room. They sit behind black tables with their notebooks out. Most of the men, hanging back, slump in their seats, faces blank.

"Three unexcused absences and you're out," the red-haired man in a white chef's jacket continues. At 350 pounds, Jimmy is a physically intimidating presence. "These are the same requirements that an employer has. We teach you life skills as well as knife skills. Courtesy, teamwork, responsibility, and personal hygiene along with academics, menu planning, and sanitation. And we'll do everything we can to help you get a job when you graduate. But listen up: We have a zero-tolerance policy for drugs. Our test can pick up a poppy seed. So if you're using, consider yourself warned. You fail and you're out. That's the rule."

Jimmy's eyes twinkle as he speaks. He's an effusive thirty-five-year-old white guy warming to his role as the master of tough love. "We keep it formal here. I'm Chef Jimmy. I'm not Big Red or Jim. I'm here to train you—for the industry. I've been out there. I know what I'm doing. And I got eyes in the back of my head, I swear to God. So don't fool around with me."

The chef pauses to let his message sink in. Like the FoodBank's commissary kitchen, where most of the training occurs, the classroom is Jimmy's theater, his bully pulpit. He's got the attention of all thirty-five black and Latino students. Even the cool guys, with gold necklaces half hidden in their hooded sweatshirts, seem riveted. "I'm a fat cat," Jimmy says, affirming more than his considerable girth. "We're all about eating here. Eating and teaching."

Suddenly, the door opens and a bulky man with a shaved head enters. "You're late," Jimmy bellows, raising his loud voice another couple of decibels. The bluster fails to obscure the chef's pleasure-loving, Falstaffian spirit. "I won't be late again, man," the student responds, respectfully.

A week before this opening session began, I had a distressing dream. In the dream, I notice among the sea of dark faces a white couple. They're both from Georgia, in the former Soviet Union, where I have lectured and made good friends. Chef Jimmy has fingered the two of them for stealing—stealing food from the FoodBank.

The FoodBank looms large in my dream as site and symbol. The Community FoodBank of New Jersey, which houses the Food Service Training Academy, occupies a vast, gritty warehouse in a run-down suburb of Newark. The Food-Bank is a nonprofit arsenal in the war against poverty. It recycles food from the banquet tables of the rich (including the U.S. Department of Agriculture) to the kitchen tables of the poor, distributing more than 20 million pounds of food and groceries annually to a half million New Jerseyans. The FoodBank's resources, which the academy uses for its cooking and feeding programs, are not under lock and key.

I ponder the connections between crime, the FoodBank, and the Georgians. Most of the workers in the FoodBank's warehouse are ex-convicts and recovering addicts; so too are more than 50 percent of the academy's students. The Food-Bank offers hope (in the form of jobs and job training), which the criminal justice system destroys. It attempts to compensate for the moral crimes of capitalism: our indifference to the vulnerable poor and the machinations of powerful interests. The Georgian connection is illuminating. An economy that was buoyant under communism, with food and employment for everyone, is now dysfunctional under capitalism. Corruption infiltrates every sector of the society. Perhaps the Georgians in my dream perceive the FoodBank as state surplus, meant to be ripped off by them.

My dream is a quagmire of ethnographic angst. Christina, the accused Georgian woman, asks me to intercede with the chef on her behalf. Her man steals, she confesses, but she doesn't. I take her trembling hands in mine and agree to plead her case. But I don't hold out much hope. Moreover, I fear that interceding for this white foreigner will seem to students of color like racial bonding. (And maybe it is.) I fear that my connection to Christina will exacerbate their suspicions of me as a white professional woman who knows nothing of their hardships. Indeed, they have reason to be suspicious. I am a privileged multicultural eater and academic globe-trotter. In my lean body lurks a fat-cat ethnographer. Now my travels have brought me to the FoodBank, where I'm indulging in a catch-up course on How the Other America Eats.

Like Chef Jimmy, I believe in teaching for change—and cooking for change. But what can a fourteen-week training program really promise? I wonder how many students will translate food service skills into personal empowerment. I wonder, too, what I might learn from their successes and their failures.

THE LORD IS HIS SHEPHERD

January–March 2004

I notice, parked outside of the FoodBank on a chilly January morning, two beat-up vans with the logo "Feed Our Sheep" in bold white letters. In smaller print are the name and address of a Newark church. Soon, FoodBank workers will help load these and other vehicles, destined for soup kitchens, day care programs, and emergency pantries. Some of the dry goods and canned goods are slightly dented. Most of the fruits and vegetables appear to be fresh. Nothing is rotten except the system that requires this desperate battle to keep hunger at bay.

The phrase "Feed Our Sheep" gives me pause. I know that the shepherd cares for his flock, protects it from hunger and want. These days, the shepherds must make do. They're at the mercy of Big Government and Big Agriculture and the big shots at the IMF and the World Bank. All the shepherds can do is plead and pray that charity will overcome venality.

Jerome is chopping red peppers and onions for pizza when I stop to chat with him. His rhythm with the knife is smooth but slow. Evenings and weekends, Jerome works in the kitchen at Goodwill House, a residence for indigent men, where he also lives. I ask Jerome how the food service course is affecting his cooking at Goodwill. "I cook better," he says. "The head cooks, they ask me questions now." Jerome mentions that he's spent time in prison, twelve years. "For doing drugs?" I ask, since that is the history of many students at the academy (and tens of thousands of poor people of color). "No, the real things," he says. "Kidnapping and armed robbery. Altogether I got seventy-five years and served a dozen."

My left shoulder is less than six inches from Jerome's right one when he drops this detail. A smart reporter would follow up immediately with questions about the crime, his defense, and the response of his family. But I'm at a loss. This information, so casually delivered, throws me off balance. "Oh, no," I exclaim, reaching for Jerome's arm, "twelve years in prison."

Jerome is accustomed to telling his story. He goes on to explain that he recently graduated from his drug recovery program and looks forward to graduating from the Food Service Training Academy. "I've made a career commitment," he says, adding that the Lord has put him on this earth for a purpose. In an essay on the first day of class, he wrote, "The highlight of my day at Goodwill is when we feed the homeless. I just love to see these poor souls sit, eat, and get their fill. I'm really starting to believe that my purpose from God is to help people, and it's being done through the Food Service Department. If this is where I belong, this is where I'll be. I love cooking, mainly when I'm helping someone."

On my way home from the FoodBank I think about Jerome's crime. I imagine him in a 7-Eleven, pulling a gun from his jeans pocket and ordering the cashier to open the register. When the cashier hands over some twenties and a handful of singles, Jerome notices two men approaching the shop. Panicked, he grabs the arm of a young boy who's lounging near the cash register and pushes the kid out the door in front of him. Two cops apprehend him in a jiffy.

Jerome is working alone, setting up the deli station for lunch. "I've been thinking about your kidnapping and armed robbery," I say, "trying to imagine it." I proceed to spin out my scenario. "No, it wasn't like that," Jerome says. In fact, he held up two elderly (white) women in their car and forced them to drive at gunpoint from Elizabeth, New Jersey, through Irvington to the Oranges—across a couple of town lines. He was nineteen. In the B movie in my head, I see the two white women and the young black man with a gun. I see race adding dozens of years to the criminal's sentence. Wrong again, or so Jerome insists. His victims were religious women who did not want vengeance. They wrote to the judge on his behalf, asking for compassion. The robber was young, they pleaded, and had had a lot of trouble in his life. He deserved a break. That was more than twenty-five years ago.

Jerome has a soft manner. Twelve years in prison seem not to have hardened the man. Volunteers who come to Goodwill enjoy hanging around him, Jerome says, especially those from church groups. Children, too. Maybe that's where religion makes a difference, he says; that and the twelve-step program. There's comfort in having the Lord as his shepherd.

Of course, Jerome is no saint. In the kitchen, he's a moody worker, a fellow used to killing time. Lately he has been complaining about not feeling well. "I'm tired," he says, referring to the regular eight-hour shift at Goodwill that supports his keep, and on some weekends an additional eight hours of "community service" as a condition of his parole. Beneath Jerome's mild surface is a temper and a history of punching people out. A few days earlier at Goodwill, when one of his superiors made an insulting remark, Jerome walked away rather than slugging the man. But the memory of the insult stings. I watch him pick over a huge batch of lettuce, throwing out wilted leaves, one every thirty seconds. At this rate, he'll be standing there until the Second Coming.

It's the eighth week of the program, and students are prepping for the ethnic food competition, which functions as their midterm exam. Jerome and his partner, Terise, have drawn Tex-Mex cuisine as their assignment. Their simple, neatly designed menu, with a black-and-white desert landscape at the top of the page, looks promising. In the menu presentation category, it might place second or third. But now they are in the FoodBank's shopping area, bickering as they scramble for ingredients. They are already two hours behind the other teams in *mise en place* for tomorrow's meal-as-exam. Jerome is worried and distracted. He is supposed to be in court later in the day to pay a $50 installment on an accumulated fine of $790. He has no income and no reserves. "What will happen?" I ask. "I'll just trust in God," Jerome replies. He's too proud to mention that his girlfriend, an editor, might bail him out.

On a bitter Saturday morning in March, the commissary's service and dining areas are set up for the first annual pancake breakfast, a benefit Chef Jimmy has organized for the FoodBank. Five hundred guests are expected, volunteers who will be sorting and packing goods in the warehouse in response to agency "orders." Back in the kitchen, Jerome teases Terise, who enjoys the distraction. He then moves to hug Toni, who brushes him off.

A few minutes later, shifting from his cut-up mode, Jerome begins singing the praises of a white woman who volunteers at Goodwill. A churchwoman, I imagine, who communicates her concern for guys like Jerome and the troubles they have. A kind woman who makes him feel cared about. Jerome marvels at her goodness. "Comin' up," he tells me, "we learned to keep separate. Black here, white there, it was better that way. But now," he continues, "I jus' feel we all connected. Tha's how it is. We all connected."

The speech at the pancake breakfast is for my benefit, and I nod in agreement. Of late, Jerome has been testing the boundaries of our connection: with a soft-shoe, mock-courtship routine, with an arm thrown lightly over my shoulders. Does Jerome identify me with that saintly white woman? Does he like the ease he feels with me? Does he dig my attention to his revelations and jive?

"Hey, Doris, m'love, how are ya today?" Jerome asks as I enter the kitchen. He opens his arms theatrically, and I move toward him, into a very gentle embrace. Jerome yearns to be good. He feels ready to love and be loved. After twenty-five years of addiction, of consuming feelings of worthlessness, he has found God and abandoned drugs and alcohol. "In my life now, there's no room for failure," he says. "I'm gonna stay here in this industry 'til I retire. I ain't lookin' to own a restaurant. Whatever God has for me, I gotta do."

BURNED

February 2004

Chef Jimmy bangs his fist on Chef Robert's metal toolbox. "It's Clint!" he roars. "I can't believe what that guy has done! Less than two months on the job and he stopped showing up. Just walked away. I used my contacts to get him the job, and now he's burned me. He's burned the program."

I remember Clint, a stocky man in his forties with a history of drug abuse and some time in prison. I happened to be in Chef Robert's office the day Clint heard about the job offer. Robert and I were talking about race, poverty, and unequal opportunity in America when Clint appeared. "I got my offer," he announced. "It's in utility, doing pots and pans, but that's okay. I'll move up." I remember Robert's response: "Great, man! I know you will."

But now Clint has just been on the phone, asking Jimmy to find him another position. "The guy's a fool," Jimmy sputters. "He blames everybody but himself." It seems Clint had complained about the money. After taxes, health benefits, union dues, and child support were deducted from his check, only $50 a week remained—not enough to make working worthwhile. That level of income leads directly to the local soup kitchen; it leads to dependence on the agencies that distribute dried pasta and canned tomato sauce from the FoodBank. But what choices does Clint have? The only "legit" road ahead is another low-paying food service job and the discipline of hard work and hope.

When Clint failed a second drug test, he pleaded for one last chance, and Jimmy yielded to his pleas. Jimmy yielded to his own wish to go more than 100 percent for a student who he thought just might make it as a food service professional. Clint graduated, but he failed the industry's ServSafe exam, a credential that is not necessary for employment but makes a difference in opportunities and earnings.

"He's burned me," Jimmy reiterates, looking straight at Robert, seeking support. "I want the program to sever relations with Clint. He said he'd come by next week, but I don't want to see his face around here again." Robert stays cool. "Did I know that Clint flunked a second drug test?" he asks Jimmy. "Somehow I don't remember that." Robert and Jimmy balance each other well. Jimmy uses his large physical presence to maintain authority with the students. But he is a passionate man, not afraid of closeness. Students feel the warmth that's inseparable from his vitality. Robert, short and rotund, is the analyst, the visionary on the team. A reader, a musician, and a natural innovator, Robert is eager to be challenged. He cultivates openness, even with an unknown food writer who dropped in one day and announced her interest in his school.

"Okay," he tells Jimmy, "if that's the way you feel. Still, I'm not sure that the program should slam the door shut on a guy in trouble. Giving people chances is what we're about," Robert says. Jimmy seems almost calm as he returns to the kitchen. When the two chefs are in synch, both feel more confident. Clint, as it turns out, resolved their differences. He never called Jimmy back, and he never visited as promised.

Teaching engages the emotions. "If we invest in students," I tell Jimmy the next day, "then their success is our success. But there's only so much that's in our control." Jimmy went all the way for Clint; and, as the head instructor, he had more on the line than Robert. Surely his anger with Clint was also anger at himself—for not reading Clint right; for hoping for too much. Had Clint called on a day other than this one, I wonder whether his confession of failure and sad call for help would have evoked the same fury from Jimmy.

Barely two hours before Clint called, Jimmy had kicked four students out of the program for poor attendance and attitude. Among the failures was Paulo, another recipient of Jimmy's generosity, who had enrolled in the academy for the second time. I was in Jimmy's office when the repentant twenty-year-old had appeared, seeking readmission. "Man, I'm glad to see you back," Jimmy greeted him. "From my heart I want to be here," Paulo responded, his eyes filled with tears. Had Paulo been conning the chef when he promised to do better, or simply conning himself?

Paulo won't show his face at the school again, I think to myself. After a second failure, how could he? But what options does he have? What other free training program in the Newark area all but guarantees a job to its graduates? Where else have people been so encouraging? I wonder what promises Paulo will make the next time to get beyond the big chef's skepticism and fear of betrayal—to reach his tenderness.

PERFECTIONIST

March 2004

"It all started when I was five years old," Tracey wrote in her in-class essay "A Memorable Meal." She remembers her grandmother cooking for the family and welcoming homeless people to her table. "I admired my grandmother for that. Watching her help people that couldn't or wouldn't help themselves made me feel good inside and blessed. I started to stick around in the kitchen and help her."

As a teenager, Tracey began honing her skills. "I am the cook of my family. When there is a gathering with friends or family, they call on me. I am a perfectionist. I strive to put smiles on people's faces when they eat my food." Driven to satisfy all of her guests, Tracey goes all-out. On Thanksgiving, for example, in addition to "stuffed turkey, pot roast, ham, lamb, veggies, and salads," she made "pound cake, banana pudding, brownies, sweet potato pie, peach cobbler, pineapple coconut cake, upside down pineapple cake, and yellow cake with chocolate frosting."

Thirty-eight-year-old Tracey, a divorced mother of two, loads up on culinary "Oscars" at the March 2004 Food Service Academy Awards. In the midsemester ethnic food competition, Tracey and her partner translate a German assignment into "New German Pride." With Tracey's savvy and ambition driving the team, they win medals for the best entrée (stuffed lamb roast) and best dessert (baked stuffed pecans), the cleanest work, and the coveted "best in show," for presentation and culinary quality. When I congratulate her at the end of the ceremony, she falls into my arms, sobbing. "Cooking is my passion," Tracey says as the tears flow. Several weeks later, at graduation, she clowns before an appreciative audience while accepting awards for leadership and academic excellence.

The Monday following graduation Tracey starts working at Magnolias, where southern cuisine is served on soft pink linens and "proper attire" is required. In welcoming Tracey into their "family," the owners exult: their new hire, an ambitious cook, is an upbeat woman with a lovely face, organizational skills, and a polished telephone manner. No wonder they promise her a long-term, hands-on tutorial in all facets of the restaurant's operation.

Four days later, however, all is not so rosy. "Imagine," Tracey tells me over the phone, "a line cook dropped a chicken breast on the kitchen floor and the chef said, 'Throw it back on the grill.' I couldn't do that," Tracey continues. "It's unsanitary and wrong." The chef told her she just didn't know how real restaurants functioned. But Tracey wasn't buying that. When she began working in the kitchen, she asked about hairnets (not used) and plastic gloves (also not used). She spotted supplies lying in cartons on the basement floor even though the law, she knew, requires that foodstuffs be stored at least six inches above the ground. Magnolias is shoddily run, Tracey has decided. "I couldn't bring my children or my friends there," Tracey says, explaining her decision to quit.

THE WAY TO A WOMAN'S HEART

April 2004

Entering the kitchen on an April morning, I confront a mosaic of white chef's hats framing black faces. A dozen students are busy: turning Betty Crocker mixes into cakes, cantaloupes into fruit salad, the previous day's baked potatoes into twice-stuffed potatoes, and chicken breasts into fried chicken. Justice is standing alone between two pairs of bakers, dreads halfway down his back, at leisure. He flashes one of his megasmiles in my direction. "I owe you an apology," I say. He looks confused. The knot in my stomach relaxes.

Apparently he's forgotten the exchange we had the morning before. Or maybe he has forgiven my condescending remarks—or dismissed them as predictable coming from someone like me. "Yesterday," I say, "when I asked about your grade on the practice certification exam, you told me you got only six wrong. Remember? I said I was certain you were putting me on. You turned to Kristen for confirmation. 'Tell her how I did,' you said. 'Tell her outta ninety questions I had only six mistakes.'"

My assumptions regarding Justice's performance didn't spring from race or gender narrowly construed. All the students remaining in the class are African Americans, and three of the top five achievers are men. It was Justice himself. Justice advertises himself as a man of the 'hood. Tall, bearded, and very black, he generates energy by clowning and teasing the ladies. Shuffling around, he hides behind banter and self-mockery. "I've been watching you play the fool," I tell Justice, "and I know you're a smart fool." He's like King Lear's fool, I tell him, inventing the role and himself. "Yesterday, when I questioned your grade on the test, it didn't occur to me that the smart fool is also a smart student." "A wise man can play the part of the fool," Justice responds, "but the fool can't play the part of the wise man."

Like millions of Americans, I have a head filled with media images of blacks growing up in Newark (or Harlem or South Central LA) who look and sound like Justice, boys and men with street smarts and fast mouths who rarely make it through high school. I wonder, does the sly game Justice plays, including his refusal to present himself as serious, constitute an invitation to a put-down? Did I react to Justice as he wanted me to—or as I was programmed to? Or is his con-artistry a calculated challenge to the likes of me: a test of whether well-intentioned white liberals can get beyond the obvious and read him correctly? These questions trouble me still. At that moment in the kitchen, however, my intention was clear. I wanted Justice to see me as I saw myself: grappling with my prejudices and my ignorance.

"Wanna know why I'm really here?" Justice asks. He leans back in his chair in the commissary dining room and scrutinizes my face. "I got tired of runnin' back and forth to prison."

Justice's father was a cook—a chef, Justice calls him—at a mental hospital, and Justice felt drawn to cooking. As a boy, he liked watching his father at ease in the kitchen. Between prison stints, Justice turned to the Food Channel for ideas. "Cookin's the way to a woman's heart," he says, "and I love women. I love wom-en," he repeats, taking his time with each word, giving each word equal emphasis. "I love women. I love women. I love women." That's Justice, playing with his script as much for his own amusement as mine.

Prison looms large in Justice's thirty-three years. He first went to jail at fifteen, for stealing. He was a kid who wanted everything he saw. But his mother kept saying no. "They'll just steal it off ya," she told him. He came out of each prison sentence more savvy about crime. He made money dealing drugs. In prison Jus-tice began reading: first the Bible and then the Koran. "I'm very studious," Justice tells me. "When I read a book in prison I read it over and over. I studied for my exam here the same way. I take nothing on face value. I question everything. Some people wanna call me a revolutionary," he boasts, "but I would say I'm a modern philosopher."

"I see no man outsida God and no God outsida man," he continues. "A lotta people choose to believe that something outside themselves has power. I don' believe that. We control our own destiny. The streets and the jails made me the man I am today. Prison is what you put into it. If you don' educate you'self you ain't gonna learn nothin'."

Justice emerged from his last incarceration in December 2003, only two weeks before the course began. "It's rough on the streets, and I don' wanna kill or be killed," he confesses. He's out, but "on the bracelet," an electronic monitoring program that requires parolees to be at home each night by six. Without a work history to show employers, Justice knows it won't be easy to land a job. He's managing now, paying the rent on his apartment and seeing his two kids, with money he saved from dealing drugs. Thinking about work, he's a realist. "Man has gotta have some pride and dignity. I'd rather sell drugs than flip burgers at McDonald's."

VOLUNTEER CHEF

March 2004

Eddy, the volunteer chef-instructor, checks the grill and the warming ovens. He pokes his head into the fruit salad and then into the walk-in refrigerator. His movements are twitchy and abrupt, like a dog with fleas. "Take this pan, quickly. No, put it here. Who's got potatoes? Get the chicken in." He harangues the students in a shrill, scratchy voice. When he spots me chatting with the pizza makers, he approaches with an officious "Can I help you?" "No," I say, "there's nothing I need."

I remember when Eddy appeared, on a Saturday in March, in the midst of the pancake breakfast fund-raiser. The FoodBank is always looking for volunteers, and he had useful skills. With a tight expression, Eddy explained to Chef Jimmy that he cooked at an assisted-living facility and had time on his hands. He wanted to be helpful, he said. I wondered then if the tension in his pale, doughy face was suppressed anger. I wondered whether the guy liked cooking. Or food. Or people.

Ever since Chef Robert began staying home with his sick mother, I've worried that the students need more supervision and feedback in the kitchen. How else will they make progress? Jimmy's hands are too full—with administration, teaching, catering, and general oversight. Now another professional chef with two decades of experience had appeared, offering his services. He was bored with his job, Eddy let us know, and was looking for new challenges.

Tracey, the student sous chef for the day, comes by to slip me a hairnet. You know how it is, she says with a raised eyebrow, reminding me that the health inspectors are on the premises and I ought to be properly attired. In the bathroom, I position the thin black hairnet over my blond frizz—it gives me a ghoulish look—and retreat to Jimmy's office. There I find Eddy, in agitated conversation with Jimmy about my presence in the kitchen. She's in the way, he must have said. And without a hairnet. "She's not a food handler," Jimmy explains, "just an observer."

"The guy's bad news," I say to Jimmy as soon as Eddy leaves, assuming that my feeling of disruption was shared by the students. "What a prick," Jimmy responds. "Two more sessions 'til this group graduates. Then I'll tell him I don't need him any more. And take the hairnet off, now!" he says. "I can't bear to look at you with that thing on."

Later, during lunch, I ask Justice, who is sporting a bright yellow T-shirt instead of chef's whites, what he thinks of the volunteer. "Well, he knows some things I don' know, so tha's good enough for me."

I'm inclined to be less generous than Justice. The visiting chef is changing the chemistry of the kitchen. His barrage of instructions, like a military incursion, threatens our collective well-being. "Our"? I'm surprised to hear myself identify with the students, and I'm grateful to the intrusive Eddy for this announcement of bonding. I think of diplomats, who are moved from country to country to prevent them from identifying too closely with the foreigners among whom they work. Paradoxically, they are relocated exactly at the moment when their imagination of the other—their empathy—opens them to deeper understandings. Once they can really do the job, it's time to leave. I ask myself: If I identify too closely with the students and staff, will I lose my perspective on their experience at the school? Will my vision blur in some respects as it sharpens in others? Where am I in the case of Eddy? Even if Jimmy shares my view of the volunteer chef, I still have Justice's comments to reckon with. It could be that Justice is not alone in his commonsense assessment—and I'm off on a psychological spin of my own.

The following day, I ask Jerome about the volunteer. A less subtle student than Justice, he gives me the response I am looking for. "He got in our way," Jerome says, "Didn' leave us do our work. It's our kitchen and he was buttin' in. He the chef from hell."

Tracey is equally direct. "He's an asshole," she says. "And arrogant. He doesn't know how to cook. He couldn't even season chicken properly. Everybody agreed the chicken had no flavor. He just took over, supervising every little thing. Treating us like we knew nothing. Condescending to us."

The students are proud of the kitchen community they have created. At this late stage in their program, an outsider, especially a nervous one with authority, is certain to screw up. The students expect a chef to act like their Chef Jimmy, someone who acknowledges their efforts and appreciates their hard-earned skills. How they are treated matters. Respect, in short supply in many of their lives, inspires them, builds self-esteem.

Timing is important. Perhaps the end of the term was the wrong moment to release a loose cannon in the kitchen. Eddy volunteered his time as a way of advancing his own stalled career. He wants a job at the school. Jimmy, short-handed in Robert's absence and sympathetic to someone he saw as a fellow professional, mistakenly opened the door.

INTERN

January–March 2004

I was in Chef Robert's office during the first week of classes when Nelson dropped in for a chat. A youthful forty-two, Nelson sported a clean-shaven head and a neat black mustache. The second student to serve as sous chef for the day, Nelson was taking the assignment seriously. The sous chef, a rotating job, plans the day's menu and supervises the students in the kitchen. His grade depends in part on their performance. He asked Robert about how the steaks for the following day's lunch should be marinated and what guides the choice of a dry or wet marinade. Unlike most of his classmates, Nelson frames questions—about menus, cooking methods, ingredients, and the art of seasoning—in a manner that invites explanations. He claims Robert's time just as any serious student would take advantage of a faculty member's office hours. I can imagine a much younger Nelson, as an art student at Brooklyn College, interrupting a professor's coffee break with a query about the department's policy on independent study. Owning a restaurant is a dream Nelson has nurtured ever since quitting his job at Home Depot. "I got tired of thinking about other people's kitchens," he tells me.

Nelson smiles as he works, and he never stops working. Light on his feet, he is magically there when another student needs a hand with a steaming-hot pot or a garbage can that doesn't want to fit through the door. If he isn't prepping or cooking or serving lunch or checking inventory in the freezer, he can be found with a mop in his hands. By midsemester, Nelson ranked among the top three students in the class.

When the chef-owner of a French bistro in Tribeca offered a two-week internship to a Food Service Academy student, Jimmy unhesitatingly chose Nelson. "I went in like a blank page," Nelson tells me at the end of his stint in New York, "without expectations. I'm like Einstein. In order for me to learn, I have to unlearn what I know."

Nelson arrived at the restaurant with a white chef's jacket, courtesy of Chef Jimmy, and a pair of black pants purchased especially for the assignment. When the restaurant's owner, Chef Mark, mentioned that black-and-white checkered pants were "more traditional," Nelson bought himself a pair. "If people give you advice and they see you don't take it," Nelson says, "they shut down." During the first week and a half of his internship, without a knife of his own, Nelson struggled to make do. He knew he needed to buy a knife, but what kind and where and at what price? Then Chef Mark offered to take the intern knife shopping at Korin's on Warren Street. "When you're on the right path," Nelson says, "everything opens up."

At the restaurant, Nelson found that most of the dishes were new to him. He prepped for Chef Mark's special *porc savoyard*, which had been written up in the *New York Times*, and got to make it twice, the second time entirely alone. He kept a notebook in his back pocket, but there was never enough time to write things down. "The batteries aren't included in this kit," Nelson says. "So you figure it out. You have to be able to function without instructions."

Back in school after the internship, Nelson continues to work at the restaurant on Sundays and two nights a week—without pay. "It's free training," he tells me, grateful for Chef Mark's kindness and support.

A day before graduation Nelson tests positive for cocaine. He was caught once before and had prevailed upon Chef Jimmy to give him a second chance. Now I wonder. The restaurant world is tough on an inexperienced student. And speed in the kitchen is essential. Were the demands of his workplace chipping away at Nelson's confidence? Was the offer of paid work that Nelson expected not forthcoming? Are his cash reserves running low—desperately low?

Chef Jimmy agrees to let Nelson graduate, on the conditions that he attend Narcotics Anonymous sessions regularly and do a month of community service. "I won't recommend him for a job unless he deals with his disease," Jimmy tells me. "This guy can go beyond line cook. He can become a chef," Jimmy continues, "and I want the credit for him when he succeeds. I want him in our network, training other graduates."

TRAINING AND CHANGING

April 2004

Waretta, who completed the Food Service Training Academy program and graduated in December 2003, was the last of her cohort to find employment. As a student, Waretta never missed a day and never shirked a task. She earned a standout grade of 95 on the national certification exam. School was Waretta's oasis. After two years in prison, she was assigned to a halfway house, where she shared a dorm room with twenty other women. In those crowded quarters, someone was always stressed and making trouble for the roommates. At the Food Service Academy Waretta found peace and a purpose.

Through Chef Jimmy's network, Waretta obtained a job at Kean University in their on-campus "diner." A break, at last! It was "good money," she says, $8.50 an hour, and, once she settled in, she thought she might be able to take a course or two—on business management and entrepreneurship. Waretta worked for five months, she tells me on a visit to the school, and managed to save $1,000. It's for the car she plans to buy in August 2004 when she is released from the halfway house; she says having a car will make her more employable. But there's a hitch: the university diner is closed from May 1 to September 1, a detail no one seems to have mentioned to Waretta when she was hired. Most employees collect unemployment during the summer; but in order to fulfill the conditions of her parole and avoid returning to prison, Waretta needs to work. "I don't need much," she says. "Maybe I'll try Burger King. That's $5.50 an hour, and I'm outta the dorm"—away from the halfway house during the day.

In the three-plus years since the food service academy opened, its leadership has changed four times. As a consequence, employment records for graduates are flimsy, even for those graduating during the past year, when Jimmy and Robert have alternated as executive chef. The chefs estimate that the school has placed roughly three-quarters of its graduates (about a hundred all told) in at least one position, a decent record for any training program. Unfortunately, there is little hard data about where most graduates are currently employed, at what salaries, or how they feel about their lives in the industry.

Clearly, Waretta, Jerome, and Justice belong to the program's target population. Jerome, the former inmate and recovering addict, has embraced God, sobriety, and cooking. Justice is a dangling man. He's the ex-con without work experience in the "straight" world: a guy with the wit—although not necessarily the will—to benefit from job training and certification. Whether Justice can forswear the financial benefits of drug dealing for the safety of legitimate, poorly paid work is an open question. Waretta, prior to her one-time conviction, worked in casinos in Atlantic City. She raised and educated two daughters who enjoy stable jobs and relationships. Her work ethic made her a strong student. Her modest expectations are well matched to a labor market of abundant low-wage opportunities.

Cooking enthralls both Nelson and Tracey. It challenges their creativity and ingenuity. Were it not for family and financial constraints, they might have applied to the Culinary Institute of America or Johnson and Wales University. Instead they each used the free course to jump-start their dreams. High motivation, self-confidence, initiative, research skills, and workplace savvy identify them as the academy's best and brightest. However, if they mean to compete with their better-trained peers, they could use a sequence of advanced courses—on subjects such as stocks and sauces, butchering, plating, and restaurant management.

The Food Service Training Academy benefits from a mix of students: the fast starters who set a standard for the others, the uncertain who catch fire, the dropouts who return, and the slackers whose poor performance provides another kind of object lesson. Competition is the way of the world, Chef Robert likes to say, and it's built into the training program. Competition is the other side of the comfort that his students experience in cooking. Watching Tracey and her team of bakers step back to admire the Black Forest cakes they have carefully decorated, I envy their satisfactions: handwork and headwork coming together, along with patience and planning, precision and collaboration. The kitchen yields to their efforts, makes them feel worthy. Some would say blessed.

The last word belongs to Jerome, who lost a dozen years to prison and twice as many to addiction. Jerome now works as a supervisor in the kitchen at Goodwill House, where he lives. He makes $11 an hour feeding "lost souls" who value a simple meal and the encouragement it represents. "Comin' here to school," Jerome tells me, "it's like God puttin' the icing on the cake. Some people they don' care what others say about them. I do. I wanna leave a good name." A week before his graduation in April 2004 he says, "I'm forty-two years old and until this program I never achieved nothin'. If I knew at the beginning what I do now, I'd have worked much harder." He learned, among other lessons, to trust himself. "Doris, m'love," he teases, "when you write about me, tell them I haven't arrived but I'm on my way."

Part 5

EATING ALONE

HOW DO YOU EAT?

Kathmandu, Nepal, 2000

I sit, squeezed between Adam and Sapana, on a narrow couch. On my lap I balance a snack plate containing half a hard-boiled egg, three rice balls stuffed with cooked vegetables, a few slices of pickled cucumber, and two pale pink rice wafers. The hard-boiled egg slithers around on the plate and drops into my lap. "It's okay," I tell Sapana, whose dark eyes register what she takes to be my distress. "These black pants won't show a thing."

At least I hope they're not showing almost two weeks of rough and tumble eating, much of it seated on cushions on the floor around Adam and Sapana's low oblong table. I cope poorly with food on the floor, especially when I'm eating with my hands, as I occasionally do here, following the custom of my daughter-in-law's country. I also cope poorly with Rahula, Adam and Sapana's year-old son, who, when he's not at his mother's breast, circles us like a sheepdog, leaving a trail of mushy bananas, chocolate, grape jam, and rice.

This evening it's important that my costume pass muster because I am on display. Sapana's parents have invited relatives to meet their son-in-law's mother. At last, they can introduce a member of the family of the American father of their first grandchild. Thus far about twenty-five people—the older women in brilliantly colored saris—have passed through the narrow living room where the three of us are perched, surrounded by eight members of Sapana's parents' household.

I twist awkwardly in my chair to smile at Sapana's diminutive aunt, who sits to Adam's left, her chair, like our sofa, flush against the wall. Turning sharply to my right, I flash a smile at Sapana's mother, who is seated to Sapana's right, also flush against the wall. The rest of the family is lined up opposite us. A passage, no more than three feet wide, leads from this "Western" living room to the "Eastern" one, a square, carpeted space furnished with bright woven cushions and a color TV.

The English term for this household, Sapana once explained to me, is "joint family." Even as I envisioned a large cut of meat, a roast with the bone still in it, I understood that she meant "joint" as in shared, fastened together. They are all joined in a tight unit: Sapana's parents, her father's brother and sister-in-law, her father's unmarried sister, Sapana's brother and sister-in-law, and her two adult sisters. Bound together yet elastic now, in their embrace of Adam, in the warmth I feel in their eyes, and in the outpouring of welcoming words whose meanings I can easily imagine.

I reach for my orange soda, wishing it were a double scotch. "My mother wants to know how you like Kathmandu," Sapana is saying. "I'm happy to be here," I respond, "happy to be in your home." Clearly this is not the occasion for sounding off about the pollution, the abominable traffic, the uncollected garbage, the power outages, the sad-eyed beggars in the streets, or the emptiness I experience without the *New York Times*. "Sapana's father is asking who lives in your house with you," Adam says, interrupting my silent conversation with myself. "Tell him I live alone," I say.

Sapana's father inspects my face. A slender man in sparkling white Nehru pants and a white Nehru jacket, he is fine featured like my movie-star-beautiful daughter-in-law. I feel the weight of the question he is about to ask. "My father wants to know how you eat," Sapana says. "We can't imagine eating alone. No one eats dinner in my parents' house until everyone who lives here is home. If my sister-in-law is delayed at hospital, they wait. Eating means eating together," she says, elaborating her father's thought.

Eating alone is easy, I want to say. I eat what I like, when I like. No one sees how much red meat I devour or how much Chardonnay I drink. I can indulge an impulse for sushi without having to lay on a fancy meal or make brilliant conversation. The *New York Times* brings six presidents and five prime ministers to the breakfast table along with Andre Agassi, Meryl Streep, V. J. Naipaul, Rudy Giuliani's wife and his mistress, and a dozen other contentious voices. I can listen to them or not, as I choose. Eating alone is liberating, I want to say.

"I have friends," I tell Sapana's father, pausing while my daughter-in-law translates. "Friends and relatives eat at my house, and I eat at theirs. I live alone," I say, "but usually I don't eat alone."

MY OWN MUERTOS

Leonia, New Jersey, 1991 and 2000

Just a few days before he died in August 1991, Eli asked me what I was planning for his funeral. He was sitting in the big round chair in my study, rail thin in his warm-up suit, his dense curly hair gone with the chemo. We were drinking coffee, and I had swiveled my desk chair around to face him. Of course, the funeral was on our list of items to deal with. Over the past few months, we had reorganized our finances and rewritten our wills. After reading Derek Humphry's *A Final Exit*, about end-of-life choices, we collected a stash of pills. Many mornings, when the sun streamed into the dining room, we discussed the needs of the house; we talked about the two exhibits of Eli's paintings that were in the works. Many evenings after turning off the lights we reviewed, in whispers and tears, segments of our twenty-four-year romance.

Still, his blunt "What are you planning?" caught me by surprise. Was Eli going to leave the concluding round of arrangements entirely to me? Or did he believe I had already made some decisions but couldn't bring myself to tell him? As it turned out, I had misinterpreted his question. Often my husband would open a discussion by grilling me on my views. "It clarifies my thinking," he would tell me, as we dove into politics or the domestic dilemma of the day. While I generally got off to a quick start, he was the more logical, passionate, and tenacious debater. He didn't need to win. He simply craved the mental gymnastics.

In the matter of the funeral, however, it took less than thirty minutes for us to agree on the essentials: a minimalist Jewish frame and comments by two close friends and three family members. Constructing a public farewell didn't hold much fascination for Eli. Not because the cancer had utterly exhausted him, although it had. Rather, he was more invested in private farewells and in the unfinished business of his career.

In the summer of 1990, just a year before he died, Eli completed the text for an illustrated volume on his work, entitled "The Secrets of Elias Friedensohn." The book, under contract with a French publisher, probed his intentions as an artist, his craft, and the zeitgeist that informed each phase of his artistic production. Enamoured of language almost as much as he was enamoured of painting,

219

Eli savored each day's writing—week after week for a solid nine months. More than he was willing to let on, Eli cared about his legacy as an artist.

The living take charge of the memory of the dead. It was Jackie, after all, who created Camelot. Although I haven't attempted to reinvent Eli, each time I explain one of his paintings or arrange an exhibit, I am in an interpretive mode. "The Secrets of Elias Friedensohn," unpublished as a consequence of a scandal at his publishers, are mine to disseminate.

In the years since Eli's death, I have been a part-time custodian of his legacy, readying paintings for shows proposed by friends and colleagues and putting together exhibits in the studio that is attached to our house. My efforts in the studio, while professional in appearance, are, for me, not about enhancing Eli's reputation in the art world. Rather, they are occasions to revisit the work and remember the man—and to celebrate with friends and family.

In December 2000, after a month's stay in Patzcuaro, a small city in central Mexico, I installed a different sort of show in the studio, and I invited twenty-five close friends to a viewing and dinner. The purpose of the event was to engineer an encounter between Eli's death paintings and the Mexican celebration of the Day of the Dead, Dia de los Muertos, celebrated on All Saints' Day and All Souls' Day (November 1 and 2).

The idea for this encounter dates back to November 1998, when I joined my cousin Marlene, a teacher of Spanish and collector of Mexican folk art, in Oaxaca. "Bring bright colors," Marlene had advised. "Your black pants and sweaters are fine, but you'll want to be in synch with the vividness of the holiday." Indeed, all over the city, bright orange marigolds, red coxcombs, and a sea of candles transformed homes, public spaces, and especially drab cemeteries. Altars laden with flowers, food, drink, photos of the dead, and other ritual objects lured the departed back into the bosom of the family. The dead visited with the living. Heartened by the presence of the dead in their midst, relatives sang and danced and rejoiced as they wept. "Eli would have been smitten by these altars," I remember telling Marlene, "by the Mexicans' manic inventiveness married to darkness."

Marlene, who always built altars with her students in the weeks before Dia de los Muertos, suggested that I build one for Eli in the studio. "I'll lend you my Caterinas, the famous lady skeletons," she said, "and my skeleton painters—you need at least one painter on Eli's altar. I'll lend you the dancing devils, the five-man orchestra, the sugar-head skeletons, and of course the painted heads of female saints that decorate loaves of bread."

Those saints got me going. They were so different from the elegant, suffering Jesus on the cross, purchased on our honeymoon in Spain, that still hangs over Eli's drawing table—different, yet connected. Made of flour and water, brightly painted, and about three inches in length, each head sits on a toothpick-like base so that it can slip easily into a crusty bread. I took home from Oaxaca three of these ladies and tucked them away in a dresser drawer. They remained there, wrapped in tissue paper, for two years. When a small artists' colony in Patzcuaro, in central Mexico, offered me a November hideaway and the chance for a second Dia de los Muertos in Mexico, I knew that the saints in the drawer would soon have their day.

Patzcuaro is almost as famous for its celebration of the Day of the Dead as Oaxaca. For the week leading up to All Saints' Day and All Souls' Day, the Plaza Grande and the Plaza Chica are flooded with artisans and their wares. Picking my way among ceramic pots, clay figures, skeletons large and small, carved wooden animals, dolls, toys, and yards of brightly woven fabric, I assembled my own Muertos collection.

Back home, I cover a seven-foot table along one wall in the studio with a deep purple cloth topped off by a hand-woven orange one from Patzcuaro. The orange cloth, with thin bands of turquoise and purple, crosses over easily from central Mexico to northern New Jersey. On this transplanted ground I position white flowers and orange candles, baskets of fresh fruit and vegetables, and round Portuguese breads blessed by my saints. Surrounding two photos of Eli are a group of his small sculptures, wooden masks, his office nameplate, and his tennis club ID. On the ledge above the table sit Eli's paintings of men counting, including one that is clearly a self-portrait. The self-portrait, which shows Eli holding a number 9 for the final chapter of "Secrets," appears soulful but mellow. Four other angst-ridden males surround the self-portrait; death is their invisible companion.

On the wall opposite the altar are professional photos of Noche de Muertos, the Night of the Dead, also from Patzcuaro: cemeteries ablaze with candlelight, graves bedecked with flowers and votive lights, and home altars somewhat like my own. The photos are simply framed and smaller than the smallest of Eli's paintings. Strung across the same wall are *papel picato*, brightly colored sheets of tissue paper with cutouts of skulls, witches, and other traditional Muertos figures. They float, like a comic version of Buddhist flags, above photographic renditions of a "real" Muertos.

The altar, with its intense bang of color, increases the temperature in the white, vaulted studio. But the real heat is generated by Eli's death paintings on the center wall, consorting with the Mexicans' whimsy-mad Muertos paraphernalia. The biggest painting, *Lament for Lost Lovers*, foregrounds four prettified circus performers with skeleton heads. A painting entitled *The Anatomy of Sharing* has a male figure and a female figure, both with skulls for heads, attempting to communicate. Masking his moralizing, Eli took potshots at a consumer society's dream of eternal youth and the pop psychology of sharing. Eli, the self-confessed maker of masks, taunted death with his rich palate and loving strokes of the brush. In the company of these Mexican artifacts with their uninhibited embrace of death, his morally invested paintings release their antic energy.

My dinner, in the spirit of the show, is playful. The pozole, straight from a hole-in-the-wall on the Upper West Side of Manhattan, sits on the dining room table like a stage set waiting to be struck. Guests, admiring the huge soup tureens, piles of shredded cabbage, green onions, chunks of lime, and dishes of chiles and red pepper, await instructions about how to proceed. "This is Mexican comfort food," I say, normal for funerals: hominy and pork stew with lots of crunch; heat *a su gusto* and citrus, too.

Eli did not know pozole, but I imagine him attacking it with zest. He loved rich stews. He shared my passion for pork. He loved crunch, and he loved surprise. Had he been with me in Patzcuaro at the funeral of Lupe's father-in-law, where pozole was cooked for hours over open fires, he might have made sketches of the outdoor kitchen and the female guests huddling in their rebozos on the rickety porch. He might even have declared himself a pozole addict. Being open to new foods, like being open to new art forms, new subjects, and unfamiliar works of art, was part of his nature.

Eli had a fiendish appetite for juxtapositions. After trips to Africa, South America, and Mexico, he taught a graduate seminar at Queens College on primitive art. The emotional force of so-called primitive forms excited him, as did their symbolic systems of representation. His satiric drawings and watercolors, with their flattened, simplified figures, have a spooky connection to the cutout witches and devils on the wall opposite the altar. Nevertheless, Eli would probably not have chosen to exhibit his death paintings in the context of a Mexican Dia de los Muertos. I can hear him saying, "It would only confuse viewers about my intentions, throw too many distractions into a limited space."

Eli is long gone. It is in my power to betray him, but not with this Mexican-themed party. The Muertos objects and altar intensify Eli's dance with death; they remind us of his black humor and wit. In the studio, surrounded by friends and family, I imagine him drifting from guest to guest, kibitzing and philosophizing. I can almost hear him discoursing on love and loss and the leveling power of death. He asks for a scotch and raises his glass. "The waiting room is where we all are," he intones, quoting from his unpublished "Secrets." "Our weariness reminds us that there is no escape from the ancient limits of time."

WHEN CHOPSTICKS ARE
NOT THE PROBLEM

Tokyo, 1995

"I'm so sorry," I tell Michi, "but my stomach is sending a message that I dare not ignore. I've been looking forward to our reunion, and especially the sea bass you promised to steam for me. 'I'm in my element with fish,' you said, sounding mystical. I almost asked you about the connection between fish and feminism. But I decided to save that conversation for dinner. And now I have to cancel. Even if I could get to your house this evening, there's no way I could do justice to the sea bass."

I hang up the phone, relieved. It's my last day in Japan. For three weeks in six cities, I've lectured and toured and been extravagantly feted. Every breakfast, lunch, and dinner has been a social event. I've knocked myself out being an attentive and lively guest. My appetite is sated. Even though an invitation to a Japanese home is uncommon and Michi is a charming, high-spirited woman, I just can't manage another evening out.

Still, I regret having to hide behind my stomach. I regret not being able to admit to Michi, as I would to an American friend, that heavy rain turns the outside world into enemy turf. If the rain weren't challenging enough, there's the complicated subway ride to Michi's place, halfway across Tokyo, which involves three changes of trains. (A taxi would be a stiff $50 each way.) The Tokyo subway system, with only a limited number of transliterated signs, is hard on a foreigner at the top of her form. On this final day in Japan, I'm functioning in a very low gear. I yearn for my own kitchen and bed.

After making my excuses to Michi, I meet with senior English majors at Tokyo Woman's Christian University, where I've been a visiting scholar for the past several days. Standing before forty impeccably groomed young women, I describe the conflicts my female students confront when they set out to "have it all"—career and family, independence and intimacy, private time and leisure. I mention one student's unwanted pregnancy, another student's boyfriend who sabotaged her plan to become a police officer, and a lesbian student's suffering and triumph in the military. I mention students dealing with day care and elder care and the likelihood of commuting marriages. When I ask how it is for young women in Japan, a long silence ensues. After prompting from their professors, three students acknowledge anxieties about the tight job market. But no one speaks about social constraints, self-doubts, or escaping for six months to the Australian outback.

Will I never learn? I'm a stranger, an American professor passing through. The students and I have one hour together. I come on with bravura, recounting confessions from a U.S. feminist classroom. My self-consciously American performance is up close and personal, like an unexpected invasion. I should have been prepared for Japanese reticence about private matters and shyness in speaking English.

Back in my suite, I finger two elegantly printed Japanese notebooks, filled with jottings on memorable Japanese meals, considerate Japanese colleagues, protocols for sampling food in department stores, and the Japanese art of gift wrapping. I reread my comments about Japanese stay-at-home wives as activist-volunteers and Japanese nursery school kids who do not fight over toys and food. What do these impressions add up to? What have I truly understood? With my academic responsibilities completed, I am free now to languish in my own head in these blessedly quiet quarters.

Ever thoughtful, my Japanese hosts at Tokyo Woman's Christian University have filled the kitchen larder with oranges, white bread for toast, jam, rice, miso soup, coffee, and chocolate. To these provisions I've added a comforting bottle of Johnny Walker Red. Making do for dinner will be no problem.

Outside, the downpour is subsiding. Streaks of light dart across the dark gray sky. Perhaps I don't have to stay in after all. It's foolish to spend this last evening at a kitchen table, washing down a meal of white toast and white rice with a couple of stiff scotches. I can grab an umbrella and a magazine and head for the Peipin Bar and Restaurant across the street. Maybe the chef will remember that I was there the night before with Hiroko Sato, a famous professor of English and American literature. Maybe some of her aura will be accorded to me.

From his station behind the sushi bar, the chef nods to me as I enter the Peipin. A single customer, a tall, thin man in his sixties, is seated at one end of the six-stool sushi bar. He has the meditative look of a man remembering a particularly precious moment with his mistress. I grab a stool at the opposite end. Repeat last night's meal, I want to tell the chef—everything just as you made it for Hiroko and me: that succulent steak, perfectly rare, the delicate salad of grated carrots mixed with bits of a creamy goat cheese, the fragrant citrus sherbet, and the strong coffee at the end.

The waitress hands me a menu, and the two of us burst out laughing. The chef laughs, too. My helplessness, in the face of the Japanese-only menu, without photographs of favorite dishes, is our common problem. Perhaps reciting "Hiroko Sato, Hiroko Sato" like a mantra will jog the chef's memory. Of course, I could say "tempura" or "sukiyaki" or "katsudon" (breaded pork cutlet), dishes I liked back in the 1960s, when Japanese restaurants were becoming commonplace in New York. Or I could make things easy for all of us by ordering sushi or sashimi. But that's too easy. Besides, not even the finest *hamachi* (yellow tail) or *toro* (white prime tuna) competes with the steak I fancy. And short of the steak, I prefer the unexpected.

"Meat," I say, opening my hands to the chef as if to suggest my openness to his inventions. The chef moves between the sushi bar and the built-in kitchen behind him with light, fluid motions. He pulls out a collection of pale purple eggplants, slices them, tosses the slices into a small wok over a very high flame, and stir-fries the eggplant for about a minute. His performance is both artful and efficient. When he sets out three wide-mouthed, shallow soup bowls, which he lines with bright green leaf lettuce, I get it. Two Japanese women who arrived shortly after I did must have ordered an eggplant dish, and now I am the beneficiary of their selection. I watch the chef divide the eggplant among the dishes. From a pot on the stove behind him, he ladles ground beef in a light broth into the bowls and adds a few drops of sesame oil. "Very tasty," I say as I dig in with my chopsticks. But no match for last night's steak.

I sip Kirin beer with the eggplant dish and begin reading a diatribe in *The Nation* on the cost to our country of Bill Clinton's sexual proclivities. This news from home can wait. Much better to watch the chef's fancy knifework as he debones sardines and lays six gorgeous fillets on a bed of daikon. These are intended for the man at the other end of the sushi bar. A regular client of the Peipin, he has "his" bottle of whiskey waiting for him. The waitress serves him a generous shot from the bottle and fills the tall glass with club soda. She then pours a whiskey for the chef from another bottle, his second drink since my arrival.

The Regular moves methodically through the sardines. I sense both his enjoyment and his habit of keeping all emotions close to the chest. His wife must find him maddening, I think to myself, unless she has long ago made a separate peace and turned to female friends and social activities for emotional satisfaction. It's what women in Japanese culture do, my female colleagues here have told me.

As the chef removes the sardine platter, he and the Regular fall into an animated conversation. Is the subject politics or economics, I wonder, or the doings of their respective children? Or have they been deliberating over the Regular's next dish? When it appears, I can't resist a grin: a plate with four Ritz crackers and a slice of smooth white cheese. Ritz crackers indeed. "Danish," the chef tells me as he presents me with a single Ritz cracker and a generous slab of cheese. "Delicious," I say, meaning it.

A young couple take a table at the front of the restaurant and give the waitress their order. Watching the chef shredding greens for their salad, I point to them and then to my chest. "Me too," I say. "Japanese salad?" he asks, wanting to be sure of my intention. The "Japanese" dimension of the salad, I understand when my dish arrives, is a nippy sesame dressing. "Bravo!" I say. "I love this salad."

When the Regular offers the chef a shot from his bottle of whiskey, the chef happily accepts. I wonder how this ritual is reflected in the bill or whether it relates to the Ritz crackers and cheese. Is the chef's pleasure a response to the courtesy or to the superior quality of the customer's brand?

"Scotch?" I ask. "No, Japanese whiskey," the chef says, and he promptly pours me a double shot from his own bottle. "Wonderful," I say, "like Dewars, one of my favorites." It's the gesture that counts, even more than the liquor. The Regular, with a slight lift of his glass, acknowledges my membership in the confederacy of drinkers. But that's the most I'll get from him. How much English does he understand, I wonder. Is his reserve, like my fatigue earlier in the day, a sometime thing?

I drink, absorbed in a review of two feminist biographies of women novelists. If I were eating sea bass at this moment with Michi, who happens to be Gloria Steinem's Japanese translator, would we be exploring the connection between feminist writers and their subjects? Would her mystical connection to fish transform our casual friendship into a deeper one? The perks of my professional world are sweet. And so are the effects of a large whiskey on top of a beer. Checking my watch, I see that I've been at the Peipin for almost two hours, the same amount of time I spent with my Japanese host the previous evening. The rain has started up again, but I don't mind. There's still time to get back to my room and make a few final notes before calling it a night.

SUNDAYS AT WHOLE FOODS

Edgewater, New Jersey, 2002

Maria is rolling up Joe's wrap as I approach the counter. I watch her hands, in clear plastic gloves, press the bulging green tortilla into a neat roll. She cuts it at an angle, revealing a landscape of intense greens and reds in an ivory field, and wraps the two halves in brown butcher paper. "What's in it?" I ask Joe, a thirty-something Latino. He reels off the ingredients—chicken salad, hummus, lettuce, tomatoes, sprouts, red pepper dressing, and a splash of balsamic. "Hey," he says, "it's Sunday. *Verdad*, Maria? I go all the way on Sunday."

My own Sunday choices are unpredictable. I'm as likely to be ascetic as excessive. Still, I've made the twelve-minute drive to the Whole Foods Market in Edgewater for just such a mouthful of flavors as well as the soothing sight of the Hudson. As Joe says *adios* to the sandwich-maker, I signal my intention to follow suit. "*El mismo, con aguagate, por favor*"—the same, with avocado, I tell Maria.

A Whole Foods addict, I unfailingly inspect the display of foods to go. Wrap in hand, I gawk at the grain salads and grilled vegetables, the samosas, arepas, lasagnas, and the ten types of tofu. In the spirit of political correctness and full disclosure, dishes are carefully labeled: forbidden (black Chinese) rice, Sicilian cauliflower salad, Vietnamese spring rolls, haricots verts with sun-dried tomatoes and goat cheese, zucchini parmesan latkes, sweet Indian carrots, and adobo enchiladas with jack cheese and cilantro. I watch the Japanese sushi chef turn out glistening broiled eel on vinegary rice. Shall I bring home a few slices of beautifully bloody London broil for dinner or half of a barbecued chicken? To escape from the burden of choice, I peruse the juice bar, but wind up ordering a decaf cappuccino from the coffee bar.

Wandering as if at leisure, no matter how anxious I am about time (wasted because I'm not writing), is an essential part of the process. I've come not just to fill up a shopping cart or enjoy quality caffeine or meet a friend for lunch. I want to see whether the flower market has white orchids and pink ginger and what kind of fruit platter can be purchased for $15. I want to check on the forty-five variations of olive oil, the lobster salad at $24 a pound, and the homemade chicken sausages made with spinach and feta, tequila black bean lime, ginger plum, and cilantro chipotle.

A glance at the votive candles and the aromatherapy section reminds me that the steam room at my health club has been out of order for more than two weeks now. Will a tube of blue chamomile shampoo provide a substitute balm for this week's frenzy? In the book aisle, all is explained: how to detox, get fit, and stay young; how to use feng shui, nutritional healing, vitamin therapy, and macrobiotic cooking as paths to well-being. In spite of myself, I caress a volume on learning to relax.

Often while making the rounds here I run into friends who, like me, identify a salad of greens and grains for lunch with the hope of healthy living. Sometimes I join them. But mostly, I like being alone in the calm of Whole Foods. I like eating alone with my fantasies for company. I like the urban-style anonymity and the suburban amenities: the green and white paper plates and the plastic knives and forks in their own clear plastic wrap; the neat trash cans, the spotless restrooms, the blond wood booths inside the market and the wrought iron tables outside.

It's about 1:00 p.m. when I settle down at an outdoor table with a view of the river and the huge sanitation plant on the other side at 145th Street and Riverside Drive, on top of which sits Riverbank State Park. The parking lot between my table and the Hudson is the price of access. Beyond the parking lot, at the river's edge, widely dispersed benches line a narrow walkway. Wild grasses edge the inland side. On the river side, clusters of black rocks slope toward the water. Waves splash rhythmically against the rocks. Soft breezes carry a whiff of salt.

For the sly art of people watching, no place beats the tables bordering the parking lot. Is the blond woman who grabs her cell phone the minute her handsome male companion takes off calling her mother, her husband, or her best friend? I eavesdrop on two Hebrew-speaking women comparing their children's private schools and a middle-aged, Spanish-speaking couple complaining about the heat. The wide glass doors of Whole Foods open automatically, releasing a moving tableau of suburbanites: the assertive Russian speakers, the dulcet Japanese speakers, and the unmistakable Jersey-speakers—all pushing overloaded carts toward their gas-guzzling SUVs.

For company, I've brought the Sunday *New York Times Book Review*. Glancing across at Manhattan and southward, I register the view as it was before 9/11: two arrogant towers shimmering in the distance. Now I push away thoughts of the diminished skyline and my sense of our diminished condition. Was the past a simpler time? Is the half century after Auschwitz easier to come to grips with than imperial America in the era of Bin Laden?

I remember Indian summer Sundays with my parents, more than fifty years ago, when we would head down to Riverside Park, about two miles south of the site opposite Whole Foods. We would take the entire Sunday *Times* with us, along with the *New York Herald Tribune* and a brown bag filled with seedless grapes, apricots, and plums. My brother and I, on roller skates, the old-fashioned metal kind we screwed onto our shoes, would race up and down a smooth hundred-yard track yelling, "Faster! Faster!"

On those uneventful family days when all the stores were closed, I would look for someone with a radio and ask how the Yankees were doing. The Yankees' only competition for my interest was not the Dodgers but Palisades Amusement Park, almost directly across the river, with its landmark roller coaster and Ferris wheel. Between the Palisades and Riverside Park, the Hudson sparkled. Back then I didn't notice the oil sludge on the surface of the water or the condoms caught among the rocks. Years later, I boasted that we could see the Hudson from my parents' apartment—by leaning out of the living room windows. But even in my adolescent, roller-skating prime, I daydreamed about other rivers: the Seine, the Mississippi, the Jordan, and the Nile.

Eleven years ago, on another heartbreakingly sunny Sunday, not far from this site, my stepdaughter Shola and I scattered four handfuls of Eli's ashes into the water. Does the river remember?

THE MOON IN MY DINING ROOM

Leonia, New Jersey, 2004

Rinpoche presses his hands together and begins the mealtime prayer. He speaks in a low singsong, in Tibetan. Adam joins him. Sapana, sitting very straight in her chair, follows silently. Rahula, age five, probably knows this prayer but doesn't participate. My eyebrows, should anyone be watching, signal amusement. More than sixty years ago, when my grandfather recited blessings, as if to himself, in a droning, Yiddish-inflected Hebrew, I averted my eyes and chattered with my cousins. Those ritual invocations were alien forms. Now, shifting my gaze between Rinpoche's serene face and Adam's uncharacteristically calm one, I strive to give the spirit its due.

We are all at our regular seats at the table. I'm at the head nearest the kitchen; Adam sits to my right, and Sapana and Rahula are on my left. Rinpoche, my son's lama and teacher, presides at the other end. Adam's place in the middle is both convenient and symbolic. He is the bridge, connecting Rinpoche, who speaks only Tibetan, to the rest of us.

Rinpoche (the term is honorific, indicating a lama who is reincarnated) wears his traditional garb: a gold-colored, sleeveless blouse with a Chinese collar and a full-length maroon wrap that drapes over his left shoulder. Adam, who has spent the day translating Rinpoche's teachings for a group of American Tibetan Buddhists in Summit, New Jersey, is wearing his own lama outfit: an eggshell-colored silk blouse, like Rinpoche's, and a long, eggshell "skirt," wrapped at the waist.

Rinpoche has been in residence here, along with the visiting family members, on and off for almost four weeks now. I've made several celebratory American-style meals during this time. Tonight, however, I'm slowing down. The leftovers from last night's dinner party, courtesy of Whole Foods, are on the table: barbecued chicken and salads of white beans, spicy corn with feta, edamame, and red peppers. A green salad and a platter of peppery turkey breast slices round out the meal. It's an ordinary family supper without pretense or ambition.

After the prayer, Adam, as is his habit, serves Rinpoche. The evening before, Adam mentioned that the Japanese contributed edamame to American cuisine and the Greeks (along with the French, Bulgarian, and Turks) have made feta a staple of American eating. Because this is Rinpoche's first trip to the West, such explanations are called for. Once the platters have been passed around, Adam plunges into an exchange with Rinpoche that seems to go on and on. Restless and somewhat irritated, I ask Adam to translate a bit so as to include Sapana and me in the conversation. "This stuff—the business side of dharma—isn't worth translating," Adam says. "But why don't you ask Rinpoche a direct question."

There's been no real conversation between Rinpoche and me since the evening a few weeks back when Rinpoche asked me if I was a Buddhist. "I'm not interested in religion," I confessed, "or ritualized systems of belief." Rinpoche is not easily put off about matters to which he has dedicated most of his fifty-one years. He responded by saying that there were things I could do that were not very ritualistic and that might yield, in Adam's phrase, greater understanding. "Thank you," I replied. "I'll keep that in mind."

"What surprises you about the U.S.?" I ask. My six-word question requires almost six minutes of interpretative work on Adam's part. Watching my son's gestures as he reformulates the question in Tibetan, I can tell that he is suggesting possible avenues of response. Rinpoche remains silent. I can't tell if he is puzzled by the notion of surprise or indifferent to this line of inquiry. "Try again," Adam suggests, adding that people often ask Rinpoche about his life in Tibet.

At another moment, I might willingly have taken that suggestion. Now, however, if there is to be a conversation, I want at least a piece of it to be on my terms. It's not Rinpoche's history that I'm after, but how he crosses cultures. On the food front he does well enough. He's a sturdily built man with a healthy appetite. At breakfast he is happy with granola (because he knows oats) and milk. He'll eat toast, if it's offered, along with his tea. He copes, somewhat awkwardly, with a knife and fork and has adjusted to our family's passion for fresh greens and tropical fruits—all new to him. He devours unfamiliar cuts of beef, chicken every which way, and vegetables that must seem to him radically undercooked. Adam has warned me not to serve fish or seafood, which Rinpoche rejects for complicated reasons having more to do with their foreignness to him as a Tibetan than with religious dogma. Shrimp he regards as ugly bugs and lobsters as murderous scorpions. Besides, one gets so little nourishment from the death of each of these souls, Adam explains, and so much more from a dead yak (the protein staple of Tibet) or a cow.

"How is the U.S. different from Tibet?" I ask. Again, Adam's version of the question goes on at length. Another long silence follows. Then Rinpoche answers. "We're all the same," Adam says for him. "Everyone is the same. There's no difference between here and Tibet. We all suffer. We all seek ways to transcend suffering."

What does one say in the face of such a simple truth—and such an absurdly reductionist view of human experience?

"We're all going to die," Adam continues, beginning the Buddhist riff about the spirit outliving the body and the importance of the afterlife and previous lives. We suffer less once we understand that the spirit lives on, that the corporal life of the body is not the only life. Again Rinpoche suggests that I might benefit from some dharma teachings. "I'm more interested in questions than answers," I say. "I'm a materialist, focused on how to live in this world rather than what might mysteriously occur in the next."

If Adam hadn't found the preceding eight hours translating for Rinpoche exhausting, I would have gone on. I would have spoken about the Food Service Training Academy, where ex-convicts and recovering addicts are trying to change their lives through cooking. I would have lamented the bad diet of the poor in America, the role of food banks in feeding the hungry, and malnutrition around the world. I would have been tempted to mention that I spend my days at the computer writing about some of these matters. But I hold my tongue.

If I'm interested in questions, Rinpoche wants to know, how come I'm not interested in questions about the afterlife? It's like the psychoanalyst's trap: if you express *x*, that must be an issue for you. If you repress the same *x*, that's also an issue. I acknowledge Rinpoche's skill in argumentation. "One hasn't the time or the energy for every question," I say. "Each of us operates out of a framework, and the framework establishes priorities. Mine are about this world and this life."

From my end of the table to Rinpoche's is roughly seven feet. But we are galaxies apart. I watch my son's juggling act. He's brilliant, but only beginning to fine-tune his performance, to erect an accessible bridge between Western rationalism and Eastern spiritualism.

We go back and forth on priorities until Adam evokes the notion "what goes around comes around" in reference to failures of generosity and compassion. Attempting to translate some comment of Rinpoche's, he compares my materialism to Saddam Hussein's cruelties. What? How? I try not to take this personally—even as I think of my nonstop shopping and feeding as meeting more than bodily needs. Still, I tell Adam that I am shocked at the crude comparison. What on earth does Rinpoche have in mind? It turns out Adam has misunderstood the lama. Without formal training in Tibetan, he sometimes fails to grasp the finer points of Rinpoche's regionally accented discourse.

When Adam first told me that Rinpoche would be joining the family party on this U.S. trip, he said, "Think about it this way: it will be like having the moon in your dining room." "Light is always welcome," I replied. I didn't add that moonlight can be eerie, especially for sun worshippers like myself. Adam, it turns out, was implying something in addition: that Rinpoche is a man *from* the moon. Born in isolated, rural Tibet, he grew up (from age seven) in a monastery. As a monk, he has been sheltered from the secular world and the ways of the postindustrial West. He exists in another space, on another planet. His discipline encourages depth of knowledge and experience within what I think of as a narrow—that is, exclusively spiritual—focus.

Clinging as I do to the affairs of this world, I miss what Rinpoche is about. I see a gracious, likable man, a person my son tells me is a brilliant teacher and a gifted doctor of Tibetan medicine. Still, the chasm between us is enormous. The otherworldly Rinpoche is also from the other side of the world. My table accommodates him better than my mind.

With the end of the six-week visit in sight, we are again at dinner. As Adam slices the loin of beef, which is pink and beautifully bloody, I find myself wondering what Rinpoche thinks of our collective passion for rare meat. I also wonder about the crunchy greens and the rice medley. More to the point, I'm conscious of a failure of hospitality with regard to my guest. Surely he would have been more pleased with white rice or some simple potatoes, along with the meat that is the Tibetan's staff of life. With Adam's encouragement, however, I've gone my merry way in cooking for the visit, making what I like, more or less. Avoiding fish and seafood for Rinpoche is not especially inhibiting. But avoiding pork, which Adam and Sapana reject as a personal discipline—because they love it—is a real sacrifice.

Adam, eager for feedback from Rinpoche about how the trip is going, sets me up to pose the question. Rinpoche's initial responses are bland: "Fine, nice, it's good." "How do you feel about American students?" I ask, pressing further. "They are willing and eager," Adam translates, "and they ask questions, while Asian students always say, 'Yes, Rinpoche, yes, Rinpoche.'"

"So it's not all the same after all," I say to Adam, who translates the comment.

When Rinpoche does not respond, I wonder whether he hasn't taken my meaning or doesn't wish to. Adam seems reluctant to pursue this any further.

I ask about the medicines that Rinpoche makes and uses in Asia. They are herbally based, following ancient traditions, Adam says, suited to certain common disorders involving blood and the organs; they also have a mind-body component and are good for ailments generated by anxiety and the like. My query, doubtless too open-ended for a brief response, leads Rinpoche to ask about my health. "Do you have any problems?" he wishes to know.

By now I've had three glasses of sauvignon blanc. "No, none at all," I say. At the table, surrounded by my clever, happy son, my loving and lovely daughter-in-law, and my delightful youngest grandchild, I am feeling no pain. When Adam asks if I'd like Rinpoche to do a consultation—listen to my pulse to see what it might reveal—I acquiesce.

Settling into the chair that Rahula has vacated, I move closer to Rinpoche and stretch out my left hand. It's a warm evening, but Rinpoche's fingers are dry and cool as he places them across my wrist. He inclines his head toward my arm, grazes my wrist with a slight pulsing motion, and remains still for about fifteen seconds. The entire procedure takes less than a minute. I no longer have my menses, Rinpoche tells me via Adam. "Well, yes, at my age I should hope not," I say. He detects some small disturbances in the liver-kidney areas—and given many decades of regularly indulging in scotch and wine, I can't say that I'm surprised. But do I have pain? No. No pains? No.

Rinpoche's doctoring, in great demand by Tibetan Buddhists in the United States who have been attending his teachings, doesn't get very far with me. Still, I don't wish to seem dismissive. Returning to an earlier part of the conversation, I ask Rinpoche whether his satisfactions with the trip came from teaching or doctoring or both. "The teacher pours water into a cup," Adam translates. "The water, like teachings, is received by students, some more successfully than others. He feels this has happened on his trip here. He feels satisfied."

"Teaching," I say, "is full of mysteries. Teaching makes me modest, even humble. I can never be sure what is received and by whom, what is retained, or what makes an impact." I tell Rinpoche about my recent meeting with a former student who remembered vividly what had transpired in my class thirty years earlier. I barely remembered the student—until the conversation. Yet here this accomplished fifty-year-old woman was insisting that the water I poured into her cup still quenched her thirst. She teaches in the field of food studies, she told me as we exchanged e-mail addresses and planned a lunch together. As I recount the incident, it occurs to me that what we don't know about this world is more interesting than what we do know. I don't say this to Rinpoche. My parrying skills are spent. Besides, the wine is making me sleepy, and the kitchen needs cleaning.

SALAD DAYS AND NIGHTS

Leonia, New Jersey, 2003–2005

The voice on the phone is light and cheery, somewhat at odds with the formal diction. I imagine a woman who used to wear white gloves to church, even in eighty-five-degree heat. "I'm your Leonia neighbor, calling on behalf of United Way," she says. "A close neighbor, actually. My husband and I can see your lovely dining room from our house on Eastview." I hesitate, at a loss for words, before promising to put a check in the mail first thing in the morning.

"How extraordinary," I announce, as if to a room full of guests. After years of observing other eaters, after intruding on their meals and conjuring their secrets, the tables have been turned on me. The dining room, which faces a rear garden, has floor-to-ceiling windows but no shades. My life at the table is an open book, it turns out, especially at night, for those with good spying equipment. I'm relieved that my caller does not live in the house directly behind my back garden fence, where I might catch a glimpse of her peering at me, but on the far side of that street. I imagine the woman and her husband, bird-watchers perhaps, pressed against their dining room window, passing the binoculars back and forth.

What do they think when they observe me eating alone, maybe three or four evenings a week, at the head of the oval table, with the *New York Times* piled neatly to my left? Do they zero in on the oversized salad of mesclun, cherry tomatoes, yellow peppers, cucumbers, jicama, and calamari, decorated with fire-engine-red peppadew peppers, oil-cured olives, and feta cheese? Do they comment to each other on the omnipresent wineglass filled and refilled with pale white wine? Do they remember Eli sitting to my right, facing the garden? Do they happen to check in when I'm entertaining a lover?

I'm not spooked; I am the spook. These neighborhood spies are too old and too genteel to be dangerous. If they are tracking my dining habits, they are probably too fixed in their ways to appreciate my game with salads. Like my mother, they probably think of salad as a pretty little plate of lettuce and tomatoes with a garnish of parsley that precedes a larger plate of meat, vegetables, and a potato or rice. They might be surprised to learn that over the past several years in my house, the eight-inch salad plate has become obsolete, as is the case in many restaurants.

In its place the eleven-inch dinner plate, plain white Wedgwood, offers itself as a canvas for salad making.

My mother, to be fair, adapted to the salad revolution of the 1970s and '80s. Born in New York in 1903, she lived to the end of the twentieth century. Her embrace of my salad-as-meal—the greens, the cooked and raw vegetables, the cubes of leftover meat or fish, the artichoke hearts and olives, served with raspberry vinaigrette—is a measure of the distance she traveled as an American eater. Your salad platter, I remember her saying, puts the whole garden right on the table. That there hadn't been a garden in our backyard since Adam was in junior high was beside the point.

I didn't pull my weight in that garden, sad to say. Weeding gave me a sore back. Squatting among the zucchini made me short-tempered. In those years, I hid behind the gendered division of inside and outside work. If Eli and Adam would give the garden their sweat labor, I'd honor it by trying out a new vegetable recipe from Craig Claiborne's *New York Times Cook Book*.

These days, my romance with salad has a different, outside labor base. Julio's is its name. At Julio's, now a Korean-owned greengrocery, Latino kitchen workers do my prepping. From Tuesday through Saturday and a half day on Sunday, a crew of four in the back kitchen wash leaf lettuce, iceberg, watercress, and spinach. They spin and cut the greens. They chop red, yellow, and green peppers; they slice carrots, cucumbers, red onions, red cabbage, and white and red radishes. They also dice scallions, grate zucchini, and divide broccoli into bite-sized florets.

When I'm shopping for myself, I fill a plastic half moon container, about eight inches in diameter and six inches high, with ingredients for three or four individual salads. If guests are coming and I'm down to the last bit of greens and red cabbage, I happily make the five-minute drive for a refill and a few extra items—maybe portobello mushrooms, sliced jicama, and asparagus or slender French green beans. The labor provided by Julio's liberates me and hundreds of other regular customers. I can devote myself to composing the salad and designing the plate.

Sometimes, on the way home from Julio's, I think about a different relationship to salad and, by extension, to cooking. I see my friend Alice, in front of her house in the Berkshires, kneeling in the dirt. Red and green leaf lettuce plants, perky from the predawn rain, beckon to her. Her hands rest on the warm, moist earth. Lingering is not Alice's mode. There's still one chapter to write for her latest manuscript (later to be a prize-winning book), on women's struggle for economic equality, which claims the first four hours of each vacation day and often the last four hours as well. But now, on her knees, carefully separating our luncheon salad from the Massachusetts soil, she breathes freely.

At lunch, following homemade borscht with sour cream, Alice serves a big platter of greens, tomatoes from the farmers' market, and a homemade potato salad. This meal, like the five others that punctuate my weekend visit, is organized down to the last green onion. Alice, a distinguished historian of women and labor, cooks the way she conducts research: with no shortcuts and no canned products. The more headwork she does, the more handwork she craves. For Alice, all phases of food preparation, from gardening to cleanup, are honorable—and therapeutic. "I like chopping onions, cleaning basil, grating cheese, and kneading dough," Alice says. "I also like washing pots in warm soapy water. That's how I relax."

I'm tempted to say that my car does for me what gardening does for Alice. Driving around, I am liberated from my computer even as I continue to work on an essay. When Alice and her husband, Bert, come to dinner at my house, I happily pick up salad basics from Julio's in Teaneck, a black olive focaccio fresh from the oven at Balthazar Bakery in Englewood, and chicken sausages with feta cheese and spinach from Whole Foods in Edgewater. Behind the wheel, and without the distractions of music or news on my car radio, I think through a missed connection or tame a meandering paragraph. While I'm waiting for a green light, my semi-conscious maneuvers through verbal traffic jams, seeking an open lane. For as long as I've been living alone, I have thought of salads, made with time-saving shortcuts, as an end in themselves: healthy, semi-spontaneous creations, uninhibited by recipes, beautiful to behold. But perhaps I'm selling my salads short. Perhaps they are also a means as well as an end: a therapeutic adjunct to writing.

My daughter-in-law, Sapana, born in Kathmandu, is intrigued by my salad mania. In Nepalese cuisine, everything is cooked. If three vegetables are served, or three different pickles, they are never assembled in a bowl or on a single serving platter. Moreover, cooked food is served hot, not at room temperature.

Initially, Sapana was puzzled by the provenance of my salads. Okay, she would tell herself, this is an American dish, with American trademarks: easy and efficient to manage, without lots of rules about what goes with what. Still, the salad choices—especially in summertime, when she visits—can be overwhelming. What goes best with baby spinach, she asks. How will I know whether to use blue cheese or feta, jicama or fennel? Sapana is surprised when I layer slices of hot turkey sausage onto chilled greens. She is even more surprised when I sprinkle lentils cooked with cumin over the sausages. Soupy curried lentils (*dal*) are the indispensable partner to white rice (*bhat*) in a Nepalese family's daily or twice-daily *dal bhat.* If my salad platter has rice, it's likely to be the dark brown, wild variety that isn't rice at all but the whole grain of a water grass, native to the Great Lakes region of the United States.

Sapana and I both relish the smooth consistency and cool taste of mango combined with cubes of roast chicken and acidic peppadew peppers. Presliced mango from Julio's is among my refrigerator staples. Slicing a mango is messy work. The skin is tenacious, and the big flat pit clings to the fruit. It takes a steady hand and an extra-sharp knife—or, in Nepal, two hands and a *chulesi*, a slim, curved knife blade affixed to a piece of wood. I remember watching Sapana's elderly aunt, seated on the kitchen floor, bending forward, with her right foot pressed against the wood base of the *chulesi.* At first, I didn't see the mango half hidden between her two hands. I thought she was in the midst of prayers or yoga. Swaying slightly from side to side, she cut a firm mango into fine slices. We use the *chulesi* to cut everything, Sapana later explained—eggplant, onions, potatoes, and mutton, too.

Tools are not a passion of mine, but collecting oddly shaped objects is. If only U.S. Customs were not so paranoid, I would ask Sapana and Adam to bring me a *chulesi.* I imagine the menacing blade perched on an embroidered cloth, protected by tall cactuses, in a corner of the dining room.

In the course of six annual visits to the United States with Adam, Sapana has become a salad maven. Like me, she enjoys the art of presentation, the light, healthy way of eating, and the chance to improvise. I expect that often on her way home from work, after a demanding day as president of a small foundation, she wishes for a Julio's of her own. But no: in Sapana's kitchen every lettuce leaf must be carefully washed and soaked in sterilized water. There isn't a home cook in Kathmandu—or her housekeeper—who would trust even a gourmet shop's treated water to be safe enough for a Western-style salad.

Since Sapana and Adam's last visit, and in her honor, I've added a South Asian flourish to my salad repertoire: *chaat.* Although the Indian term *chaat* ("to lick" in Hindi) includes many kinds of snacks, I use it in the narrow sense, meaning snack mix: a golden crunch of salty, spicy, slender fried noodles, *kala namak* (a black, sulfurlike salt), and small nuts. In Kathmandu, Sapana serves a Nepalese version of *chaat* with drinks. I wonder whether my daughter-in-law will enjoy this Asianization of the salad. From her perspective, will a sprinkling of *chaat* on top of sautéed mushrooms or eggplant—instead of parsley or almonds—make my salad more or less American?

It's still light at 8:00 on a mid-June evening when I bring dinner to the table. Delicate bay scallops from the fish market in Hackensack top off this evening's combination of arugula, roasted fennel, and Jersey tomatoes. While I've held back on *chaat*, thinking it would overwhelm the scallops, I go all the way with bottled peppadew peppers. Four or five of these gently vinegared gems, each the size of a large grape and cut into quarters, brighten all the tastes around them. Firm in the mouth rather than slippery like roasted red peppers, they add both texture and color. The flashy red counts. If peppadews were dull green, I might never have noticed them to begin with.

Functioning on autopilot, I head for my regular place at the table. But then I reconsider. I could take Eli's former seat, facing the garden. But there I'll be a sitting duck for the spies. Or I could position myself with my back to the garden, denying them and facing Eli's *Grass Goddess*. The large, satiric oil painting shows a voluptuous naked woman wearing lime green stockings and bright pink pumps. She is held aloft by two odd-looking fellows—their bodies painted gray like hers—who resemble circus performers. With a marijuana plant in her left hand, the Grass Goddess, my outlaw gardener, strikes a triumphant pose. The rainbow logo behind her promotes "Gorton's Finest Grass Seeds." While the painting was inspired by early-twentieth-century advertising cards promising eternal youth and beauty, it actually mocks our culture of falsity. Beneath Eli's witty surface is a dark view of human nature and skepticism about simpleminded nostrums for change.

For me, however, Eli's sensuality trumps his moralism, and his *Grass Goddess* speaks volumes. Unlike our current political and corporate leaders, who are clothed in hypocritical rectitude, the undressed Grass Goddess scoffs and teases. There's no piety overlaying her corruption. The chair opposite the painting beckons. I take my seat across from the *Grass Goddess*, a bemused celebrant, with my salad of scallops, arugula, fennel, and tomato as my song, my offering.

The goddess's naked crotch, her own garden of earthly delights, draws my gaze, and I laugh till the tears come. "Lovely dining room" indeed! To think that the spies might have been interested in my solo habits or salad arts—in me. What kind of vanity (or exhibitionism) prompted that notion? The spies are simply doing what every meter reader, plumber, house painter, and visitor does in my house: inspecting the naked bodies for edification and thrills.

HAPPY MARKET

Leonia, New Jersey, 2004

Pete, my plumber, stares glumly at his coffee. He is in what I think of as his office at the corner table of Happy Market, angled toward the front door. Next to him, two Latino day workers remove freshly made fried egg sandwiches from tinfoil and settle into their breakfast. I hesitate before approaching Pete. His body language signals that he's still half in the sack. However, the half that's up and running sends what passes for a welcoming glance in my direction. He waits, his long torso slumped over the small round coffee bar, for my opening sally.

I stand tall but feel like slumping. With the election only a month away, the polls show Bush's lead widening over Kerry. The details, including ugly Republican pronouncements that electing a war hero turned war critic is an invitation to terrorist attacks, sit like spoiled eggs in my stomach. I won't lay my anguish on Pete, who probably doesn't lose sleep over electoral politics. Fifty now, Pete was too young to be sent to Vietnam. When his generation argued over the war, he stayed silent and stoned. At least that's what I've been led to believe.

"Open for business?" I ask. "Yeah—got a problem?" he responds. Sure, I've got a problem, but it's not in Pete's line of work. I'm so restless some mornings I could scream. Even Trader Joe's French roast, my usual home brew, tastes bitter in the predawn darkness. Like Pete, I crave distraction.

Happy Market rewards me with a choice of six coffees for ninety-nine cents a cup and nonstop small dramas for free. I watch a landscaper check his watch and pull down his baseball cap before pouring himself a giant-sized hazelnut coffee. I watch a Korean man in a white shirt pick up a Korean-language newspaper and a yogurt before heading into the city. I watch a lean, redheaded runner still breathing hard as she examines the packaged sushi. And I watch Jinny sing out "Good morning" as each customer arrives while ringing up sales at the front register. My mind starts to work, and I berate myself for not bringing my notebook.

Pete tells me he's leaving Leonia. I wonder whether his move is connected to the return to town of his ex-wife. Fifteen years ago, she moved out, leaving him and two small boys. I'm sure she had her reasons. Recently I ran into her at the nail salon. "It takes two," she said, referring to their failed marriage.

Since selling his three-story house, Pete has been camping with his parents. Happy Market is his salvation. He says his parents are making him nuts. "Each morning my father puts out three coffee cups and waits for me to tell him where I'm going and when I'll be home for dinner. The only way to survive," Pete says, "is to get out before he's down in the kitchen with the coffee, waiting."

Even before returning to his boyhood bedroom, Pete had the Happy Market habit. For years, customers have been hunting him down before 8:00 a.m. here at the convenience store in the middle of town. No day goes by, he says, without a clogged second-floor toilet. Volunteer firefighters with a furnace in trouble find Pete easily during his office hours. So do his pals in the ambulance corps. I know. I've lined up more than once to get my kitchen sink on his schedule.

I know because I am developing the Happy Market habit. A couple of times a month, sometime between 6:00 and 7:00 a.m., the *New York Times* fails me. It's not about whether the front page reveals or hides the latest count of the world's damaged and dead or whether there's a breakthrough in funding AIDS victims in Africa. The news, hopeful or awful, can't provide what I need.

After Eli died I joined the "Early Birds" at my tennis club. Monday through Friday at 5:45 a.m., I'd be among the first of our middle-aged gang to arrive. "Use the coffeepot on the left," Mary would instruct me from her command post behind the front desk. "Let me know if it's strong enough." "It's as good as ever," I would say.

It wasn't just the coffee that boded well. Mary's solicitousness and her half-whispered complaints about the club owners and their smelly cats jolted me into consciousness. The pro, with whom I had taken lessons since the mid-1970s, gave me the same tough workout as he gave the guys. My male partners offered compliments and hugs. We all compared notes about elbows and ankles, memorable meals, and the travails of our adult children. In addition, an hour on the court did wonders for my adrenaline. Win or lose, I returned home ready for yogurt, granola, and a day's work. When my knee rebelled and I stopped playing in the summer of 1997, I didn't give up the club. Every weekday morning for a year I drank Mary's brew with the Early Birds and hung out for an hour. Separating from tennis was like a prolonged farewell to a lover.

To get over my loss, I joined a nearby spa. Two weeks later, in the sauna, I met the wife of an Early Bird player, who invited me to join her writers' group. That connection, along with a drive of less than five minutes to the gym, still justifies my membership. Unfortunately, I soon discovered what I have always known: that I hate exercise almost as much as I hate the spa's weak coffee. Still, I'll drop in on sunny afternoons when I'm likely to have the place to myself. A relaxing twenty minutes in the whirlpool is balm to my back and spirits; then, if I'm lucky, I'll give my Spanish a workout with Maura, the housekeeper in the women's locker room, who was once a college teacher in El Salvador.

Jinny, a perky Korean woman in her mid-twenties, has the early-morning shift at Happy Market. Effortlessly efficient, she never misses a greeting or a good-bye. She also manages to keep tabs on the Latino sandwich makers, the multiple pots of coffee, the guys picking up and delivering newspapers, and the lottery ticket machine that sits between the cash register and the ATM. "This job is better than being stuck alone at home," Jinny tells me. "So many customers are regulars. I know what size coffee they buy and what brand of cigarettes. It's a game for me."

Jinny's game and mine are not quite the same. She focuses on individual preferences and predictability while I look at the big picture: the amazing diversity of my suburban community of nine thousand and the ways in which a small Korean-owned convenience store meets the needs of these different eaters on the run. While I rarely buy food at Happy Market, I often kill time surveying the options. These include the omnipresent bagels (whole, plain or sliced with cream cheese or butter), along with hard rolls, prepared cakes and cookies, a dozen varieties of sandwiches and wraps, and franks in a spinning grill, available with or without chili. Lately they've added sushi, three soups, salads in plastic boxes, fresh fruit, Jell-O, and the special "house" yogurt with honey, granola, and dried fruit.

When I comment to the Korean owner, a slender man in his late thirties, that there seem to be more choices every week, he nods enthusiastically. The limits of his spoken English embarrass him. But they do not prevent him—or his wife, who has similar language anxieties—from mastering this business. How have they managed to anticipate the preferences of blue- and white-collar workers, housewives, high school athletes and senior citizens, natives and immigrants from near and far? Doggedness? Market research? An entrepreneurial gene? Can this savvy about ordinary American eating be packaged and taught? I'd better watch what I seem to be wishing for. Replication is the road to Burger King.

The unflappable Jinny, who was in the United States for only three months when she began working, is completely in synch with the morning routine. Unlike her bosses, Jinny speaks idiomatic American English, which she learned in Indonesia, at an international (American) school. I imagine her school resembling ours in Leonia, where the students' first languages are forty in number. (Korean, Spanish, Japanese, and Russian are the most common, followed by Arabic and Italian.) Still, I wonder: does Jinny experience the mixing and occasional blending of our suburban cultures as an oddity (so unlike Korea, where she went to college and met her husband) or as characteristically American?

My question to Jinny is the question I ask myself each day, whether or not I visit Happy Market. Is this vibrant diversity—once confined to big cities and the two coasts—the quintessential feature of American culture? At Happy Market, small things help focus my thinking. For example, in this Christmas season, the tree at the front of the shop seems to grow out of a rack devoted to Haribo Gold-Bears and other fruit-flavored snacks marketed to eight-year-olds. The tree, with lights and colored baubles, is inverted to fit the space: shaved off at the bottom and wider at the top. Surrounding the tree on either side are store lights in the form of Korean lanterns, yellow, orange, lime green, and red. The lanterns, which are more noticeable before and after the Christmas season, make their own wry symbolic statement. Behind the candy racks I catch sight of snow shovels and ice scrapers that have been laid in for the bad weather, along with chemically treated logs. Is there a fine logic at work determining the inclusion of objects in this display? Do the owners have a brother-in-law in New York with a similar store who advises them on matters of buying and selling?

Speculation is as entertaining as knowing—sometimes more so. I remember being surprised one morning when a bearded American construction worker in his thirties, with a bandana and a couple of earrings, picked up an Italian-language newspaper. Of course, there's a chance that the fellow was only temporarily working in construction while financing a graduate degree in Italian Renaissance history, and reading *America Oggi* was a way of keeping his Italian current. More likely, the paper was for his mother or grandmother. If on another occasion he chooses the *Irish Times*, which Happy Market also carries, I may have to revise my thinking.

But I won't revise my enthusiasm for this quirky convenience store and its unique place in my town. Until a few years ago, I would have avoided a shop with a smile stenciled between the words "Happy" and "Market." I hate the empty good cheer of smile stickers. I never say, "Have a good day." Nowadays, however, with so much misery and evil pressing in upon us, I'm more open to unexpected solace. I take in what is offered at Happy Market: from the earnest multiethnic sensibility to Jinny's friendly question, as she accepts my dollar, about the doings of my family in Asia.

At 6:30 a.m., settling onto Pete's empty barstool, I ask the Latino worker sitting next to me *"de donde vienes,"* where he's from. He points to the woven Guatemalan bag I'm carrying, with my *New York Times* in it, and says, *"Mi pais,"* my country. We haven't made a real connection. Real connections require years of labor and love. It's just a simple, welcome moment of openness. Two minutes later, the Guatemalan turns away from me to shake hands with two *compañeros.* I see the light breaking over the avenue. A few more sips of coffee and I'll head home to work.

EPILOGUE: MY BOOK OF MAPS

Leonia, New Jersey, August 2005

Four months ago, in South Africa, I had a dream about this book. When I awoke, I wrote in my notebook:

Once again I am a graduate student at Yale. In a cramped, gloomy office, one of my professors is admonishing me to pay attention to the reading list. You'll have four chances to prove yourself, he says. Out in the corridor, I hear that a poetry reading is about to begin at Yale Chapel. Everyone in American studies will be there. After a brief hesitation, I head off in the direction of the chapel.

Suddenly the scene changes. I'm driving a car, which turns into an open truck. The steering wheel is high above my head. I strain as I stretch upward, just barely grasping the wheel. The truck lifts off the ground. I'm flying, fifteen feet over the city. I feel the wind at my back and the sun on my face. I'm not going to crash. My panic dissolves into exhilaration.

In the final sequence of the dream, I'm on the ground again, in New Haven. I show the same unsympathetic professor a volume of street maps of Johannesburg—maps that are connected to my explorations of food and politics in that city and elsewhere. I tell him that the book is important for scholarship in American studies and that it illuminates my history as an American. "Irrelevant," he says, dismissing the work—and dismissing me. I am furious. The guy is dead wrong. I know the significance of maps.

Food does not appear in this dream of anxiety and feverish excitement. At Yale, more than four decades ago, eating and drinking were normal, life-sustaining (and sometimes life-enhancing) activities for students of American culture, but they were not subjects for serious study. Food was out of bounds for Americanists—as were women's lives, sexuality, and the movies. High culture was our business. In the dream I avoid the lecture at the chapel, where poetry, history, and politics are worshiped along with God. I'm in flight, on another path, toward an unknown destination.

I know as soon as I awaken that, in this dream of mine, flying is one stand-in for eating as an approach to culture, and maps are another. Whether those in authority like it or not, I have taken hold of this supremely enticing subject. It not only grabs my attention as an observer and critic of American society but also helps to explain my life. Still, I am anxious. Willy-nilly, I have abandoned the familiar land route, and I can barely control my vehicle.

The flying machine and the book of maps, the former unbounded and the latter very grounded, are the yin and yang of my education as an eater. Clearly, flying represents the emotional energy that drives my adventures in eating: the need to cut loose from home and (some) received traditions, to open myself to other people and worlds, and to experience shifts in my thinking and being. The flying machine, my comic dream of freedom, speaks to the restless, risk-taking, and unconventional side of the journey.

Maps speak to the practical, tangible, and self-protective side of my history as an eater. I don't skydive. I move around, picking and choosing my subjects among sites, ceremonies, cuisines, individual ingredients, and relationships. Maps illuminate the origins of my journey, some ordinary and unlikely directions I've taken, and connections along the route. With a map, I can retrace my steps when necessary. And I can prepare for potholes, blockades, bad visibility, and roads that lead nowhere.

My book of maps points to lessons—in culture, history, and personal relations—offered by merchants and waiters and companions at the table. Taking my cues from others, I observe how food both separates people and brings them together. I scrutinize my own food baggage. I expose the tug-of-war between old habits and new perspectives; and I acknowledge the constraints of my class, culture, gender, and imagination. I use maps and make maps; they are my guide and the spine of my story.

My book is finished now, but I have hardly exhausted my supply of maps. A group of Hudson Valley, New York, pickle makers, who are regulars at local farmers' markets, attract buyers from many ethnic groups. As I begin talking with them, I'm reminded of connections between Jewish deli and kimchi. Have my past and present merged in these pickle jars? Shouldn't I map that connection? At the Youth Consultation Service Kids' Café in Newark, eight-year-olds who are addicted to pizza and fries are being taught to enjoy salads and fresh fruit. It's a war, the teachers tell me; and that war zone is only a twenty-minute ride from my home in New Jersey. I am also returning to Kathmandu; this time, the site I'll be mapping is The Organic Village, a combined market, boutique, and café catering to eco-tourists and expats that my son and daughter-in-law are developing.

At The Organic Village, where chemical-free eating is a privilege of the privileged, I imagine settling myself on a stool at a wooden table under a bamboo roof. After inspecting the menu, I'll order *yomari*, a sesame dessert, and a *tongba*, fermented millet beer that is said to double milk production for lactating mothers. As I sip the hot, bitter drink and chew on the sweet, my adrenaline will surge. I'll grab my pen and make notes on the scene. All the while I'll be wondering where this organic story intersects with my own. Perhaps I'll figure it out, eating as I go.